For Supplementary
   List
      by Barnet

See:

Numismatist

Apr 1943 et seq.

also Index of names
Feb 1944 et seq.

See Numis Scrapbook
   Feb - Mar 1959 for
Fuld list
See Fuld photo plates

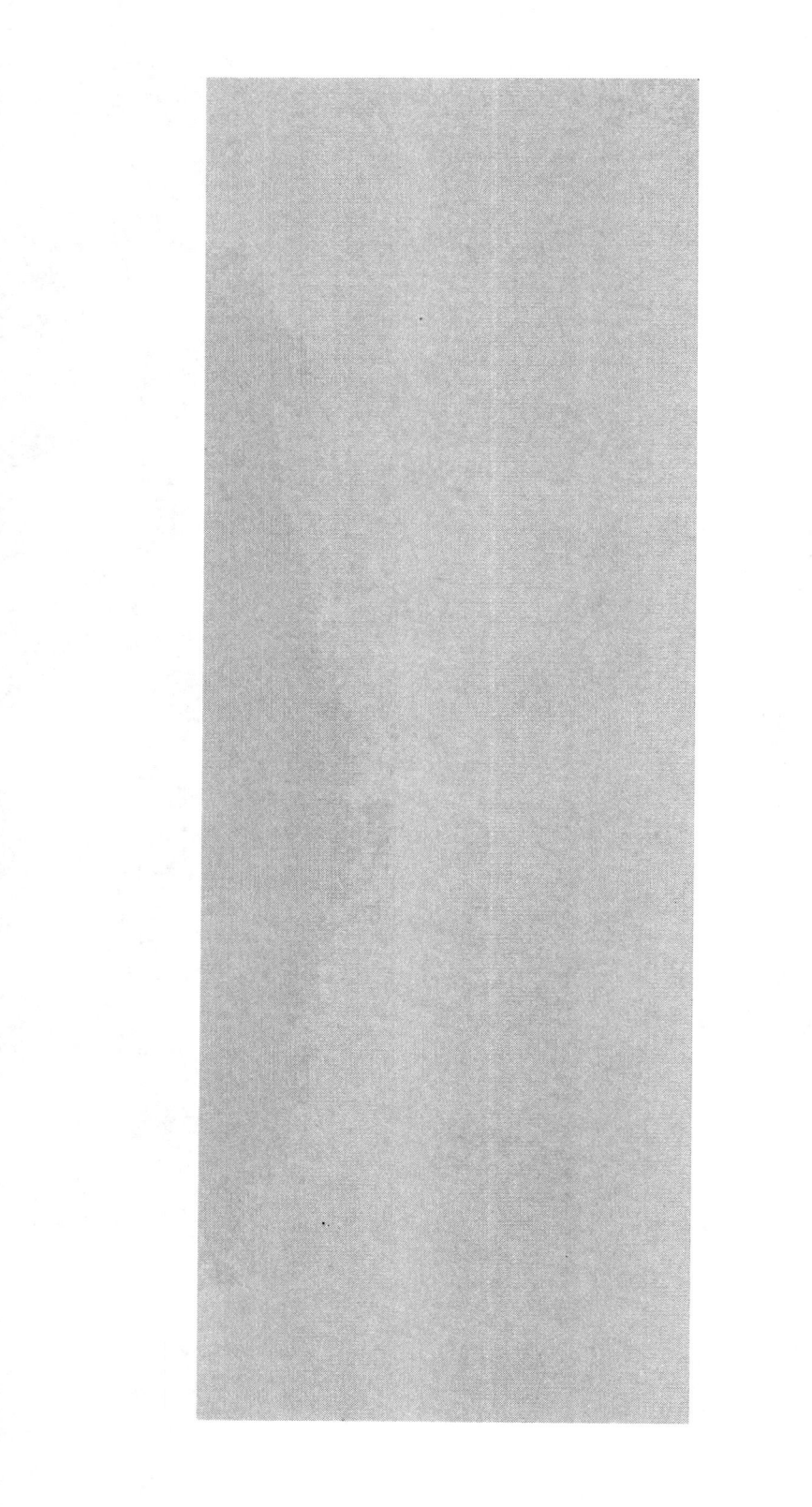

Civil War Tokens
AND
Tradesmen's Store Cards

A tentative list of the Civil War tokens, and store cards issued by the merchants of the United States, and used as money during the period from 1861 to 1864.

George Hetrich, M. D.
Birdsboro, Pa.

Julius Guttag
16-18 Exchange Place
New York City

1924

THE small coins, known to collectors as tokens, issued during the Civil War, have been neglected in the past, and have not received the attention of the collectors which they deserve. They represent a very important period of the history of our country, and should receive more attention from the American collectors for this reason, if for no other. It seems that the main reason for this neglect has been due to the lack of an adequate list of the different varieties printed in a convenient form, and the compilers trust this want the present volume will fill.

A little attention given these coins will repay the collector. An interest in these pieces is soon aroused and easily maintained, and it will not be very long before one discovers that the addition of a new variety to his collection will be attended with as much satisfaction as the acquisition of a new variety of the more pretentious series of United States coins.

Early in 1862 all metallic currency was gradually withdrawn from circulation. Citizens, anticipating the possible increase in value of all metals, commenced hoarding gold, silver and even copper to such an extent that in a short time there were no metallic coins of any denomination in circulation. Tradesmen were thus forced to issue a medium that would supply the place of small coins, and the first of these coins issued on account of the lack of the proper Government currency made their appearance in Cincinnati in the Fall of 1862. In the Spring of 1863 New York followed this example. The first to be made in New York was the Lindenmueller currency, of which a million pieces were struck. William H. Bridgens, the die-cutter, then issued the Knickerbocker currency, which consisted of numerous varieties, and were struck in large quantities.

The issue of similar pieces became general throughout the Eastern and Middle Western States, until it was estimated that not less than 25,000,000 of these private tokens were in general circulation, which must have included between seven and eight thousand varieties.

These little coins filled the wants of the trades-people, and were accepted as a means of exchange for the value, which usually was one cent. They undoubtedly were a source of great relief and convenience; but their irresponsible character soon attracted the attention of the Federal Authorities. It is said that the Third Avenue Railroad of New York requested Lindenmueller to redeem a large number of his tokens, which they had accepted in the course of business, but this he laughingly refused to do. The railroad had no redress, and it is not improbable that incidents of this character forced the Government to put a stop to their issue. This was done by the passage of an act of Congress in 1864, forbidding private individuals to issue any form of money.

The work of preparing such a list of tokens issued between 1861 and 1864, inclusive, is of such a magnitude that it is preposterous to think of being able to get a complete list on the first effort; nor is it within the bounds of reason to think that no errors have crept in this work. For such errors the compilers ask the indulgence of the collectors, and request that they be notified if any errors are found. The compilers further wish the collectors to assist them in making any future edition more complete, by notifying them of any new varieties that may be found in their collections.

The first attempt to print a list of these coins was made by the 'Coin Collectors Journal' during 1882 and 1883, and was chiefly founded on the Groh collection, now the property of The American Numismatic Society of New York, which no doubt is the largest collection of these coins ever brought together. This list was made the basis upon which Mr. Edgar H. Adams performed that monumental work, the results of which he published in the 'Coin & Metal Bulletin' from April, 1916, to March, 1917. This Bulletin was unfortunately discontinued before the complete list was published. Through the courtesy of Mr. Adams the present compilers were privileged to freely use his manuscript, and by adding such varieties as were found in their private collections they are able to present to the collectors of this series a list, which we hope will be an assistance, and trust give an impetus to the collecting of these coins.

Much assistance has been rendered by several collectors of these tokens, and the compilers take this opportunity to express their appreciation to Waldo C. Moore and Howland Wood, to whose efforts the Ohio series owes its completeness; besides the unselfish devotion of Francis A. Livingstone has materially added to the completeness of the remainder of the list. The splendid plates that show the different dies used in compiling this list represent the individual work of Edgar H. Adams.

This list should be self-explanatory, but to assist the amateur collector it should only be necessary to say that the compilers have left sufficient space to the left of the number column, so that a collector can check such varieties as he may find in his individual collection; the first column gives the number of the coin, by which number this coin should hereafter be identified; the second column gives the die number of obverse in the token list, or it gives the inscription on the obverse of the store cards, and these inscriptions are all lined or spaced, for collectors will find several coins of the same series with the same inscription, but differently spaced. This method will give collectors the means by which they can differentiate these coins and give them their proper number; the third column either gives the number of the reverse die, or describes the inscription found on reverse, which is also spaced. The fourth column describes the variety of the metal, and the fifth column describes the character of the edge—plain or reeded. All tokens have plain edges with the exception of three varieties, but among the store cards there are about as many reeded as plain edges.

The abbreviations used are the same as found in all numismatic works:

C^1—Copper
Br—Brass
N^2—Nickel
C-N—Copper Nickel
W-M—White Metal
G—Gold
S—Silver
L^3—Lead
Z—Zinc

(1) The compilers include under the head of Copper that metal which previous authors have designated under the title of Composition.

(2) The German Silver metals are included under Nickel, for the compilers find that medallists and collectors differ among themselves in differentiating between these two metals.

(3) Some of the New York series of tokens and store cards are struck in a dark metal, which we have designated under Lead.

ERRATA

When the collector receives this list, kindly make the following corrections, before assorting his collection according to this book:

Change the reverse die of Nos. 1 and 2 to No. 143 instead of No. 147.

Change the reverse die of Nos. 784 and 785 to No. 346 instead of No. 342.

Change reverse die of No. 4940 to 427 instead of 327.

Change obverse of No. 5189 to read "Cafe Autenreith/85/Chatham/St/N-Y/1863."

√ Change reverse die of No. 5194 to 180 instead of 178.

Change reverse die of No. 5196 to 291 instead of 290.

Change reverse die of No. 5196 to 293 instead of 291.

Change reverse die of No. 5240 to 645 instead of 336.

Change reverse die of No. 5498 to 645 instead of 336.

Change reverse die of No. 5774 to 645 instead of 336.

Change the obverse of 6089 to read—'right hand sceptre points to 'G' of 'agent' instead of 'left hand.'

Change reverse die of No. 6201 to 274 instead of 'same.'

Change reverse die of No. 6345 to No. 403 instead of 404.

Change reverse die of No. 10416 to 535 instead of 435.

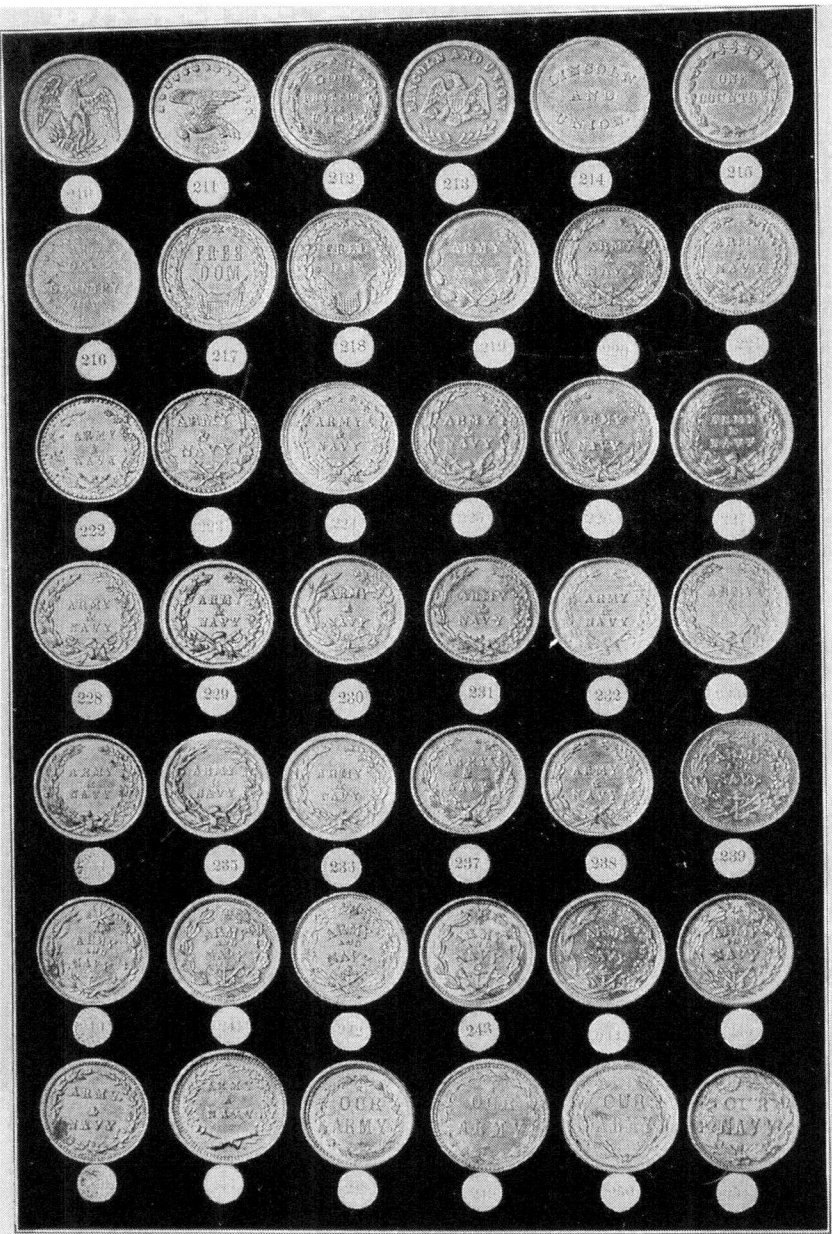

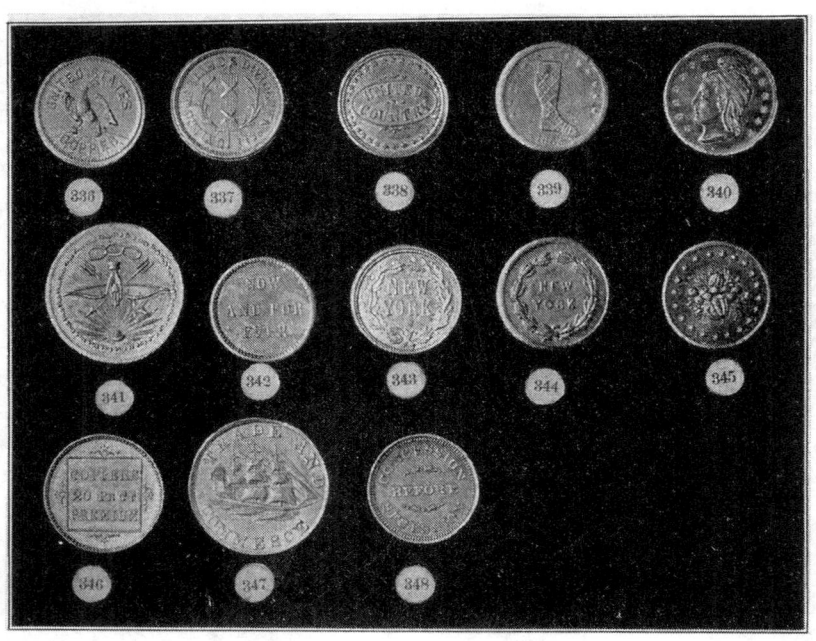

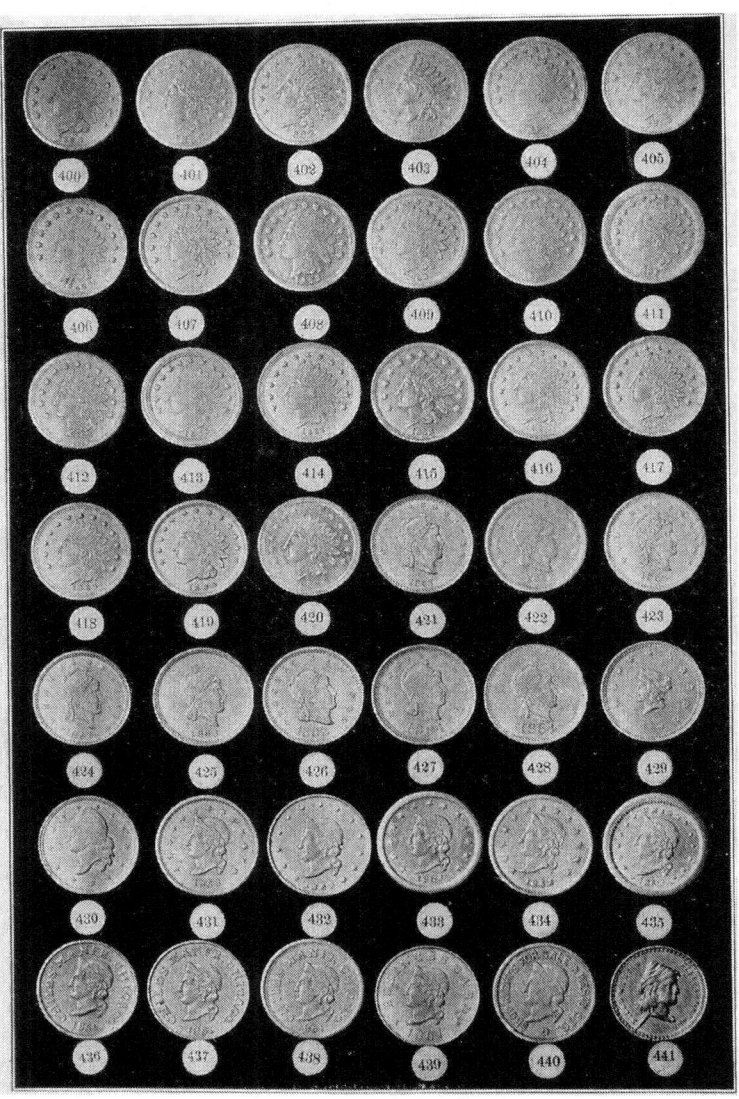

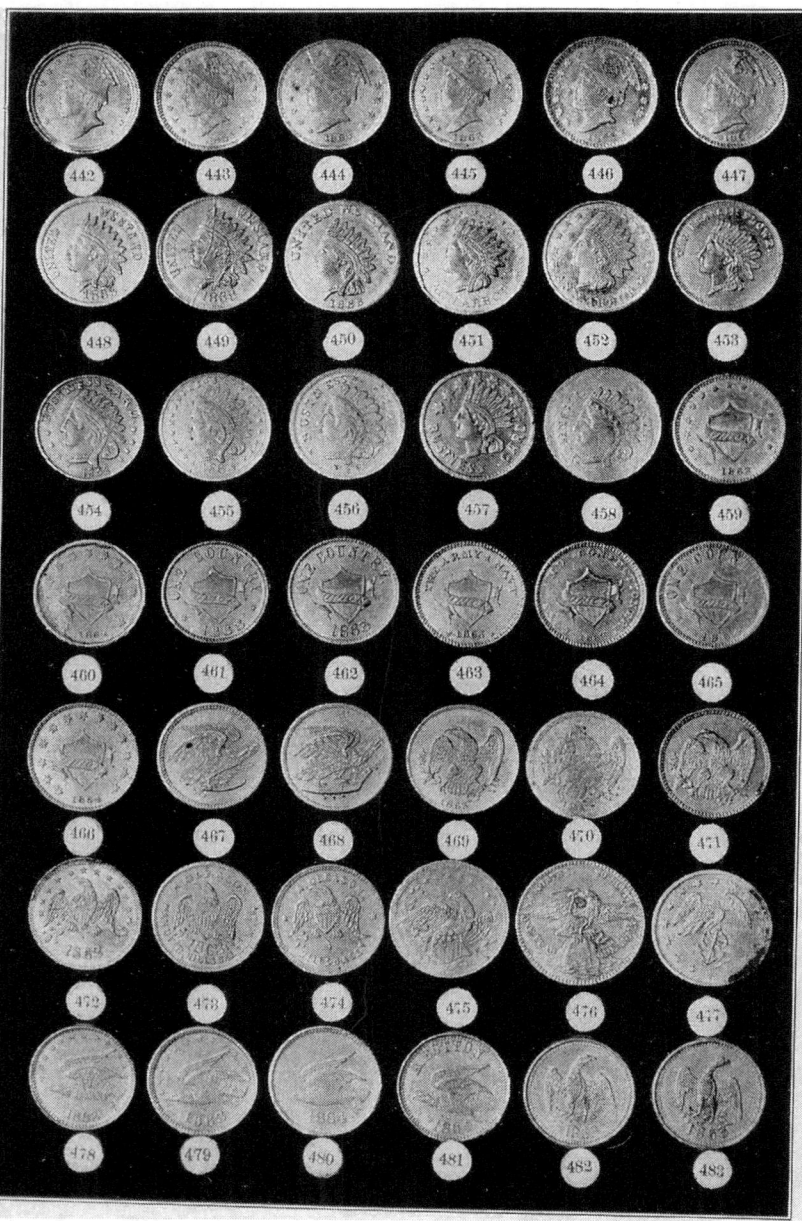

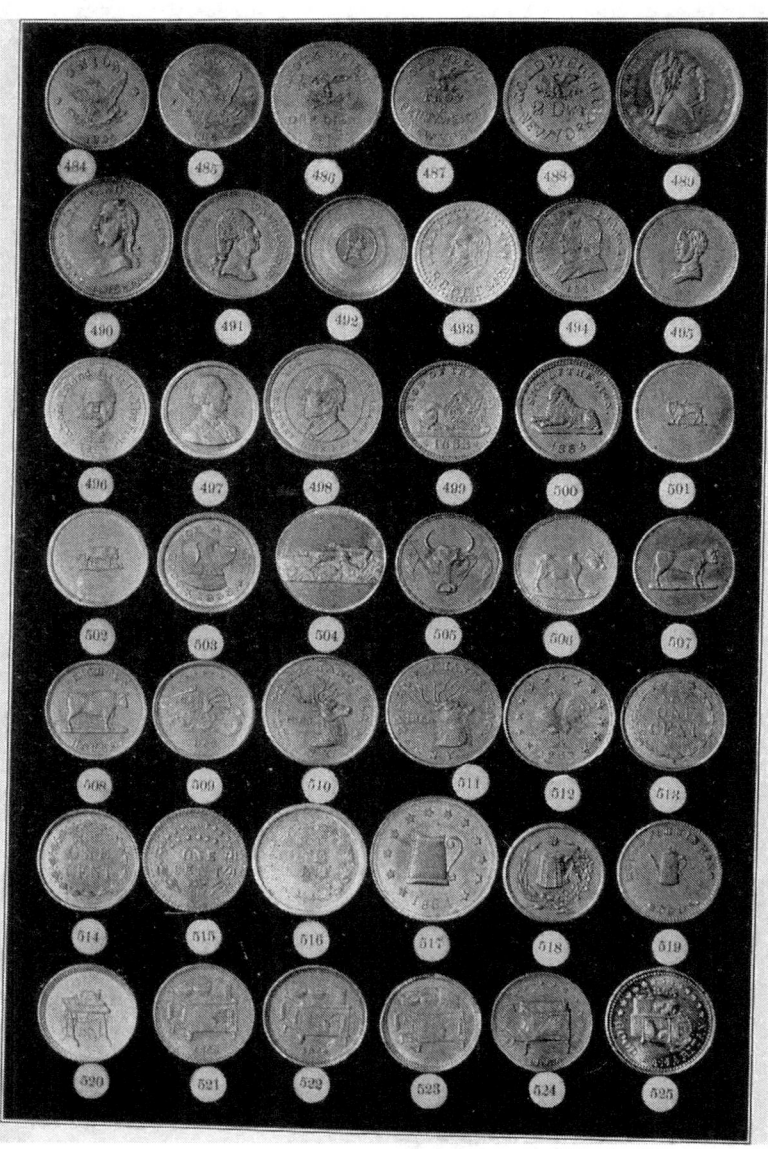

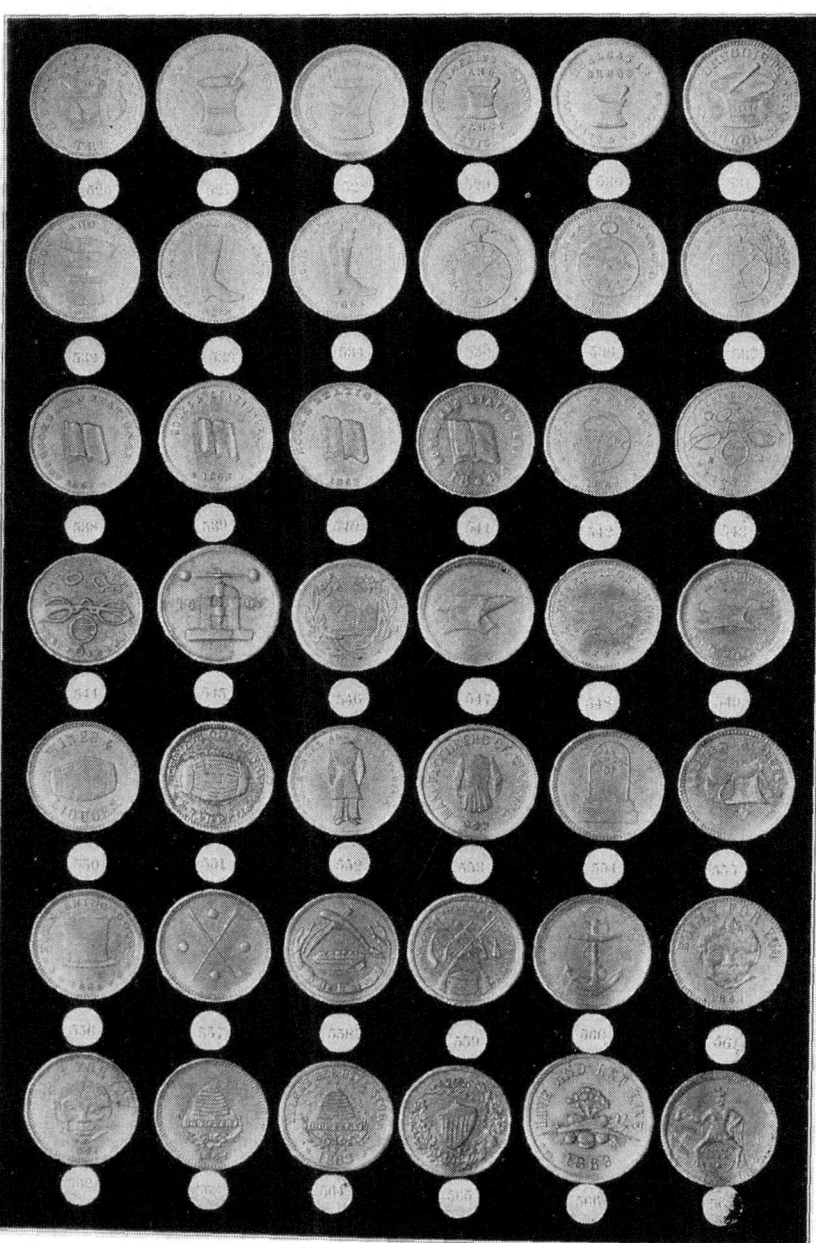

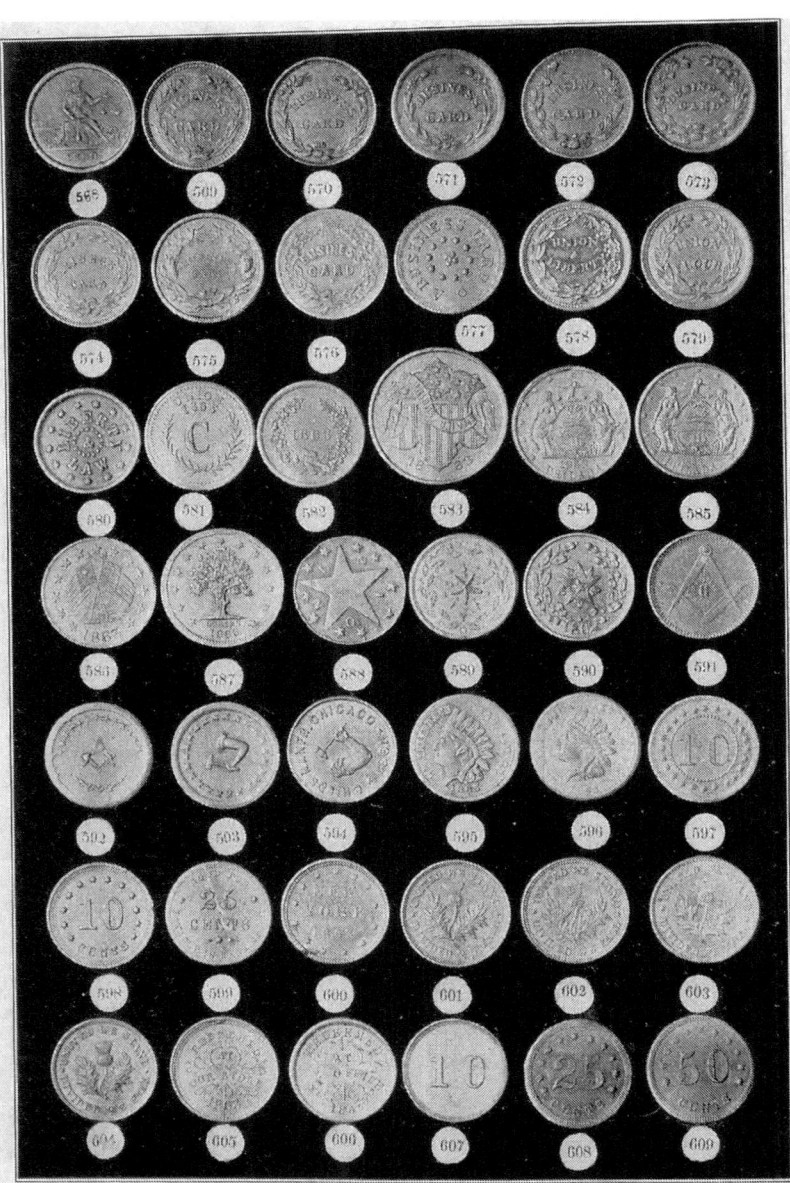

Reprinted from
Numismatic Scrapbook Magazine
October, 1954

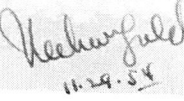

Subject Index of Adam's Photographs in Hetrich and Guttag "Civil War Tokens and Tradesman's Cards"

By

GEORGE FULD, Cambridge 39, Mass.

MELVIN FULD, Baltimore 9, Md.

EDWARD H. DAVIS, Waterbury 10, Conn.

The elaborate listing of Civil War pieces in Hetrich-Guttag is in two series: Patriotic Tokens and Store Cards.

Numbers 1 up to 1342 cover patriotic tokens with their obverse and reverse numbers being indicated by an independent set of numbers, from 1 up to 672, which are shown in photographs done by Edgar H. Adams. It is with this series of photographs that this article deals. The symbols are both patriotic (including portraits) and commercial. The inscriptions are mainly patriotic but include some commercial (Tradesman, Masonic, Wilson, Walker, Street & Number, Child's, Thierbach, Business Card, etc.) From numbers 2001 up to 10,506, store cards are covered—some with a token symbol on one side, and others with commercial symbols on both sides.

When the photographs were originally taken, Hetrich & Guttag intended numbers 1 through 348 to be the obverses and reverses of the patriotic series and those numbered 400 through 613 to be of the store card series. Subsequently, however, as Hetrich & Guttag did more research on their listings, they found other tokens unknown originally, so additional Adams numbers 614 to 672 were included as photographs of these new varieties. This new series threw like subjects out of chronological order, and consequently the reader finds it necessary to look in several places for a given obverse and/or reverse.

There has never been published (to our knowledge) an index of these Adam's photographs, and this present undertaking deals with the photographs as originally printed and includes no varieties found since 1923. The senior authors of this article are currently preparing a new set of photographs including all new varieties, and would appreciate hearing from anyone who has any new varieties, so that the new listing may be as complete as possible.

H. & G. — Index of Photos (Adams)
Subject Index

The master subjects are basically:
 (a) Designs as first preferred,—listed under 4 classes, namely: Animals, Objects, Patriotic Symbols and Persons: usually with legend.
 (b) Dates — major legend, with or without design.
 (c) Numerals — major legend, with or without design or inscription.
 (d) Legends only, without design except incidental decoration.
 (e) Supplement in Tables — Indian Head, Liberty Head.

Store cards are mainly listed under objects and in tables.

Procedure:

In general, observe the coin first for the chief distinguishing mark,—in terms of the Master Subjects listed above. Then turn to that in the index and note the secondary feature.

In the Tables:

For Indian Head and Liberty Head—the simplest proceedure is as follows:

Note general sub-classification:
 For Indian: Feathered Crown, Feathered Headdress
 For Liberty: Head Band (Fillet), Liberty Cap, Winged Hat
 1. Check direction of facing. (All Indians are Left.)
 2. Look for Legend (on obverse). Locate in Table, check for Date and/or Stars.
 3. If no legend, look for Date. Then check for Stars.
 4. If no legend, or Date, look for Stars.

An asterisk (*) indicates that a date is given on the coin.

Animals

Bull 502
Cock (to L) *512
Dog (to R) *503
 Good for a scent
Eagle .. *116-*18, 119-120, 208-10
 *211, 213, 336, 467-68, *469,
 470-71, *472-*73, 474-477,
 *478-*88, *614, *639-41, *643,
 645, 654, *657, *670
Lion (to L) 501
Lion, Sign of (to L) *500
Lion, Sign of (to R) *499
Ox (to R) 506-7
Ox Brighton House 508
Ox head & flag 505
Sea Horse (to L) *509
Serpent - Beware *307
Sporting design with 2
 pointer dogs 504
Staghead (to R)
 Exchange P. *510-511

Dates

1863 329
1863 wreath, anchor
 X cannon 327-28
1863 in wreath 582

Numerals

1 Cent - Good for	302-03
1 - I O U	610
1 - Wilson Medal	306
5 cents	664
8 Sign of the	*624
10	607
10 in ring	597
10 Cents - in ring	598
25 Cents - in star ring	608
25 Cents - Good for	599
50 Cents - in star ring	609

Legends (Lettered — with no Object or Symbol — except Incidental Decoration)

All Work Warranted	*536
America wreath	324
Ann Arbor	451-52, 531
Apoth. weight — one dram	*486
Army & Navy wreath	221, 246
wreath anchor X swords	239-45
wreath X cannon	247
wreath X swords	219-38
Army & Navy, The — Shield & Union	*463
B & K	545
Beware	*307
Books and Stationery	*538-*541
Boots and Shoes made to Order	533, *534
Brighton House	508
Bully for you	*561-*62
Business Card	84, 439, *454-55, 456, *457, 458
Business Card — wreath	*569, 570-76, 637-8, 655
(surrounded by stars)	577
Button, A. Flying Eagle	*481
C L R wreath; anchor; X swords	331
Childs Mfgr. Chicago	436-38, *594, *612-*13, *618
Child's One Penny Barrel	551
Concession before Secession	348
Constitution — Scroll	*192
Constitution and the Union	260
Constitution for ever	176-77
Constitution - It must, etc.	314
Copper 20%	346
Dealers in Drugs, Hardware & Saddlery	530
Dix — If anybody, etc.	317-23
Drugs & Medicine	528
Drugs & Medicines	*532
Druggists — Ann Arbor	531
Dry Goods, Groceries & C	*619
E Pluribus Unum	*583
Excelsior	558
22 & 23 Exchange Place, N.Y.	*510-*11
Exchange wreath	326
Federal Union, The — It must	*133-34, 158-64
For Our Country Common Cause	105
For Public Accommodation	29
Freedom-wreath shield flags	217-18
Furnishing Goods	556
Gleason, A. Manfr. Hillsdale, Mich.	*639
God protect the Union — wreath	212
Gold Weight Troy & 2 Penny Weight	487
Gold Weight 2 DWT	488
Good for 25 Cents payable in Bank Bills	599
Good for a Scent	*503
Good Samaritan	*525, *636
Hardware and Tools	549
Hardware Dealer	*542
Hardware, Iron Stoves	548
Hero of Pea Ridge	135
Horrors of War Blessing of Peace	*187
Horter	*587
House Furnishing Goods	519
If anybody — see "Dix"	
Industry	*138
Industry-Bee hive	*563-*64
Iron, Nails and Glass — Hardware Dealer	*542
Knickerbocker Currency	186
Lager Beer	567
Liberty	*34-*37
Liberty and No Slavery	28
Liberty in wreath	*170-71
Liberty & Law	580

Lincoln and Union — Eagle	213
Lincoln and Union	214
Little Mack	109
Live and Let Live	*566
McClellan— Medal for One Cent	304
Manufacture of Clothing	553
Military Necessity	332
Millions — see One Cent Not — also Indianhead	
Millions for Contractors	81
Money makes the Mare go	*185
New York — stars	*600
New York — wreath	343-44
New York — shield	*145
No Compromise with Traitors	335
No North No South	476
North Star — star	182
Not One Cent—See One Cent	
Now and Forever	342
O K — 13 link ring	181
One Cent — wreath	194
One Cent — shield	193, 195
One Cent — Good for	302-03
One Cent — Good in shield	147
One Cent — I O U	300-01, 610
One Cent — Medal	304-05
One Cent — Not—stars	515
One Cent — Not—wreath	268-96, 516, 653
One Cent — shield	515
One Cent — Not (L. Roloff)	290-01, 513-14
One Cent — Not —for Tribute	297-98
One Cent — Not —for the widow	299
One Cent — Pay the bearer	*196
One Country	155-57, 215-16 *416, *462
One Country — Shield	*465
One Dime — see Patriotic Symbols, Eagle	
Our Army — Eagle	119, 120
Our Army wreath	248-50
Our Card wreath	205-07
Our Cent	195
Our Country wreath shield	165-67
(See also Union on shield)	

Our Little Monitor	172-73
Our Navy — wreath	251-53
Our Union — shield	198-99
Our Union — wreath shield	*146
Pay the Bearer One Cent	*196
Peace clasped hands	325
Peace maker — cannon	*126
Penny saved is	133
Perfumes, Notions & Fancy Articles	529
Periscopic Spectales	543-44, 625-26
Philda	*584
Philda Jacobus	*585
Pistols, Guns, Rifles & C. Made & Repaired	559
Pluribus — see E Pluribus	
Prescriptions Accurately Compounded	527
Pro Bono — Shield & Star	*140
Proclaim Liberty	315-16
Pure Copper	616
Quick Sales and Small Profits	552
Redeemed at	*605-06
Redeemed — Face	493
Reinnerung of 1863	*180
Remembranct of 1863	*178, *180
Remembrance War of 1861-2-3	*179
Saddles, Bridles	555
Shop Rights for Sale	440
Sigel, F	135-136
Sign of the Lion	*499, *500
Sign of the 8	*624
Silver Mine Token E	654
The Prairie Flower	453
The Triumph	*526
W. Thierbach, 142 Elm St.	*595, *596
Time is Money	*137
Toys & Confectionery, Shield & Union	*464
Trade & Commerce	191, & 347
Trademan Currency	147
Tylers' Beehive Store	*564
Union — See also Objects, Stars; also Patriotic, Eagle, Shield	
Union	*25-*27, 435 *620, *627, *641
Union — across shield	*459-66

Union and Liberty 82
Union — Eagle ... *116, *484-485
Union Flour 579
Union For Ever 645
Union for Ever — shield ... *256
                          *257, *258
Union Forever wreath
   X swords 200-01
Union Forever wreath
   shield 202-03
Union on shield 121-22
Union-shield 123
Union within Star 588
Union-wreath 330
Union-wreath C *581
Union, The — wreath 197
Union, The Federal
   It Must etc. *133-34
Union, The Forever — wreath
   X swords 204
Union, The God protect —
   wreath 212
Union, The Liberty wreath 578
Union, The Must and
   shall be preserved ... 106-07
Union, The Must and
   shall — Jackson 310-13
United Country 338
United States—Capitol *168, *169
United States Copper —
   Eagle 336
United States of
   America *141-*142, *143-*144
United we stand divided
   we fall 38, 83, 337, 441,
          448-50, 601-04, 648-50
Value me as you please —
   wreath 334
Watches and Jewelry
   Repaired 537
Wilon Medal 1 306
Wines & Liquors 550

Objects (Chiefly Store Cards)
Anchor 560
Anchor X Cannon *327, *328
Anvil 547-49
Arm & Hammer in Star ring 593
Arm & Hammer — Child's .. *594
Barrel 550-51
Basket in star ring 345
Bee hive *138, *563-64
Beer Mug in star ring *517
Beer Mug wreath 518
Billiard balls & cues 557
Book *538-41
Boot 533-*34
Cannon crossed *128
Cannon (to R)
   flag Peace Maker *127
Cannon (to L)
   stars balls *124
Cannon (to R)
   flag Peace Maker *126
Cannon (to L)
   flag Peace Maker 125
Clasped Hands 325
Clock — see Watch
Clothes — see Suit
Coat of Arms — Philada *584-85
Coffee Pot — see Tea Pot
Cup in double star — large 651
Denture 558
Eye (with rays) 3 links
   on IOOF symbol 341
Eye glass — see Spectacles
Flower in wreath *590
Forceps — see Denture
Fruit 345
Fruit — Live & let live *566
Guns and Pistols — crossed 599
Hat *556
Hose — see Sock
Masonic — see Square
Monitor 172-773, *174-75
Monument — wreath 630-31
Mortar & Pestle *532, 527-31, 623
Mug — see Beer Mug, Cup
Musket — see Gun
Padlock *542
Philada Ct. of arms *584-85
Pistol — see Gun
Press 545
Pumpkin — see Basket
Rifle — see Gun
Saddle 555
Scales 546
Scroll — Constitution *192
Sewing Machine 520
Shield — Union
   through it *459-*466

Ship 191, 347
Sock Surrounded by Stars .. *399
Spectacles 543-44, 625-26
Square & Compass 183, 592
Square & Compass G ... 184, 591
Star in wreath 308-09, 589,
*590, 667
Star in star ring —
  North Star 182
Star in star ring Union 588
Star enclosing shield *140
Star shield with wreath 308
Stocking — see Sock
Stove *521-22, 523, *524
Stove Good Samaritan *525, *636
Stove Triumph *526
Suit of Clothes 552-53
Tea Pot 519
Teeth — see Denture
Thistle 601-04
Tombstone 554
Tree *587
Vegetable — see Fruit
Warrior *157
Watch 535, *536, 537

Patriotic Symbols
Capitol *168-69
Columbia - seated (to L) *189-90
Eagle anchor star ring 477
Eagle (to R) on Cannon *118
Eagle Flying (to L) *117, *478-80
Eagle Flying (to L)
  A Button *481
Eagle Flying (to R) .. *657, *670
Eagle Flying stars (front) *211
Eagle Gold Weight (to R) 487-88
Eagle on Globe—
  Union Forever 645
Eagle on Globe—
  U.S. Copper 336
Eagle on Shield (to R) .. 467-68
Eagle on Shield (to L) 475
Eagle on Shield
  with streamer *141-44
Eagle over Shield —
  wreath — Union 121-22, *123
Eagle Serpent No North
  No South 476
Eagle Spread *469-70, 471

Eagle Spread Gleason .. *473-74,
*639
Eagle Spread One Dram .. *486
Eagle Spread Our Army .. 119-20
Eagle Spread Silver
  Mine Token 654
Eagle Spread Stars .. *116, *472,
*611, *640, *643
Eagle Spread Union ... *208-09,
*494-85, *614, *641
Eagle Standing — Spread .. 210,
482-83
Fasces 337
Flag(s)
  Crossed *586
  Crossed with rays — Union *139
  Stand of guns 262, *263
  Stand of guns
    liberty cap & Cannon 264-67
  Stand by the Flag *154
  The Flag of etc. .. *148-53, 155
  Wreath 156
Indian Head — see Table at end
  of Index
Justice, seated with scales .. *568
Liberty Head — see Table at end
  of Index
Shield
  Anchor within—New York *145
  E. Pluribus Unum *583
  Flags, liberty cap, wreath 255
  Good for One Cent 147
  in Star *140
  in Star ring *254
  in Star in wreath 308
  in wreath 261
  in wreath Constitution ... 260
  Our Union 146
  Union — see legends, Union
    across shield with Streamers
      *141-44
  Tradesmens Currency 147
  Union — star 259
  Union for ever *256-58
  Union One Country—
    see Legends
  Union in wreath 565
Persons — (note Unspecified below)
Bell, John of Tennessee
  (to L) 498

Burnside, General (Front) Rhode Id First		496
Douglas, Stephen, (to L)		115
Franklin (to L)		*494
Franklin (to R)		114
Grant (to L)		113
Greeley — see Seymour		
Jackson, — The Union Must (to L)		106-07
"Knickerbocker" — standing (to L)		*185-186
"Knickerbocker" — sword (to R)		188
Lincoln (to R) Abraham		104
Lincoln - name - (to L)		495
Lincoln & Union		214
Lincoln & Union eagle		213
Lincoln President (to L)		*100
Lincoln Redeemed (to L)		493
Lincoln with stars (to L)		*102
Lincoln with stars (to R)		*103
Lincoln The First in (to L)		*101
Mercury - see Table - Liberty Head		
McClellan (to L)	108, *109-10,	111
McClellan Medal (to R)		112
McClellan For our Country (to L)		105
(Roman Warrior) (to L)		157
Seymour - small - (to R)		497
Sigel (to L)		135-36
Washington bust (to R)		658
Washington Dry Goods & Groceries (to R)		*619
Washington in circle (to R)		492
Washington with name (to R)		491
Washington Pater Patriae (to L)		94
Washington Born — quarter (to L)		95
Washington (Large) President (to L)		490
Washington (Large) President (to R)		489
Washington in Star in Circle		87
Washington with stars (to R)		88, *89-93
Washington with stars and flags (to R)		*96-7
Washington with stars and wreath (to R)		*98
Washington United We Stand (to R)		*648
Washington Mounted Standing (to L)		*129-32
Washington Token (to R)		*99
Unspecified		
Face (to L)		495
Face (to R) (supposedly Seymour)		497
Face front, Bully for you		*561-62
Face front Horrors of War		187
Head (to R)		441
Person Mounted, horse rearing (to L)		*133-34
Person Mounted, horse Exigency (to R)		137
Person Sitting on cask		567

TABLE — LIBERTY HEAD

Face	Head Dress	Style Head Band	Legend	Date	Star	Number	Note
L	Head Band	IIII	Business Card	*		439	SC
L	Head Band	Plain	Childs Manuf'r.			436-38, 612-13	SC
L	Head Band	IIII	Childs Manuf'r.	*		618	
L	Head Band	Plain	Shop Rights for Sale			440	
L	Head Band	IIII	Union	*	*	25-27	
L	Head Band	Plain	Union	*	*	435, 620, 627	
L	Head Band	IIII		*	*	21, 431, 433-34, 628, 632-44	
L	Head Band	Plain		*	*	20, 432, 633	
L	Head Band	IIII			*	429	
R	Head Band	Plain		*	*	33	

TABLE — INDIAN HEAD

Face	Head Dress	Style Head Band	Legend	Date	Star	Number	Note
L	Feather Crown	. . . .		*	*	45-46	
L	Feather Crown	. . . .			*	39-40, 42-44	
L	Feather Crown	: : : :			*	41	
L	Feathered Band	. . .	Ann Arbor		*	451-52	
L	Feathered Band	Stars	Business Card			458	SC
L	Feathered Band	Solid	Business Card	*		84	SC
L	Feathered Band	Stars	Business Card	*		456	SC
L	Feathered Band	Stars	Business Card	*	*	454	SC
L	Feathered Band	IIII	Business Card	*	*	455	SC
L	Feathered Band	Plain	Business Card		*	457	SC
L	Feathered Band	Fort Lafayette	Millions for Contractors	*		81	
L	Feathered Band	Liberty	The Prairie Flower			453	
L	Feathered Band	Plain	W. Thierbach	*		595	SC
L	Feathered Band	Star	W. Thierbach	*		596	SC
L	Feathered Band	. . . . .	Union and Liberty	*		82	
L	Feathered Band	Plain	United We Stand	*		83, 448, 450, 649	
L	Feathered Band	Plain	United We Stand	*		449 shattered die "H" above Date	
L	Feathered Band	Plain	United We Stand	*		650 Shattered	
L	Feathered Band	Solid				85	
L	Feathered Band	Liberty				86	
L	Feathered Band	Liberty		*	*	47, 647 L Roloff Large Size	
L	Feathered Band	Liberty		*	*	58-60, 63-64, 67-68, 400-02, 404-20, 615-17, 622, 629, 634-35, 642, 656, 659-63, 668, 671-72	
L	Feathered Band	Key. Phild.		*	*	80	
L	Feathered Band	-o- -o- -o-		*		61-62	
L	Feathered Band	. . . .		*	*	49-57, 65-66, 646	
L	Feathered Band	: : :		*	*	72	
L	Feathered Band	Stars		*	*	48, 403	
L	Feathered Band	ΛΛΛΛ		*	*	69	
L	Feathered Band	Plain		*	*	70-71, 73-78, 652, 655-56, 669	

TABLE — LIBERTY CAP

Face	Head Dress	Style Head Band	Legend	Date	Star	Number
L	Liberty Cap	Stars	Liberty	*		29
R	Liberty Cap	Plain	For Public Accomodation	*	*	34-37
L	Liberty Cap	Plain	Liberty and No Slavery	*		28
L	Liberty Cap	Braid		*	*	11
L	Liberty Cap	Plain		*	*	7, 10
L	Liberty Cap	Stars		*	*	1-6, 8-9, 13-19, 22-24
L	Liberty Cap	Plain			*	340
L	Liberty Cap	Stars			*	430
R	Liberty Cap	Plain	United We Stand Divided We Fall	*		38
R	Liberty Cap	Plain	United We Stand, etc.			441
R	Liberty Cap	Braid		*		425, 428
R	Liberty Cap	Braid		*	*	421-24, 426-42
R	Liberty Cap	Plain		*	*	31-32
L	Winged Hat			*	*	30, 443-46, 621
L	Winged Hat				*	442
L	Winged Hat			*		447

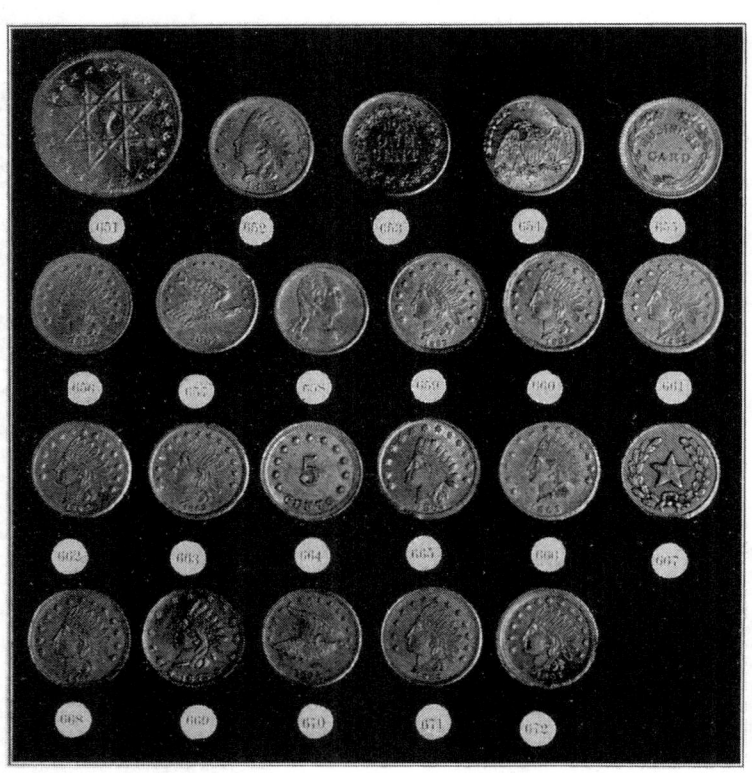

CIVIL WAR TOKENS

Check	Number	Obverse	Reverse	Metal	Remarks
	1	1	143	C	
	2	1	143	Br	
	3				
	4				
	5				
	6				
—	7	1	165	C	
	8	1	165	Br	
	9	1	165	N	
	10	1	165	C-N	
	11	1	165	W-M	
	12	1	165	S	
	13				
	14	1	274	C	
	15	1	274	Br	
	16	1	274	N	
	17				
	18	1	274	W-M	
	19				
—	20	1	301	C	
	21	1	301	Br	
	22	1	301	N	
	23	1	301	C-N	
	24	1	301	W-M	
	25	1	301	L	
	26	1	301	S	
	27				
—	28	1	338	C	
	29	1	338	Br	
	30	1	338	N	
	31	1	338	C-N	
	32	1	338	W-M	
	33	1	338	S	
	34				
	35	2	204	Br	
	36				
	37	3	268	L	
	38				
—	39	4	212	C	
—	40	4	212	Br	
	41	4	212	N	
	42				
	43	5	5	C	Obverse incused
	44				
—	45	5	200	C	
	46				
	47	5	201	C	
	48				
—	49	5	227	C	
	50				

Check	Number	Obverse	Reverse	Metal	Remarks
—	51	5	228	C	
	52				
—	53	5	229	C	
	54				
	55	5	232	C	
	56				
—	57	5	233	C	
	58				
—	59	5	234	C	
	60				
—	61	5	235	C	
	62				
—	63	5	236	C	
	64				
	65	6	152	C	
	66				
—	67	6	221	C	
—	68	6	221	C	Obverse die break
—	69	6	221	C	Reverse die break
	70	6	221	Br	
	71				
—	72	6	231	C	
	73				
—	74	6	314	C	
	75	6	314	Br	
	76				
	77	6	315	C	
	78				
	79	6	316	C	
—	80	6	334	C	
—	81	7	220	C	
—	82				
—	83	8	238	C	
	84	8	238	Br	
	85	8	238	N	
	86	8	238	C-N	
	87	8	238	W-M	
	88	8	238	S	
	89				
—	90	9	223	C	
	91				
	92	9	267	C	
	93				
—	94	10	298	C	
	95				
—	96	11	223	C	
	97				
—	98	11	252	C	
	99				
—	100	11	267	C	
	101				
—	102	12	306	C	
—	103	12	306	Br	
	104				

Check	Number	Obverse	Reverse	Metal	Remarks
—	105	13	224	C	
	106	13	224	Br	
	107				
	108	13	237	C	
	109				
—	110	13	295	C	
	111	13	295	Br	
	112				
—	113	14	220	C	
	114				
—	115	15	220	C	
	116				
—	117	16	325	C	
	118				
—	119	16	343	C	
	120	16	343	Br	
	121				
—	122	17	202	C	
	123				
	124	17	202	N	
	125	17	202	C-N	
	126				
·	127				
—	128	17	225	C	
	129	17	225	Br	
	130	17	225	N	
	131				
	132	17	225	W-M	
	133				
—	134	18	179	C	
	135	18	179	Br	
	136				
	137	19	Blank	C	
	138				
	139	19	19	C	Obverse incused
	140				
	141	19	194	C-N	Obverse struck over a C-N cent
	142				
—	143	19	325	C	
	144				
	145	19	325	N	
	146				
	147	20	209	C	
	148				
—	149	21	206	C	
	150				
—	151	22	279	C	
	152				
—	153	23	224	C	
	154	23	224	Br	
	155				
—	156	24	224	C	
	157	24	224	Br	
	158				

Check	Number	Obverse	Reverse	Metal	Remarks
	159	25	206	C	
	160				
	161	26	206	C	
	162				
—	163	26	207	C	
	164				
	165	26	208	C	
	166				
—	167	27	197	C	
	168				
—	169	27	205	C	
	170				
	171	27	207	C	
	172				
	173	27	208	C	
	174				
—	175	28	202	C	
	176				
—	177	28	255	C	
	178	28	255	Br	
	179				
	180				
	181	28	255	S	
	182				
	183	28	355	C	
	184				
	185	29	29	C	Obverse incused
	186				
—	187	29	186	C	
	188				
—	189	29	187	C	
	190				
—	191	29	336	C	
—	192	29	336	Br	
	193	29	336	N	
	194	29	336	C-N	
	195	29	336	W-M	
	196	29	336	S	
	197				
	198	30	340	C	
	199				
—	200	31	252	C	
	201				
—	202	32	251	C	
	203	32	251	Br	
	204				
	205	32	251	C-N	
	206	32	251	W-M	
	207	32	251	S	
	208				
	209	33	297	C	
	210				
—	211	33	298	C	
	212				

Check	Number	Obverse	Reverse	Metal	Remarks
—	213	34	264	C	
	214				
—	215	35	248	C	
	216				
	217				
—	218	35	248	C-N	
	219				
	220				
—	221	36	250	C	
	222	36	250	Br	
	223	36	250	N	
	224	36	250	C-N	
	225	36	250	W-M	
	226	36	250	S	
	227				
—	228	36	254	C	
	229	36	254	Br	
	230	36	254	N	
	231	36	254	C-N	
	232	36	254	W-M	
	233	36	254	S	
	234				
—	235	37	248	C	
	236	37	248	Br	
	237				
	238	37	248	C-N	
	239	37	248	W-M	
	240	37	248	S	
	241				
	242	38	38	C	Obverse incused
	243				
—	244	38	222	C	
	245				
—	246	39	258	C	
	247				
	248	39	258	C-N	
	249				
—	250	40	250	C	
	251				
	252	40	257	C	
	253	40	257	Br	
	254	40	257	N	
	255	40	257	C-N	
	256	40	257	W-M	
	257				
—	258	41	249	C	
	259	41	249	Br	
	260	41	249	N	
	261	41	249	C-N	
	262	41	249	W-M	
	263				
—	264	41	257	C	
	265	41	257	Br	
	266	41	257	N	

Check	Number	Obverse	Reverse	Metal	Remarks
—	267	41	257	C-N	over US cent
	268	41	257	W-M	
	269	41	257	S	Struck over a U. S. dime
	270				
	271	42	219	C	
	272	42	219	Br	
	273	42	219	N	
	274	42	219	C-N	
	275	42	219	W-M	
	276				
	277	42	250	C	
	278	42	250	Br	
	279	42	250	N	
	280	42	250	C-N	
	281	42	250	W-M	
	282				
—	283	42	257	C	
	284				
—	285	42	333	C	
	286	42	333	Br	
	287	42	333	N	
	288	42	333	C-N	Struck over a C-N cent
	289	42	333	W-M	
	290	42	333	S	Struck over a U. S. dime
	291				
—	292	43	251	C	Die Break
	293	43	251	Br	
	294	43	251	N	
	295	43	251	C-N	Struck over a C-N cent
	296	43	251	W-M	
	297	43	251	S	Struck over a U. S. dime
	298				
—	299	44	134	C	
	300				
—	301	44	250	C	
	302				
	303	44	257	C	
	304				
	305	44	258	C	
	306				
—	307	45	119	C	
	308				
—	309	46	120	C	
	310	46	120	Br	
	311	46	120	N	
	312	46	120	C-N	Struck over a C-N cent
	313	46	120	W-M	
	314				
	315	46	165	C	
	316	46	165	Br	
	317	46	165	N	
	318	46	165	C-N	Struck over a C-N cent
	319	46	165	W-M	
	320	46	165	S	Struck over a U. S. dime

Check	Number	Obverse	Reverse	Metal	Remarks
	321				
	322	46	338	C	
	323	46	338	Br	
	324	46	338	N	
	325	46	338	C-N	Struck over a C-N cent
	326	46	338	W-M	
	327	46	338	S	Struck over a U. S. dime
	328				
—	329	47	341	C	
	330				
—	331	48	296	C	
	332	48	296	Br	
	333				
	334	49	145	C	
	335				
	336				
	337				
	338	49	145	W-M	
	339				
	340	49	260	C	
	341				
	342	49	260	N	
	343	49	260	C-N	Struck over a C-N cent
	344	49	260	W-M	
—	345	49	269		
	346	50	87	C	
	347				
	348				
	349	50	87	C-N	Struck over a C-N cent
	350				
	351				
—	352	50	143	C	
	353				
—	354	50	269	C	
	355				
	356				
	357	50	269	C-N	Struck over a C-N cent
	358				
	359				
	360	51	280	C	
	361				
—	362	51	281	C	
	363				
—	364	52	280	C	
	365				
	366	52	280	N	
	367				
	368				
—	369	52	344	C	
	370				
—	371	53	276	C	
	372				
—	373	54	284	C	
	374				

15

Check	Number	Obverse	Reverse	Metal	Remarks
	375				
	376	55	285	Br	
	377	55	285	N	
	378	55	285	C-N	Struck over a C-N cent
	379	55	285	W-M	
	380				
←	381	56	143	C	
	382				
	383				
	384				
	385	56	143	W-M	
	386				
	387	56	144	C	
	388	56	144	Br	
	389	56	144	N	
	390				
	391				
	392				
	393	56	269	C	
	394				
	395	56	273	C	
	396	56	273	Br	
	397	56	273	N	
	398				
	399				
	400				
	401	56	274	C	
	402	56	274	Br	
	403	56	274	N	
	404				
	405				
	406				
	407	56	283	C	
	408				
←	409	57	283	C	
	410				
	411				
	412	57	283	C-N	Struck over a C-N cent
	413				
	414				
←	415	58	210	C	
	416				
	417	58	345	C	
	418				
	419	59	210	C	
	420				
	421	59	345	C	
	422				
	423	60	68	C	
	424				
	425	60	414	C	
	426				
←	427	61	247	C	
	428				

16

Check	Number	Obverse	Reverse	Metal	Remarks
—	429	62	246	C	
	430				
	431	63	220	C	
	432				
—	433	63	265	C	
	434				
—	435	64	265	C	
	436	64	265	Br	
	437				
—	438	65	265	C	
	439	65	265	Br	
	440				
	441	66	66	C	Obverse incused
	442				
—	443	66	265	C	
	444	66	265	Br	
	445				
—	446	66	266	C	
	447				
—	448	67	196	C	
	449	67	196	Br	
	450				
	451	68	345	C	
	452				
	453	68	495	C	
	454				
	455	69	334	C	
	456				
—	457	70	271	C	
	458	70	271	Br	
	459	70	271	N	
	460				
	461				
—	462	71	270	C	
	463	71	270	Br	
	464				
—	465	72	275	C	
	466				
—	467	73	270	C	
	468				
—	469	74	278	C	
—	470		Die Break		
	471				
	472	74	278	L	
	473				
—	474	75	224	C	
	475				
	476	75	286	C	
	477				
	478	75	335	C	
—	479	75	335	Br	
	480	75	335	N	
	481	75	335	C-N	Struck over a C-N cent
	482	75	335	W-M	

Check	Number	Obverse	Reverse	Metal	Remarks
	483	75	335	S	
	484				
	485	75	337	C	
	486				
	487				
	488				
	489	75	337	W-M	
—	490	75	337	S	
	491				
	492				
	493	76	98	Br	
	494				
	495				
	496	76	98	W-M	
	497				
	498				
	499	76	143	Br	
	500	76	143	N	
	501				
	502	76	143	W-M	
	503				
—	504	76	144	C	
	505	76	144	Br	
	506				
	507	76	144	C-N	Struck over a C-N cent
	508	76	144	W-M	
	509	76	144	S	Struck over a U. S. dime
	510				
	511				
	512				
	513				
	514	76	342	W-M	
	515				
—	516	77	276	C	
	517				
—	518	77	304	C	
	519				
	520	78	277	C	
	521				
	522	79	79	C	Obverse incused
	523				
—	524	79	282	C	
	525				
	526				
	527	79	282	C-N	Struck over a C-N cent
	528				
	529				
	530	80	95	C	
	531	80	95	Br	
	532				
	533				
	534	80	95	W-M	
	535				
	536				

Check	Number	Obverse	Reverse	Metal	Remarks
	537	80	104	Br	
	538				
	539				
	540				
	541				
	542				
	543	80	113	Br	
	544				
	545				
	546	80	113	W-M	
	547				
	548				
—	549	81	299	C	Large planchet-23 M.M.
	550	81	299	C	Smaller planchet-20 M.M.
	551	81	299	Br	
	552				
	553	81	299	C-N	Struck over a C-N cent
	554	81	299	W-M	
	555	81	299	S	Struck over a U. S. dime
	556				
—	557	82	215	C	
	558				
—	559	83	256	C	
	560				
	561	84	195	C	
	562				
	563	85	216	C	
	564				
—	565	85	288	C	
	566				
	567	86	195	C	
	568				
	569	87	143	Br	
	570	87	143	N	
	571				
	572	87	143	W-M	
	573				
	574				
	575				
	576	87	144	N	
	577				
	578	87	144	W-M	
	579				
—	580	87	269	C	
	581				
	582	87	272	C	
	583				
	584				
	585				
	586				
	587				
	588	87	273	W-M	
	589				
	590				

Check	Number	Obverse	Reverse	Metal	Remarks
	591				
	592				
	593				
	594	87	274	W-M	
	595				
—	596	88	335	C	
	597	88	335	Br	
	598	88	335	N	
	599	88	335	C-N	Struck over a C-N cent
	600				
	601	88	335	S	
	602				
	603	89	89	C	Obverse incused
	604	89	89	C	
	605				
	606	89	89	N	
	607	89	89	C-N	
	608				
	609				
—	610	89	146	C	
	611	89	146	Br	
	612				
	613				
	614	89	146	W-M	
	615	89	146	S	
	616				
	617	89	202	Br	
	618				
—	619	89	335	C	
	620	89	335	Br	
	621	89	335	N	
	622	89	335	C-N	
	623	89	335	W-M	
	624				
	625	90	343	C	
	626				
—	627	91	343	C	
	628				
—	629	92	202	C	Die Break
	630				
—	631	92	255	C	
	632				
	633	92	255	N	
	634				
—	635	93	306	C	
	636				
	637	94	217	C	
	638				
	639	94	335	C	
	640				
	641	95	211	C	
	642				
—	643	96	326	C	
—	644	96	326	Br	
	645	96	326	N	

Check	Number	Obverse	Reverse	Metal	Remarks
	646	.			
	647	96	326	W-M	
—	648	96	326	S	Struck over a U. S. dime
	649				
—	650	97	325	C	
	651	97	325	Br	
	652				
	653	98	Blank	W-M	
	654				
	655	98	144	W-M	
	656				
	657	98	274	Br	
	658				
—	659	98	308	C	
	660				
	661	99	186	C	
	662	99	186	. Br	
	663				
	664				
	665	99	186	W-M	
	666				
	667	99	187	C	
—	668	99	187	Br	
	669	99	187	N	
	670	99	187	C-N	Struck over a C-N cent
	671				
	672	99	187	S	Struck over a U. S. dime
	673				
	674				
	675	99	336	Br	
	676				
	677	99	336	C-N	Struck over a C-N cent
	678	99	336	W-M	.
	679				
	680				
	681				
	682				
	683	100	118	C-N	Struck over a C-N cent
	684				
	685				
	686	100	146	C	
	687				
	688	100	146	N	
	689	100	146	C-N	Struck over a C-N cent
	690	100	146	W-M	
	691		.		
	692	100	181	C	
	693				
	694	100	217	C	
	695				
	696	100	217	N	
	697	100	217	C-N	Struck over a C-N cent
	698	100	217	W-M	
	699				

Check	Number	Obverse	Reverse	Metal	Remarks
	700				
	701				
	702				
	703	100	324	C-N	Struck over a C-N cent
	704				
	705				
	706	100	335	C	
	707				
—	708	101	218	C	
	709				
	710				
	711	101	218	C-N	
	712				
	713				
	714				
	715				
	716				
	717	101	335	C-N	Struck over a C-N cent
	718				
	719				
	720				
	721				
	722	102	118	N	
	723	102	118	C-N	Struck over a C-N cent
	724				
	725				
	726				
	727				
	728	102	132	N	
—	729	102	132	C-N	
	730				
	731				
—	732	102	146	C	
	733				
	734	102	146	N	
	735				
	736				
	737				
—	738	102	181	C	
—	739	102	181	Br	
	740				
	741				
	742	102	181	W-M	
	743				
	744	102	217	C	
	745				
	746	102	217	N	
	747				
	748				
	749				
	750				
	751				
	752				
	753	102	218	C-N	

Check	Number	Obverse	Reverse	Metal	Remarks
	754				
	755				
	756	102	331	C	
	757				
	758				
	759	102	331	C-N	
	760	102	331	W-M	
	761				
—	762	103	213	G	Plated
	763	103	213	S	Plated
	764	103	214	G	Plated
	765				
	766	104	113	C	
	767				
	768				
	769				
	770				
	771	104	261	W-M	
	772				
	773				
—	774	104	263	Br	
	775				
	776				
	777	104	263	W-M	
	778				
	779	105	Blank	S	Struck over a U. S. dime
	780	105	105	C	Obverse incused
	781				
	782	105	144	C	
	783				
—	784	105	342	C	
	785				
	786				
	787	105	342	C-N	Struck over a C-N cent
—	788	105	Similar to 342	C	
	789				
—	790	106	307	C	
	791				
	792	107	228	C	
	793				
—	794	107	305	C	
	795				
—	796	108	186	C	
	797	108	186	Br	
	798				
	799				
	800				
	801	108	186	S	
	802				
—	803	108	187	C	
	804				
—	805	108	336	C	
—	806	108	336	Br	
	807				

Check	Number	Obverse	Reverse	Metal	Remarks
	808	108	336	C-N	
	809	108	336	W-M	
	810				
—	811	109	304	C	
	812	109	304	Br	
	813				
	814				
	815	109	304	W-M	
	816				
—	817	110	226	C	
	818				
	819	111	211	C	
	820				
	821	111	261	C	
	822				
	823	111	262	G	Plated
	824	111	262	S	Plated
	825				
—	826	112	193	C	
	827	112	193	Br	
	828				
	829	112	193	L	
	830	112	193	S	
	831				
—	832	114	333	C	
	833				
—	834	115	157	C	
—	835	115	324		
—	836	116	310	C	
	837				
—	838	116	334	C	
	839				
	840	117	329	C	
	841				
	842	118	157.	C	
	843	118	157	Br	
	844	118	157	N	
	845				
	846	118	157	W-M	
	847	118	157	S	
	848				
—	849	118	324	C	
	850	118	324	Br	
	851				
	852	118	324	C-N	Struck over C-N cent
	853	118	324	W-M	
	854	118	324	S	
	855				
	856	119	253	C	
	857				
—	858	121	231	C	
	859				
—	860	121	266	C	
	861				

Check	Number	Obverse	Reverse	Metal	Remarks
←	862	121	310	C	
	863				
	864	121	334	Br	
	865				
	866	122	335	C	
	867				
	868	123	237	C	
	869				
	870	123	337	C	
	871	123	337	Br	
	872	123	337	N	
	873	123	337	C-N	
—	874	123	337	W-M	
—	875	123	337	S	
	876				
—	877	124	230	C	
	878				
—	879	125	154	C	
	880				
	881	126	331	C	
	882				
	883	127	255	W-M	
	884				
—	885	128	332	C	
	886				
—	887	129	203	C	
	888				
	889	129	203	S	
	890				
	891	130	167	C	
	892				
—	893	130	203	C	
	894				
	895	130	203	C-N	
	896				
—	897	130	310	C	
	898				
	899	130	311	C	
	900				
	901	130	313	C	
	902				
—	903	131	202	C	
	904	131	202	Br	
	905	131	202	N	
	906				
	907	131	202	W-M	
	908				
	909	132	132	C	Obverse incused
	910				
	911	132	202	C	
	912				
	913	132	202	C-N	
	914				
	915	132	218	C	

25

Check	Number	Obverse	Reverse	Metal	Remarks
	916				
—	917	133	198	C	
	918	133	198	Br	
	919	133	198	N	
	920	133	198	C-N	Struck over a C-N cent
	921	133	198	W-M	
	922	133	198	S	Struck over a U. S. dime
	923				
—	924	133	199	C	
	925				
	926				
	927	133	199	C-N	Struck over a C-N cent
	928	133	199	W-M	
	929	133	199	S	Struck over a U. S. dime
	930				
—	931	135	256	C	
	932	135	256	Br	
	933	135	256	C-N	Struck over a C-N cent
—	934	135	256	W-M	
	935	135	256	S	Struck over a U. S. dime
	936				
—	937	135	258	C	
	938	135	258	Br	
	939				
	940	135	258	C-N	Struck over a C-N cent
	941	135	258	W-M	
	942	135	258	S	
	943				
—	944	135	333	C	
	945	135	333	Br	
	946				
	947	135	333	C-N	Struck over a C-N cent
	948	135	333	W-M	
	949	135	333	S	Struck over a U. S. dime
	950				
	951	136	258	C	
	952	136	258	Br	
	953	136	258	N	
	954	136	258	C-N	Struck over a C-N cent
	955	136	258	W-M	
	956	136	258	S	
	957				
	958	137	155	L	
	959	137	155	L	Reeded edge
	960				
—	961	138	295	C	
	962	138	295	Br	
	963	138	295	N	
	964				
	965				
	966	138	295	L	
	967				
	968	138	337	C	
	969	138	337	Br	

Check	Number	Obverse	Reverse	Metal	Remarks
	970	138	337	N	
	971	138	337	C-N	
	972	138	337	W-M	
	973	138	337	S	
	974				
—	975	139	309	C	
—	976	139	309	Br	
	977				
—	978	140	344	C	
	979	140	344	L	Reeded edge
	980				
—	981	141	289	C	
	982				
	983	141	291	C	
	984	141	291	Br	
	985	141	291	L	Reeded edge
	986				
—	987	142	269	C	
	988				
	989				
	990	142	269	C-N	Struck over a C-N cent
	991				
	992	142	291	C	
	993				
—	994	142	293	C	
	995				
	996				
	997	143	274	N	
	998				
	999				
	1000				
	1001	143	338	W-M	
	1002				
	1003				
	1004				
	1005	144	342	W-M	
	1006	145	260	C	
	1007				
	1008				
	1009				
	1010	145	269	W-M	
	1011				
	1012	146	146	C	Obverse incused
	1013				
	1014				
	1015	146	218	N	
	1016	146	218	C-N	
	1017				
—	1018	146	335	C	
	1019				
	1020				
	1021	146	335	C-N	
	1022				
—	1023	147	336	C	

Check	Number	Obverse	Reverse	Metal	Remarks
	1024	147	336	Br	
	1025				
	1026	148	320	. C	
	1027	148	320	C	Reverse die similar to Die No. 320—ring around 'Dix' looks like a string of beads
	1028	149	319	C	
	1029				
	1030	150	225	C	
	1031				
—	1032	150	239	C	
	1033				
—	1034	150	242	C	
	1035				
	1036	151	243	C	
	1037				
	1038	151	318	C	
—	1039	150a	318	C	
—	1040	151	319	C	
—	1041	150a	319	C	
	1042	151	320	C	
—	1043	151	321	C	
	1044				
	1045	152	242	C	
	1046				
—	1047	152	310	C	
	1048				
	1049	152	312	C	
—	1050	152	317		
	1051	152	322	C	
	1052				
	1053	152	323	C	
	1054				
—	1055	153	322	C	
	1056	154	154	C	Obverse incused
—	1057	155	323	C	
	1058				
—	1059	156	216	C	
	1060				
	1061	157	324	C	
	1062	157	324	Br	
	1063				
	1064	157	324	C-N	Struck over a C-N cent
	1065	157	324	W-M	
	1066	157	324	S	Struck over a U. S. dime
	1067				
—	1068	158	239	C	
	1069				
—	1070	158	242	C	
	1071				
—	1072	159	241	C	
	1073				
	1074	160	242	C	
—	1075	160	245	Br	
—	1076	160	244	C	

Check	Number	Obverse	Reverse	Metal	Remarks
	1077				
	1078	161	243	C	
	1079				
—	1080	161	245	C	
	1081				
	1082	162	241	C	
	1083				
—	1084	162	243	C	
	1085				
	1086	163	240	C	
	1087				
—	1088	163	244	C	
	1089				
	1090	164	240	C	
	1091				
	1092	165	273	C	
	1093	165	273	Br	
	1094	165	273	N	
	1095				
	1096	165	273	W-M	
	1097				
	1098	165	274	C	
	1099	165	274	Br	
	1100	165	274	N	
	1101				
	1102				
	1103				
—	1104	166	266	C	
	1105				
	1106	167	167	C	Obverse incused
—	1107	167	266	C	
	1108				
—	1109	168	231	C	
	1110				
	1111	168	231	L	
	1112				
	1113	169	334	C	
	1114				
—	1115	170	201	C	
	1116				
—	1117	171	330	C	
—	1118	171	330	Br	
	1119				
	1120	172	312	C	
	1121				
—	1122	172	314	C	
	1123				
—	1124	172	328	C	
	1125				
—	1126	173	327	C	
—	1127	173	X	C	
—	1128	174	252	C	
	1129	174	252	Br	
	1130	174	174	Br	Obverse incused

Check	Number	Obverse	Reverse	Metal	Remarks
	1131				
—	1132	174	256	C	
	1133				
	1134				
	1135	174	256	C-N	Struck over a C-N cent
	1136	174	256	W-M	
	1137	174	256	S	Struck over a U. S. dime
	1138				
—	1139	175	251	C	
	1140	175	251	Br	
	1141				
	1142	175	251	C-N	Struck over a C-N cent
	1143	175	251	W-M	
	1144	175	251	S	Struck over a U. S. dime
	1145				
—	1146	175	253	C	
	1147	175	253	Br	
	1148	175	253	N	
	1149	175	253	C-N	Struck over a C-N cent
	1150	175	253	W-M	
	1151	175	253	S	Struck over a U. S. dime
	1152				
—	1153	176	287	C	
	1154				
—	1155	177	180	C	
	1156				
—	1157	177	290	C	
	1158				
—	1159	177	292	C	
	1160				
	1161	177	292	C-N	Struck over a C-N cent
	1162				
	1163	177	293	C	
	1164				
—	1165	178	215	C	
	1166				
—	1167	178	288	C	
	1168				
—	1169	178	294	C	
	1170				
	1171	180	291	C	
	1172				
	1173	180	293	C	
	1174				
	1175	180	202	C	
	1176				
—	1177	181	335	C	
	1178				
	1179				
	1180	181	335	C-N	Struck over a C-N cent
	1181				
	1182				
—	1183	182	339	C	
	1184				

Check	Number	Obverse	Reverse	Metal	Remarks
—	1185	183	259	C	
	1186				
—	1187	184	202	C	
	1188	184	202	Br	
	1189				
	1190	184	202	C-N	
	1191				
	1192				
	1193	184	335	C	
	1194	184	335	Br	
	1195	184	335	N	
	1196	184	335	C-N	
	1197	184	335	W-M	
	1198				
—	1199	185	186	C	
	1200				
—	1201	185	336	C	
	1202	185	336	Br	
	1203				
	1204				
	1205	185	336	W-M	
	1206				
	1207	186	186	C	Obverse incused
	1208				
—	1209	186	300	C	
	1210				
—	1211	186	302	C	
	1212				
	1213				
	1214				
	1215				
	1216	186	302	S	
	1217				
—	1218	186	303	C	
—	1219	186	303	Br	
	1220				
	1221	186	303	C-N	Struck over a C-N cent
	1222				
	1223				
—	1224	186	645	C	
	1225				
	1226				
	1227				
	1228	186	645	W-M	
	1229				
—	1230	187	645	C	
	1231	187	645	Br	
	1232				
—	1233	188	230	C	
	1234				
—	1235	189	347	C	
	1236				
	1237				
	1238	189	347	C-N	Struck over a C-N cent

Check	Number	Obverse	Reverse	Metal	Remarks
	1239	189	347	W-M	
	1240	189	347	S	Struck over a U. S. quarter dollar
	1241	189	347	S	Struck over an English shilling
	1242				
—	1243	191	346	C	
	1244				
	1245	192	348	C	
	1246	192	348	Br	
	1247	192	348	N	
	1248	192	348	C-N	
	1249				
	1250	192	348	S	
	1251				
	1252	202	Blank	C	
•	1253				
	1254	206	208	C	
	1255				
—	1256	218	335	C	
	1257				
	1258	218	335	C-N	
	1259				
—	1260	222	264	C	
	1261	222	264	Br	
	1262				
	1263	222	264	C-N	Struck over a C-N cent
	1264	222	264	W-M	
	1265	222	264	S	Struck over a U. S. dime
	1266				
	1267	236	Blank	C	
	1268				
	1269	248	251	C	
	1270	248	251	Br	
	1271				
	1272	248	251	C-N	Struck over a C-N cent
	1273	248	251	W-M	
	1274				
—	1275	252	264	C	
	1276				
	1277				
	1278	252	264	C-N	Struck over a C-N cent
	1279				
	1280				
	1281	273	338	C	
	1282	273	338	Br	
	1283	273	338	N	
	1284				
	1285				
	1286	274	338	C	
	1287	274	338	Br	
	1288	274	338	N	
	1289				
	1290				
—	1291	300	336	C	
	1292				

Check	Number	Obverse	Reverse	Metal	Remarks
	1293				
	1294	302	336	W-M	
	1295				
	1296	303	303	C	Obverse incused
	1297				
	1298	319	319	C	Obverse incused
	1299				
	1300	336	645	N	
	1301				
	1302	336	645	W-M	
	1303				
	1304				
	1305	611	628	N	

ALABAMA

Huntsville

NUMBER	OBVERSE	REVERSE	METAL	EDGE
2001	White & Swann/Huntsville/Ala	607	C	Pl
2002	Same	"	C	R
2003	Same	"	Br	Pl
2004	Same	"	Br	R
2005	Same	"	N	Pl
2006	Same	"	N	R
2007				
2008				
2009	Same	'15' instead of '10'	C	Pl
2010	Same	Same	C	R
2011	Same	"	Br	Pl
2012	Same	"	Br	R
2013	Same	"	N	Pl
2014	Same	"	N	R
2015				
2016				
2017	Same	'25' instead of '10'	C	Pl
2018	Same	Same	C	R
2019	Same	Same	Br	Pl
2020	Same	Same	Br	R
2021	Same	Same	N	Pl
2022	Same	Same	N	R
2023				
2024				
2025				
2026				
2027				
2028				
2029				
2030				
2031				
2032	Same	'35' instead of '10'	C-N	R
2033				
2034				
2035				
2036				
2037				
2038				
2039	Same	'50' instead of '10'	N	Pl
2040				
2041	Same	Same	W-M	Pl
2042				
2043	Same	'$5.00' instead of '10'	C	Pl
2044	Same	Same	C	R
2045	Same	Same	Br	Pl
2046	Same	Same	Br	R
2047	Same	Same	N	Pl
2048	Same	Same	N	R
2049				
2050				

ALABAMA—Continued

Huntsville—Continued

NUMBER	OBVERSE	REVERSE	METAL	EDGE
2051				
2052	Same	608	C	R
2053				
2054				
2055				
2056				
2057				
2058	Same	609	C	R
✗ 2057	"	404	CN	Pl

CONNECTICUT

Bridgeport

2100	'A. W. Wallace's' above—'Variety/ bakery' in centre—'Bridgeport Ct' below.	121	C	Pl
— 2101	same	Same	Br	Pl
2102				
2103	E. W. Atwood/dealer/in/books/ newspapers/&c.	6	C	Pl
2104	same	168	C	Pl
— 2105			Br	"

Norwich

— 2106	Weller's/News/depot/Norwich	610	C	Pl
2107	Same—no star at side	610	C	Pl

Waterbury

2108	New York Store/Waterbury/Conn/ South Main St.	Redeemable/in sums of/5 cts/or more/in postal currency Millinery/and/fancy goods/	C	Pl
✗ 2109	same	1862	C	Pl
2110				

Willimantic

2111	Dr. O. G. Keitteridge/Willimantic/ C. T./1864/Main St.	493		Pl
2112				
2113	Arch Saloon/No. 10/O. Rudd	493		Pl

ILLINOIS

ALTON

NUMBER	OBVERSE	REVERSE	METAL	EDGE
2115	Walter & Smith, Alton, Ills. Good for 10 cts.	John Stanton, Cincinnati, Stamps and Brand Cutter.	Br	Pl
— 2116	Same as preceding Good for 25 cents	Same	Br	Pl
2117				

AURORA

— 2118	Ira H. Fitch/Dealer in/Leather Harness/&c/Broadway, Aurora, Ills.	485	C	Pl
2119				
— 2120	Gates & Trask/Dealers/in/Watches/Jewelry/&/Silverware / Aurora, Ills	575	C	Pl
2121	Same	Same	N	Pl
2122				

BELVIDERE

— 2123	George B. Ames/Dealer in/Drugs/Books &c/Belvidere, Ills.	Mortar and pestle in centre 'George B. Ames' above with 13 stars—'1863' below.	C	Pl
— 2124	Same	Same	Br	Pl
2125				

BLOOMINGDALE

2126	C P Sedgwick & Co/Variety/Goods/Bloomingdale/Ills.	102	C	Pl
2127	Same	Same	Br	Pl
2128	Same	Same	C-N	Pl
2129	Same	Same	W-M	Pl
2130		100		
2131				
2132	Same	181	C	Pl
2133				
2134				
2135	Same	217	C	Pl
2136				
2137				
2138	Same	218	C	Pl
2139				
2140				
—2141	Same	335	C	Pl
2142				
—2143	Same	Same	C-N	Pl
2144				

ILLINOIS—Continued

CAIRO

NUMBER	OBVERSE	REVERSE	METAL	EDGE
2145	R. C. Culley/Watchmaker/&/Jewelry/Cairo, Ills.	Blank Reverse	C	Pl
2146				
2147	D Ford/Watchmaker/and/Cairo/Ills.	442	C	Pl
2148	Same	Same	Br	Pl
2149	Same	561	C	Pl
2150	Same	Same	Br	Pl
2151	Same	Blank Reverse	C	Pl
2152	Same	Same	Br	Pl
2153				

CHEMUNG

2154	Wm. Moore/Dealer/in/Dry Goods/Groceries/&c&c/Chemung Ills	25	C	Pl
2155	Same	434	C	Pl
2156				
2157	B. A. Wade & Co/Dealers/in/Dry Goods/Groceries/&c/Chemung, Ills.	206	C	Pl
2158	Same	594	C	Pl
2159				

CHICAGO

2160	Baierle's Chicago Saloon	Beer mug in wreath Good for one.	Br	Pl
2161				
2162	Barker & Illsley/Hardware/Nails/&/Stoves/277 State St/Chicago	575	C	Pl
2163	Same	Same	N	Pl
2164				
2165	Good for 5 cents, G. Bauerschmidt.	518	Br	Pl
2166				
2167	Ira Brown/Book Dealer/61/West Kinzie/St/Chicago.	25	C	Pl
2168	Same	27	C	Pl
2169	Same	431	C	P
2170				
2171	J. J. Brown/Grocer/171/West/Harrison St/Chicago/Ill	575	C	Pl
2172				
2173	'A. Chandler/393/State St' in centre 'Watches, Clocks & Jewelry' above—'Chicago' below.	25	C	Pl
2174	Same	485	C	Pl
2175	Same	568	C	Pl
2176	Same	611	C	Pl
2177	Childs Die Sinker & Engraver/117½/Randolph/St/Chicago.	432	C	Pl
2178	Same	436	C	Pl
2179	Same	484	C	Pl
2180	Same	568	C	Pl

ILLINOIS—Continued

CHICAGO—Continued

NUMBER	OBVERSE	REVERSE	METAL	EDGE
— 2181	Same as preceding—Two ornaments below instead of one.	436	C	Pl
— 2182	Same	437	C	Pl
— 2183	Same	439	C	Pl
— 2184	Same	612	C	Pl
— 2185	Same	Same	Br	Pi
2186	Same	Same	N	Pl
— 2187	"	568	C	"
— 2188	Childs / Manufacturer / of / Advertising/coin/Chicago, Ills.	206	C	Pl
--2189	Same	209	C	Pl
—2190	Same	433	C	Pl
—2191	Same	611	C	Pl
—2192	Same	Same	N	Pl
— 2193	ʌ	644	C	Pl
2194	Same as Die No. 594	Dealer in/nails/stoves/crockery/&/paints.	C	Pl
—2195	Same as Die No. 436	553	C	Pl
2196				
2197	City Brewery/Manfr/of/Lager/Beer/Stock/& cream/ale	25	C	Pl
2198				
2199				
— 2200	R. H. Countiss/Grocer/&/Tea Dealer/Clark St. Cor/Van Buren/Chicago.	575	C	Pl
2201				
— 2202	R. H. Countiss/Grocer/Cor/of/State & North/&/Cor. Clark &/Van Buren/Sts/Chicago, Ill.	575	C	Pl
2203	Same	Same	N	Pl
2204				
— 2205	Dodd's Elgin Dairy/Pure/Milk/57/West/Madison/St.	25	C	Pl
—2206	Same	436	C	Pl
—2207	Same	484	C	Pl
—2208	Same	485	C	Pl
2209				
2210				
— 2211	D Dryer & Co/Groceries/&/provisions/359 Canal St.	457	C	Pl
2212				
2213	F. N. Dubois SilverWare/Badges & Metal/Manufactury/P O Box 1899/Chicago, Ill.	306	C	Pl
—2214	Same	575	C	Pl
2215				
—2216	Edwards/Fine/Watches/&/Jewelyr/Clark St/Chicago Ill	575	C	Pl
		575	C	Pl
2217				

ILLINOIS—Continued

Chicago—Continued

NUMBER	OBVERSE	REVERSE	METAL	EDGE
2218	'A. W. Escherrich' above—'Chicago/Illinois/1861' in centre—'404 St. Clark St' below	457	C	Pl
2219	'A. W. Escherich 1861 Engraver' around border—'404/S Clark/ C Ill.' in centre	475	C	Pl
2220	'A. W. Escherich Wire Workers 1861' around border—'404/S Clark/Chicago/Ill.' in centre	576	C	Pl
2221	Same as 2218 obv	576		
2222	Flagg Cheap Store/Boots/&/Shoes/181/Lake St/Chicago, Ill.	575	C	Pl
2223				
2224	Flagg & McDonald/Boots/&/Shoes/181/Lake St/Chicago, Ill.	575	C	Pl
2225	Same—wider space between 'Flagg' and 'Chicago' and between 'Ill' and 'McDonald'	575	C	Pl
2226				
2227	James Foster, Jr & Co, Opticians 46 Clark St Chicago Ill			
2228		419 / 420 / 420 / Blank	C-N / C / C-N / Br	Pl / R / R / R2
2229	Freedman & Goodkind/Dry/Goods/&/Millinery/171/Lake St/Chicago.	206	C	Pl
2230	Same	436	C	Pl
2231	Same	439	C	Pl
2232	Same	485	C	Pl
2233				
2234	'Freedman, Goodkind & Co' around border—'Dry/Goods/135/Lake St/Chicago, Ill' in centre.	575	C	Pl
2235	'Freedman, Goodkind & Co' around border—'Dry/Goods/171/Lake St/Chicago, Ill' in centre.	575	C	Pl
2236				
2237	P Gaffney/Grocer/&/Tea/Dealer/150/N. Halstead St/Chicago.	575	C	Pl
2238				
2239	New York/Meat/Market/F. Gall/Chicago/N 92 Milwaukee Ave	505	C	Pl
2240	Same	Same	Br	Pl
2241				
2242				
2243	C. E. Gerts & Co/Brush/Factory and Store/204/Randolph St/Chicago.	575	C	Pl
2244	Same	Same	N	Pl
2245				
2246	Haas & Powell/Butcher / North Market.	209	C	Pl
2247	Same	436	C	Pl

ILLINOIS—Continued

Chicago—Continued

NUMBER	OBVERSE	REVERSE	METAL	EDGE
2248	Same	485	C	Pl
2249				
2250	Harley & Johnson/Trunks/&/Valises/94/Mil. Ave. Chicago.	Trunk in centre— 'Harley &Johnson/one price'above-'Clothing/94 Milwaukee Ave' below.	C	Pl
2251	Harley & Johnson/Trunks/&/Valises/Wholesale & Retail/94/Mil. Ave./Chicago, Ill.	Same	C	Pl
2252	Wm Harley / Trunks / &/Valises/94/Mil. Ave./Chicago.	'Wm. Harley/one price' above—trunk in centre—'Clothing/94 Milwaukee Ave.' below.	C	Pl
2253	Same as preceding — larger letters.	Same	C	Pl
2254				
2255	R. Heilbroner/Fancy/Dry/Goods/217/S. Clark St/Chicago, Ill.	575	C	Pl
2256	Same	Same	N	Pl
2257				
2258	W. A. Hendrie/Watches/Clocks/&/Jewelry/35 S Clark St/Chicago Ill	575	C	Pl
2259	Gilbert Hotchkiss	572	Br	Pl
2260	S. A. Ingram Chicago Ill, Watches and Clocks.	329	C	Pl
2261	Same	400	C	Pl
2262	Same	J. A. Hughes Cincinnati O—Metallic Cards' within wreath.	S	Pl
2263	"	670	C	Pl
2264	Judd & Corthell/Boots/&/Shoes/106/Lake St/Chicago, Ill.	575	C	Pl
2265	Same	Same	N	Pl
2266				
2267	O. Kendall's Sons & Co/Bread/Good/for/one/loaf.	20	C	Pl
2268	Same	Same	Br.	Pl
2269	Same	433	C	Pl
2270	Same	594	C	Pl
2271	Same	Same	Br	Pl
2272				
2273	F. A. Leavitt/Family/Grocery/355 State St/Chicago, Ill.	575	C	Pl
2274	F. A. Leavitt Family Groceries Crockery &c. Wholesale & Retail 355 State St Chicago Ill	Same	C	Pl
2275				
2276	March & Miner/Military/Clothers/33 & 35/Lake St/Chicago.	408	C	Pl
2277	Same	414	C	Pl

ILLINOIS—Continued

Chicago—Continued

NUMBER	OBVERSE	REVERSE	METAL	EDGE
2278	Same	418	C	R
2279	Same	Similar to 453—dated '1863'	C	Pl
2280	Same	Same	C	R
2281	Same	Same	Br	R
2282	Same	Same	C-N	R
2283	"	" 420	C-N	R
2284	A Meyer/ Rag Stor/Chicago/Ill/S Clark, St 377.	457	C	Pl
2285				
2286	C. E. Meyer/196 Randolph St. Mug in centre	Good for/One glass/Beer..	Br	Pl
2287				
2288	Good for 5 cts, G. R. Meyer	House flagpole and flag flying, surrounded by trees	C	Pl
2289				
2290	'J U / Mingers/saloon' in centre—'Boarding house 33 Canal St' around border	457	C	Pl
2291				
2292	Oppenheimer & Metzer/Jewelry/&/Watch / Materials / 104 / Lake St / Chicago/Ill.	575	C	Pl
2293				
2294	Wm. Ostendorf/210 / Randolph / Street/Chicago.	Good for/one glass/Beer	Br	Pl
2295				
2296	Passage certificates/From/Liverpool/To/Chicago/No 6/Clark St.	Bank Drafts/For / I and/Upwards/on the/Royal Bank of/Ireland/1861	C	Pl
2297				
2298	Same as Reverse of No. 2296.	436	C	Pl
2299				
2300	W G Peck/Grocer/192 State St/Chicago	25	C	Pl
2301	Same	436 437	C	Pl
2302 A	Same	438	C	Pl
2303	Same	485	C	Pl
2304	Same	568	C	Pl
2305	Same	612	C	Pl
2306	Same	613	C	Pl
2307	W. R. Prentice/Family/Grocer/75/Canal St/Chicago. Ill	575	C	Pl
2308				
2309	H Regensburg/Grocery/&/Bakery/No 30/N. Wells. St. Chicago.	457	C	Pl
2310				
2311	Great Western Market/Wm/Reinhart/158/Randolph/W./Chicago.	505	C	Pl
2312				

ILLINOIS—Continued

Chicago—Continued

NUMBER	OBVERSE	REVERSE	METAL	EDGE
2313	Wall Papers/81/Randolph St/ Chicago/F. E. Rigby.	206	C	Pl
2314		426		
2315	Same	484	C	Pl
2316	Same	485	C	Pl
2317	Same	568	C	Pl
2318				
2319	'Deutsches Gast & Boarding Haus' around border—'J. F./Siechler/ Larabee/St/near Claybourne Ave/ Chicago' in centre.	84	C	Pl
2320	Same	567	C	Pl
2321				
2322	C & S Stein/Dry Goods/Store/177/ Lake St/Chicago Ill.	209	C	Pl
2323	Same	439	C	Pl
2324	Same	485	C	Pl
2325	Same	568	C	Pl
2326	Same	613	C	Pl
2327		426		
2328	W Treleaven/Gold Pen/Maker/&/ Jeweler/150 Lake St/Up Stairs/ Chicago. ILL	575	C	Pl
2329				
2330	C. Winsauer/Gunsmith/N. 111 S. Wells/St/Chicago. Crossed swords & Guns	559	C	Pl
2331				

DeKalb

2332	I. L. Ellwood/Hardware / Tin, Stoves/DeKalb, Ill.	99	C	Pl
2333	Same	Same	Br	Pl
2334				
2335	I. L. Elwood/Hardware/De Kalb. Ill.	25	C	Pl
2336	Same	485	C	Pl
2337	Same	568	C	Pl
2338				

Dixon

2339	Ed Weibezahn/Dealer/in/Groceries/& Dry/Goods/Dixon. Ill.	25	C	Pl
2340	Same	594	C	Pl

Durand

2341				
2342	H. L. Mosely/Durand/Ills.	Groceries/Harware/Crockery/Notions	C	Pl
2343	" "			

ILLINOIS—Continued

Elgin

NUMBER	OBVERSE	REVERSE	METAL	EDGE
— 2344	M. Mc.Neil/Dealer/in/Dry Goods/ Groceries/Boots &/Shoes/Elgin. Ill.	614	C	Pl
2345				
2346				

El Paso

— 2347	P H Tompkins/Dealer/in/Dry Goods/Groceries/&c/El Paso, Ill.	435	C	Pl
— 2348	Same	594	C	Pl
2349				

Freeport

2350	D S Bogar/Farmers Store/Dry/ Goods/Groceries/Freeport/Ills.	25	C	Pl
2351	Same	433	C	Pl
2352	Same	614	C	Pl
— 2353		21	C.	Pl
2354	D. S. Brewster/Dealer/in/Butter/ Eggs &c/Freeport, Ill.	594	C	Pl
— 2355	Same	614	C	Pl
— 2356	J D Diffebaugh/Confectioner/ and/Dealer in/Fruit/Freeport/Ill	21	C	Pl
2357	Same	206	C	Pl
2358				
— 2359	W. P. Emmert/Hardware/Stoves Iron/&/Tin ware/Freeport Ills	206	C	Pl
2360	Same	209	C	Pl
— 2361	Freeport Brewery / by / Helena / Hertrich/Adams/St/Freeport. Ill.	157	C	Pl
— 2362	Same	483	C	Pl
2363				

Lacon

2364	Ellsworth & Halsey/General/Merchandise/ & / Goods / for / Ladies / wear/Lacon, Ills.	410	C	Pl
— 2365	Same	Same	C	R
2366	Same	Same	C-N	R
2367	" "	" "	Br	R
2368	" "	420	C	R
2369				
2370				

La Salle

— 2371	Adame & Hatch/Dry/Goods./Carpets/Boots &/Shoes/La Salle, Ill.	25	C	Pl
2372	Same	209	C	Pl
2373				

ILLINOIS—Continued

Lena

NUMBER	OBVERSE	REVERSE	METAL	EDGE
— 2374	W. J. Bollinger/Dealer/in/Hardware/Iron & Nails/Lena, Illinois. Padlock	206	C	Pl
2375				
2376				
— 2377	M. Weaver/Dealer in/Dry Goods/ & Groceries/ Lena, Ill.	26	C	Pl
— 2378	Same	27	C	Pl
— 2379	Same	206	C	Pl
— 2380	Same	209	C	Pl
2381				

Lodi

| 2382 | C. H. Taylor/Stoves/Fine/Table &/ Pocket/Cutlery/Lodi, Ill. | 209 | C | Pl |
| 2383 | | | | |

Marengo

| — 2384 | H. G. Skinner/Agt./Dealer in/ Groceries/& Provisions/Marengo/ Ill. | 206 | C | Pl |
| 2385 | | | | |

Mendota

| — 2386 | A. Erlenborn/Dealer/in/Groceries &c./Main Street/Mendota/Ills. | 209 | C | Pl |
| 2387 | | | | |

Naperville

— 2388	Robert Naper/Dry/Goods/ Groceries/&c/Naperville, Ills.	419	C	R
2389	Same	Same	Br	R
2390	Same	Same	C-N	R
2391				

Ottawa

— 2392	A. & H. Alschuler/Ottawa. Large rosette in centre.	209	C	Pl
— 2393	Same	553	C	Pl
2394				

Palatine

| — 2395 | Dean & Slade/Dry Goods/ Hardware &c./ Palatine, Ill. | 483 | C | Pl |
| 2396 | | | | |

Paris

— 2397	Collins Bros/Druggists/Paris,/Ill.			
2398	Same	68	C	Pl
2399	Same	418	C	R
2400		Same	Br	Br

ILLINOIS—Continued

Paris—Continued

NUMBER	OBVERSE	REVERSE	METAL	EDGE
— 2401	Same	615	C	Pl
2402				
2403	Same	419	C	R
2404	″	420	C	R
— 2405	A. C. Connely's/Dry/Goods/Store/Paris, Ill.	68	C	Pl
— 2406	Same	418	C	R
2407	″	418	Br	R
2408		420	C	R
2409	Same	555	C-N	R
— 2410	Same	617	C	Pl
— 2411	James Miller/Dry/Goods/Store/Paris, Ill.	453 with 1863 date	C-N	R
		413	C	Pl
— 2412	Same	418	C	R
— 2413	Same	Same	Br	R
2414	″	634	C	Pl
2415	Same	453	C-N	Pl
2416				
— 2417	Penoyer & Larkin/Grocers/&/Commission/Dealers/Paris, Ill.	412	C	Pl
— 2418	Same	418	C	R
— 2419	Same	Same	Br	R
— 2420	″	68	C	Pl
2421	Same	473	C-N	R
2422	″	413	C	R
— 2423	Sisk & Whalen/Restaurant/E. Side Pub. Sq./Paris, Ill.	420	C	R
		418	C	R
— 2424	Same	Same	Br	R
2425	Same	Same	Z	R
2426	Same	Same as Die No. 453—dated 1863	C-N	R
2427		420	C	R

Peru

— 2428	Lininger & Bro/Dealers/in/Dry Goods/Notions/Boots & Shoes/Peru, Ill.	206	C	Pl
— 2429	Same	594	C	Pl
2430				

Pontiac

| — 2431 | Dehner & Maples/Dry/Goods/Groceries/Crockery/&c/Pontiac, Ill. | 25 | C | Pl |
| 2432 | | | | |

Rockford

— 2433	A. J. Davis/Grocer/Rockford Ills	21	C	Pl
— 2434	Same	25	C	Pl
2435	Same	209	C	Pl
2436				

ILLINOIS—Continued

Rockford—Continued

NUMBER	OBVERSE	REVERSE	METAL	EDGE
2437	Holmes & Norton/Druggists/Rockford/Ill. Mortar and pestle	206	C	Pl
2438	Same	208	C	Pl
2439		Small eagle 1863	C	
2440	Hope & Clow/Stoves/Hardware/Iron &/Rockford, Ill. Padlock.	20	C	Pl
2441	Same	209	C	Pl
2442	Same	433	C	Pl
2443				
2444	William Knapp / Artesian / Well / Driller/Rockford, Ill.	27	C	Pl
2445				

Rockton

2446	V. A. Lake/Grain/Dealer/Rockton, Ill.	404	C	R
2447	"	420	CN	R

Sandwich

2448	W B Castle/Druggist/Sandwich/Ills.	532	C	Pl
2449				
2450	Sandwich/Bank/W B Castle/Sandwich/Illinois.	Deposit / Exchange / and / Loan/Office.	C	Pl
2451	Same	Same	Br	Pl
2452	"	Deposit	C	
2453	A. G. Greenman/Druggist/Sandwich/ILL. Mortar and pestle.	532	C	Pl
2454				
2455				

Springfield

2456	J. C. Yager/Trunk/Maker/Springfield, Ill.	329	C	Pl
2457	Same	Henry Jenkins/Wholesale Louis Mo	C	Pl
2458	Same	Jos Zanone/ice/cream saloon/285/Central Av	C	Pl
2459		670	C	

Sycamore

2460	Lott & Warner/Dry Goods/Groceries/&c/Sycamore, Ills.	209	C	Pl
2461	Same	485	C	Pl
2462	Same	618	C	Pl
2463	Same	436	C	Pl

ILLINOIS—Continued

Waukegan

NUMBER	OBVERSE	REVERSE	METAL	EDGE
— 2464	J L Loveday & Co/Dry Goods/and Groceries/Waukegan, Ill.	603	C	Pl
2465				
— 2466	J. L. Loveday & Co/63/Washington St/Waukegan/Ill.	619	C	Pl
2467	Same	Same	Br	Pl
—2468	Same	Same	W-M	Pl
— 2469	Kingsley + Whipple, Waukegan	2.6	C	Pl
— 2470	D. P. Millen/Dealer/in/Boots/& Shoes/Waukegan/Lake Co/Ill	27	C	Pl
— 2471	Same	620	C	Pl
2472				

Woodstock

— 2473	M. D. Stevers/Grain/Dealer/Woodstock, Ill.	483	C	Pl
		402	C	R

INDIANA

Albany

2501	Allegre & Wroughton/Dealers/in/Dry Goods/&/Groceries/Albany Ind.	442	C	Pl
2502				

Alexandria

2503	Wolfe & Sherman/Staple & Fancy/Dry Goods/Alexandria, Ind.	416	C	R
2504	Same	Same	C	Pl
2505	Same	419	C	R
2506	Same	Same	C-N	R
2507				
2508				
2509				

Anderson

2510	J. P. Barnes/Dealer/in/Stoves/&/Tinware/Anderson, Ind.	521	C	Pl
2511	Same	560	C	Pl
2512				
2513	T & N C McCullough/Dealers/in/Hardware/Anderson/Ind.	542	C	Pl
2514				
2515				

INDIANA—Continued

Avilla

NUMBER	OBVERSE	REVERSE	METAL	EDGE
2516	Baum Walter & Co/Dealers in/ Dry/Goods/Groceries/Avilla Ind	416	C	R
2517	Same	Same	Br	R
2518	Same	Same	Z	R
2519	Same	420	C-N	R
2520				

Battlecreek

2521	Wm. Brooks/Hardware/and/ Stoves/Battle Creek/&/Elkhart.	121	C	Pl
2522	Same	484	C	Pl
2523	Same	485	C	Pl
2524				
2525				

Bethel

2526	Thompson & Wiley/Dealers/in/Dry Goods/and/Groceries/Bethel Ind	470	C	Pl
2527	Same	621	C	Pl
2528				

Bowling Green

2529	O. H. P. Ash/Cheap/Cash/Store/ Bowling Green, Ind.	407	C	Pl
2530	Same	417	C	Pl
2531	Same	418	C	R
2532	Same	Same	Br	R
2533	Same	Same	Z	R
2534	Same	419	C-N	R
2535				
2536	Ash & Black/Cash/Store/Bowling Green.	414	C	Pl
2537	Same	418	C	R
2538	Same	Same	Br	R
2539				
2540	Same	419	C	R
2541				

Brazil

2542	Connely's/New/York/Store/Brazil, Ind.	418	C	R
2543	Same	418	Br	R
2544				
2545	Same	622	C	Pl
2546				

Brooklyn

2547	Cox & Landers Dry Goods Clothing Boots & Shoes, Brooklyn, Ind.	420	C-N	R
2548				

INDIANA—Continued

Brookville

NUMBER	OBVERSE	REVERSE	METAL	EDGE
2549	H. Linck/Dry/Goods/Groceries/&/Hardware/Brookville Ind	68	C	Pl
2550	Same	405	C	Pl
2551	Same	418	C	R
2552	Same	418	Br	R
2553				
2554	Same	Same as 453—dated '1863'	C-N	R
2555				

Brownsburg

2556	G. W. Nash/Drugs / Medicines /Wines/Liquors/Notions/&c/Brownsburg, Ind.	623	C	R
2557				
2558	Same	Same	Z	R

Brownstown

2559	S S Early & Co/Dealers/in/Dry Goods &/Groceries/Brownstown/Ind.	425	C	Pl
2560				

Butler

2561	J Lutes/Dealer in/Dry Goods/and/Groceries/Butler/Ind.	442	C	Pl
2562				

Cadiz

2563	'C. Bond' above—Crossed square and compasses in centre—'Druggist/Cadiz, Ind.' below.	416	C	R
2564				
2565	Same	Same	Z	R
2566				
2567	Hiatt & Showalter/Dry/Goods/Groceries/&c/Cadiz, Ind.	416	C	Pl
2568	Same	Same	C	R
2569	Same	Same	Br	R
2570	Same	Same	Z	R
2571	Same	419	C-N	R
2572				

Centerville

2573				
2574	Gentry's/Grocers/Centerville/Ind.	419	C	R
2575	Same	Same	Br	R

INDIANA—Continued
Columbia City

NUMBER	OBVERSE	REVERSE	METAL	EDGE
2576	Gaffney & McDowell/Liquors/Cigars &c/Columbia City/Ind.	463	C	Pl
2577				
2578	Harley & Linvill/Hardware/Stoves/&/Tinware/Columbia City/Ind.	425	C	Pl
2579	Same	521	C	Pl
2580				
2581	W W Kepner & Son/Dry Goods/&/Groceries/Columbia City/Ind.	425	C	Pl
2582				
2583	Dr C. Kindermann/Druggist/&/Book/Seller/Columbia City Ind	580	C	Pl
2584	Same	419	C-N	R
2585				
2586				
2587	S. S. Lavey/Watchmaker/&/Jeweler/Columbia City, Ind.	Dealer/in / Watches / & / Jewelry.	C	Pl
2588	Same	419	C-N	R
2589				
2590	John C. Washburn/Dry Goods/&/Groceries/Columbia City/Ind.	479	C	Pl
2591				

Como

2592	Jacob Groyen/Grocer / Main St/Como, Ind.	467	C	Pl
2593	Same	Same	W-M	Pl
2594	Same	518	C	Pl
2595				

Corunna

2596	Sam'l Beck/Dealer / in / Butter Eggs/Hides and/Pelts / Corunna / Ind.	446	C	Pl
2597	Same	446	Br	Pl
2598	Same	621	C	Pl
2599				
2600	Ira W Bowen/Dealer/in/Drugs/medicines/Groceries/&/Hardware / Corunna, Ind.	471	C	Pl
2601	Same	532	C	Pl
2602				
2603	John Childs/Dealer/in/Dry Goods/Groceries/&c/Corunna,/Ind.	426	C	Pl
2604				
2605	J L & G F Rowe/Dealers/in/Dry Goods/Groceries &c/Corunna,/Ind.	425	C	Pl
2606	Same	426	C	Pl

INDIANA—Continued

Corunna—Continued

NUMBER	OBVERSE	REVERSE	METAL	EDGE
2607	Same	427	C	Pl
2608	Same	447	C	Pl
2609				

Danville

2610	Craddick&Homan/Dealers / Books/ Stationery / Tobacco / & / Cigars / Danville, Ind.	419	C	R
2611				
2612	S. A. Russell/Merchant/Danville/Ind.	419	C	R
2613	Same	Same	Br	R
2614	Same	Same	C-N	R
2615	Same	Same	Z	R
2616	Same	420	C	R
2617				
2618				

Dublin

2619	A. Jenks/Dealerin/Dry/Goods/&/Groceries/Dublin, Ind.	416	C	R
2620				
2621				
2622	Same	419	C-N	R
2623				

Elkhart

2624	J. Davenport & Son/Dealers/in/Dry Goods/Ind/Elkhart.	Variety of 6	C	Pl
2625				
2626	C. T. Greene & Co/Grocers/&/Provision/Dealers/Elkhart Ind	Variety of 6	C	Pl
2627				
2628	Boot and shoe in centre—'John Guipe' above — 'Dealer/Elkhart, Ind' below	209	C	Pl
2629	Same	438	C	Pl
2630	Same	485	C	Pl
2631				

Fortville

2632	J. H. Thomas / Dealer / in / Dry Goods/Groceries &c/Fortville/Ind.	425	C	Pl
2633	Same	442	C	Pl
2634	Same	479	C	Pl
2635	Same	563	C	Pl
2636				

INDIANA—Continued

Ft. Wayne

NUMBER	OBVERSE	REVERSE	METAL	EDGE
2637	C. Anderson/Dealer/in/Groceries/ &/Provisions/Ft Wayne. Ind.	465	C	Pl
2638				
2639	A D Brandiff & Co/Hardware/&/ Stoves/Ft Wayne/Ind.	521	C	Pl
2640				
2641	W. H. Brooks Jr/Wholesale/Dealer in/Wall &/Window Paper / Ft Wayne/Ind.	463	C	Pl
2642	Same	466	C	Pl
2643	Same	480	C	Pl
2644	Same	539	C	Pl
2645	Same	563	C	Pl
2646				
2647	Phoenix Grocery/T. K. Brackenridge/Groceries/ &/ Provisions / Ft Wayne/Ind.	463	C	Pl
2648				
2649				
2650	I. Lauferty/91/Columbia / St / Ft Wayne/Ind.	552	C	Pl
2651				
2652	P. Pierr/Dry Goods/&/Groceries/ Ft Wayne/Ind	425	C	Pl
2653				
2654	S. Schoerpf & Co/Wholesale/Druggists/Ft Wayne/Ind.	532	C	Pl
2655				
2656				

Franklin

2657	Hulsman & Alexander / Saloon / Sale/& / Livery / Stable / Franklin, Ind.	419	C	R
2658				
2659	Same	419	C-N	R
2660				

Fremont

2661	G. W. Follett/Dry/Goods/Groceries/Boots, Shoes / & / Hardware/ Fremont, Ind.	416	C	R
2662				
2663	Same	419	C	R
2664	Same	Same	Br	R
2665				
2666				

Goshen

2667	'Democrat Job Printing Office' around border—'W. A. Beane/ Goshen/Ind.' in centre.	436	C	Pl

INDIANA—Continued

Goshen—Continued

NUMBER	OBVERSE	REVERSE	METAL	EDGE
2668				
2669				
2670	J. L. Kindig/Dry/Goods/Merchant/ Goshen, Ind.	419	C	R
2671	Same	Same	Br	R
2672	Same	Same	C-N	R
2673	Same	Same	Z	R
2674				
2675	'Hascall, Alderman & Brown' around border—'Dry/Goods / Groceries/&c/Goshen/Ind.' in centre.	436	C	Pl
2676				
2677	Wm. H. Lash & Co./Dry/Goods/ Groceries/&c/Goshen. Ind.	436	C	Pl
2678				
2679	Joseph Lauferty Clothier Cheapside Block Goshen Ind.	552	Br	Pl
— 2680	Lawrence & Noble/Stoves / & / Hardware/Goshen. Ind. Padlock below.	438	C	Pl
2681	Same	438	Br	Pl
2682				
— 2683	C G March/Wholesale/Grocers &/ Druggist/Imp. of/Liquors & Cigars/Goshen, Ind.	436	C	Pl
2684				

Granville

2685	C. Crooks & Co./Dry/Goods/Hardware/Boots / & / Shoes / Granville. Ind.	416	C	R
2686	Same	Same	Br	R
2687	Same	Same	N	R
2688	Same	Same	Z	R
2689	Same	420	C-N	R
2690				

Greenfield

2691	Carr Ryon & Co/Dry/Goods/ Greenfield, Ind	419	C	R
2692	Same	Same	Br	R
2693				
2694				

Greenboro

| 2695 | Baldwin & Sweet/Dealers / All Kinds/of/Groceries/Greenboro Ind; | 501 | C | Pl |
| 2696 | | | | |

INDIANA—Continued

Hagerstown

NUMBER	OBVERSE	REVERSE	METAL	EDGE
2697	E. & L. Small/Dealer/in/Dry/Goods/Boots/&/Shoes/Hagerstown Ind.	400	C	Pl
2698	Same	412	C	Pl
2699				
2700	Same	418	C	R
2701	Same	Same	Br	R
2702	Same	Same	Z	R
2703	Same	453—dated '1863'	C	R
2704	Same	Same	N	R
2705				

Hartford City

2706	Jas. Lyon/Dry/Goods/Groceries/Boots/& Shoes/Hartford City, Ind.	416	C	R
2707	Same	Same	Br	R
2708				
2709	Same	419	C-N	R
2710	Same	420	C	R

Huntington

2711	Wm Bickel/Dealer/in/Books Toys/and/Notions/Huntington/Ind.	463	C	Pl
2712	Same	591	C	Pl
2713				
2714	Bippus & Morgan/Dealers/in/Hardware/Huntington/Ind.	522	C	Pl
2715	Same	563	C	Pl
2716				
2717	Sam, Buchanan/Dealer/in/Agricultural/Implements/Huntington/Ind.	478	C	Pl
2718				
2719	Jesse Davies/Dealer/in/Drugs/and/Medicines/Huntington/Ind	532	C	Pl
2720	Same	539	C	Pl
2721	J. H. Insworth & Co/Dealers/in/Dry Goods/&/Groceries/Huntington/Ind.	479	C	Pl
2722				
2723	Schafer & Bro Druggists and Apothecaries Huntington Ind	532	C	Pl
2724				

Indianapolis

2725	Alvord, Caldwell & Alvord/wholesale/Grocers/68/ E Wash St/Indianapolis.	416	C	R
2726	Same	Same	Br	R
2727	Boston Store/Dry/Goods/10/E. Wash. St/Indianapolis.	416	C	R

INDIANA—Continued

Indianapolis—Continued

NUMBER	OBVERSE	REVERSE	METAL	EDGE
2728	Same	Same	Br	R
2729				
2730	C E Geisendorff & Co/Wool/Dealers/&/Man'frs.	Hoosier Woolen/Factory/Indianapolis, Ind	C	Pl
2731	Same—name of firm in small letters.	Same	C	Pl
2732				
2733	G W Geisendorff & Co/Wool/Dealers/&/Man'frs	Same	C	Pl
2734	G W Geisendorff & Co/Domestic/Staple/and/Fancy Goods/61 and 63 West/Washington/Indianapolis.	Hoosier Jeans/and/Home made/Woolen Goods/ of every/variety / always / on hand.	C	Pl
2735				
2736	M H Good/wholesale/&/retail/dry/goods/Indianapolis.	412	C	R
2737	Same	416	C	R
2738	Same	Same	Br	R
2739	Same	420	C-N	R
2740				
2741	City/Shoe/Store/J B Grout/3 & 5/W. Wash. St/Indianapolis.	412	C	R
2742	Same	416	C	R
2743	Same	Same	Br	R
2744	Same	Same	Z	R
2745				
2746	J C Hereth/saddler/89/E. Wash St/Indianapolis	416	C	R
2747	Same	Same	Br	R
2748				
2749	Same	420	C-N	R
2750				
2751	City/Grocery/C L Holmes/Indianapolis	416	C	R
2752	Same	Same	Br	R
2753	Same	Same	Z	R
2754	Same	419	C-N	R
2755				
2756	J B Johnson/Grocer/&/Produce/Dealer/Indianapolis	416	C	R
2757	Same	Same	Br	R
2758				
2759	Same	419	C-N	R
2760				
2761	Charles Kuhn/Butcher/107/Mich/St/Indianapolis	416	C	R
2762	Same	Same	Br	R
2763	Same	Same	Z	R
2764	Same	419	C-N	R

INDIANA—Continued

Indianapolis—Continued

NUMBER	OBVERSE	REVERSE	METAL	EDGE
2765				
2766	J F Lenour/Druggist/No 5/Bates/House/Indianapolis	419	C-N	R
2767				
2768	Same	623	C	R
2769	Same	Same	Br	R
2770	Same	Same	Z	R

The Lenour cards are a die error—they were intended for the Senour cards, as they were no doubt used during the Civil War as change. We have catalogued them in their alphabetical order.

NUMBER	OBVERSE	REVERSE	METAL	EDGE
2771	Joseph Mc Creery/No 85/East/Washington St/Ind'pls/Ind	Stoves/cutlery/glass & Queensware/wholesale/&/retail	C	Pl
2772				
2773	Moritz Bro & Co/Clothiers/cloths/cassimeres/&/vestings/Indianapolis	416	C	R
2774	Same	Same	Br	R
2775				
2776	Same	419	C-N	R
2777				
2778	R R Parker/sells/ladies/and gents/furnishing/goods/30 W/Washington St/Indianapolis Ind	Half length figure shows shirt labeled 'Parkers / shirts/ will fit' 'H. H. Parker' above—'Indianapolis' below.	C	Pl
2779				
2780	Pomeroy Fry & Co/iron/merchants/Indianapolis	416	C	R
2781	Same	Same	Br	R
2782	Same	Same	Z	R
2783	Same	419	C-N	R
2784				
2785	Roll & Smith/carpets/&/Wall paper/16 Ill St/Indianapolis	416	C	R
2786	Same	Same	Br	R
2787				
2788	Same	419	C-N	R
2789				
2790	Roos & Schmalzried/Butchers/Indianapolis	416	C	R
2791	Same	Same	Br	R
2792	Same	Same	Z	R
2793	Same	420	C-N	R
2794				
2795	J F Senour/Druggist/No 5/Bates/House/Indianapolis	416	C	R
2796	Same	Same	Br	R
2797				

INDIANA—Continued

Indianapolis—Continued

NUMBER	OBVERSE	REVERSE	METAL	EDGE
2798				
2799	Same	623	C	R
2800				
2801	One glass/Soda/water/at//3 Senour's/ Drug Store.	623	C	Pl
2802				
2803	Smith & Taylor/No / 20 / / Toy Store/No 20/Washington St Indianapolis	423	C	Pl
2804				
2805	M Spencer/Grocer/202/E Wash ST/Indianapolis	416	C	R
2806	Same	Same	Br	R
2807	Same	Same	Z	R
2808	Same	419	C-N	R
2809	Same	419	C	R
2810	MRS A Thomson & Son/Stationers/ No 7/Penn/St/Indianapolis	416	C	R
2811	Same	Same	Br	R
2812	Same	Same	Z	R
2813				
2814	Same	419	C-N	R
2815				
2816	Tyler's/Bee Hive / Dry Goods /2 West/Washington St/Indianapolis	564	C	Pl
2817				
2818	Voegtle & Metzger/No 83/East/ Washington /Street / Ind'pls/Ind	Manufacturers/of/stoves/ tin ware/ Stamped ware/ &/Japaners.	C	Pl
2819				
2820	Weaver & Maguire / Grocers/ cor/ Ill St, & Ind/ Ave/Idianapolis.	416	C	R
2821	Same	Same	Br	R
2822	Same	Same	Z	R
2823				
2824	Same	419	C-N	R
2825				
2826	J B Wilson/Dealer/in/Hardware/ &/Cutlery/Indianapolis.	416	C	R
2827	Same	Same	Br	R
2828	Same	Same	Z	R
2829				
2830	Same	419	C-N	R
2831				
2832	A D Wood/Hardware/Merchant/ Indianapolis Small square & Compasses	416	C	R
2833	Same	Same	Br	R
2834				

INDIANA—Continued

Indianapolis—Continued

NUMBER	OBVERSE	REVERSE	METAL	EDGE
2835				
2836				
2837	Wayland, Jamestown, Ind *(handwritten)*			

Jonesboro

2838	Robt Gooder/Dry/Goods/&/Groceries/ Jonesboro Ind	419	C	R
2839	Same	Same	Br	R
2840	Same	Same	C-N	R
2841	Same	Same	Z	R
2842				

Kendallville

2843	Beyer Meyer & Bro/wholesale/&/retail/Druggist/Kendallville	532	C	Pl
2844				
2845	M M Bowen/Dealer/in/Groceries/Provision/&/Segars / Kendallville Ind	446	C	Pl
2846				
2847	Bosworth & Witford/Dealers/in/Groceries/&/Provisions / Kendallville	428	C	Pl
2848	Same	Same	Br	Pl
2849				
2850	W & J R Bunyan/Dealers in/Drugs / Medicines / Paints Oils/Kendallville Ind	463	C	Pl
2851	Same	621	C	Pl
2852	J F Corle Dealer in/Dry Goods &/Groceries/Kendallville Ind	471	C	Pl
2853	Same	480	C	Pl
2854				
2855	S C Evans / Dealers / in / Dry Goods/Groceries &c/Kendallville/Ind	421	C	Pl
2856	Same	Same	Br	Pl
2857	Same	426	C	Pl
2858	Same	463	C	Pl
2859				
2860	G C Glatte/Dealer/in/Groceries/Provisions/&c/Kendallville/Ind	471	C	Pl
2861				
2862	J H Gotsch/Dealer/in / Clocks/Watches/&/Jewelry / Kendallville Ind	537	C	Pl
2863	Same	Same	Br	Pl
2864				
2865	E Graden/Livery &/Sale/stable/Kendallville Ind	446	C	Pl

INDIANA—Continued

Kendallville—Continued

NUMBER	OBVERSE	REVERSE	METAL	EDGE
2866				
2867	Jacobs & Co / Dealers / in / Dry Goods / & Clothing / Kendallville Ind	422	C	Pl
2868	Same	471	C	Pl
2869				
2870	Jones & Mosher's/Bakery/&/Provision/store/Kendallville/Ind	466	C	Pl
2871	Same	Same	Br	Pl
2872				
2873	J J Joyce/Dealer/in/Groceries/&/Provisions/Kendallville/Ind	550	C	Pl
2874				
2875	J Lants/Dealer/in/Boots &/Shoes/Kendallville/Ind	534	C	Pl
2876				
2877	J M Loomis/Dealer/in/Dry Goods/and/Groceries/Kendallville/Ind	422	C	Pl
2878	Same	Same	Br	Pl
2879	Same	426	C	Pl
2880	Same	Same	Br	Pl
2881	Same	446	C	Pl
2882	Same	447	C	Pl
2883				
2884	F W Mesing/Dealer/in/Groceries/&/Liquors/Kendallville/Ind	550	C	Pl
2885				
2886	Miller & Crow/Dealers/in/Groceries/&/Provisions/Kendallville/Ind	563	C	Pl
2887				
2888	G S Rowell & Son/Produce/Dealers/Kendallville Ind	428	C	Pl
2889				
2890	Same	621	C	Pl
2891				
2892	Steer & Bowen/Dealers/in/Hardware/Kendallville/Ind	542	C	Pl
2893	Same	Same	Br	Pl
2894				
2895	Joseph Thew/Manufr/Dealer in / Boots / & Shoes / Kendallville Ind	534	C	Pl
2896				
2897	W S Thomas/Dealer / in / Dry Goods/&/ Groceries / Kendallville Ind	471	C	Pl
2898				
2899	D S Welch/Dry Goods/and/Groceries/Kendallville/Ind	463	C	Pl
2900	Same	471	C	Pl

INDIANA—Continued

Kendallville—Continued

NUMBER	OBVERSE	REVERSE	METAL	EDGE
2901	Same	Same	Br	Pl
2902	Same	446	C	Pl

Kokomo

2903	J V Cullen/Dealer/in/Groceries/Kokomo/Ind	442	C	Pl
2904				
2905	Haskell & Co/next/door to/Jay & Dollman/Kokomo/Ind	Go to the / Prarie/Store/ for/Dry Goods.	C	Pl
2906				
2907	I N Patterson/Druggist/Kokomo/Ind Mortar and pestle	532	C	Pl
2908				

La Porte

2909	L Eliel/Clothier/No 1/Teegarden Bl'k/ La Porte Ind	438	C	Pl
2910				
2911	J Faller & Son / Watchmakers/and/Jewelers/La Porte Ind	6	C	Pl
2912	Same	116	C	Pl
2913	Same	Same	Br	Pl
2914	Same	121	C	Pl
2915				
2916	'Jas Lewis & Co' above—Bee hive in centre—'La Porte Ind' below	438	C	Pl
2917				
2918	J M Neuburger/Clothier / Ball's/Corner/La Porte Ind	206	C	Pl
2919				
2920	Neuburger & Hamburger/Clothiers/No 1/Union Bl'k/ La Porte/Ind	439	C	Pl
2921				
2922	W W Wallace/Wholesale/&/Retail/Grocer/La Porte Ind	439	C	Pl
2923				
2924	L D Webber/Stoves/&/Hardware/La Porte Ind	439	C	Pl

Ligonier

2925	O Arnold/Druggist / and/Grocer/Ligonier/Ind	532	C	Pl
2926				
2927	Barney Bro/General/Dry Goods/Ligonier/Ind	428	C	Pl
2928	Same	459	C	Pl
2929	Same	461	C	Pl
2930	Same	Same	Br	Pl

INDIANA—Continued

Ligonier—Continued

NUMBER	OBVERSE	REVERSE	METAL	EDGE
2931				
2932	J C Best/Hardware/Stoves/Tinware/&c/Ligonier Ind	521	C	Pl
2933	Same	542	C	Pl
2934				
2935	J Decker/Groceries/and / Provisions/Ligonier/Ind	423	C	Pl
2936	Same	Same	Br	Pl
2937	Same	460	C	Pl
2938	Same	425	C	Pl
2939	S Mier & Co/Dry Goods/Clothing &/Produce/Dealers / Ligonier/Ind	422	C	Pl
2940	Same	426	C	Pl
2941	Same	Same	Br	Pl
2942	Same	428	C	Pl
2943				
2944	Geo C Nill/Drugs/Groceries/Stationery &c/Ligonier/Ind	528	C	Pl
2945	Same	Same	Br	Pl
2946				
2947	E Reeve / Groceries / Crockery/Glassware/Ligonier/Ind	425	C	Pl
2948				
2949	Straus Brothers / General / Dry Goods/Clothing &/Produce/Dealers/Ligonier Ind	423	C	Pl
2950	Same	Same	Br	Pl
2951	Same	425	C	Pl
2952	Same	480	C	Pl
2953				
2954	C G Vail/Dry Goods/Groceries/&c/Ligonier/Ind	425	C	Pl
2955				
2956				
2957	J C Zimmerman/Dry Goods/Clothing &c/Ligonier/Ind	425	C	Pl
2958	Same	461	C	Pl
2959	Same	Same	Br	Pl
2960				

Lisbon

2961	C D Baughman & Bro/Dealers/in/Dry Goods/and/Groceries/Lisbon/Ind	534	C	Pl
2962				

Logansport

2963	Booth & Sturges/Dealers/in/Boots/and/Shoes/Logansport/Ind	534	C	Pl
2964				

INDIANA—Continued

Logansport—Continued

NUMBER	OBVERSE	REVERSE	METAL	EDGE
2965	M H Gridley/Logansport/Ind Eagle in glory	536	C	Pl
2966				
2967	A Kendall Dealer in groceries & flour Logansport Ind	480	C	Pl
2968				
2969	King & Reed/Dealers/in/Stoves/&/Tinware/Logansport Ind	524	C	Pl
2970	Krug & Reed/dealers/in / stoves/&/tinware/Logansport/Ind	524	C	Pl
2971	Mc Donald & Co/Dealers/in/Dry Goods/Carpets/Logansport/Ind	442	C	Pl
2972				
2973	A J Murdock Dealer in Dry Goods & Groceries Logansport Ind	480	C	Pl
2974				

Lynn

NUMBER	OBVERSE	REVERSE	METAL	EDGE
2975	Elliot & Hinshaw/Dry/Goods/&/Lynn/Ind	419	C	Pl
2976	Same	Same	C	R
2977				
2978				
2979	Same	420	C-N	R
2980				
2981	J A Hinshaw/Dry/Goods/&/Groceries/Lynn Ind	411	C	R
2982	Same	418	C	R
2983	Same	Same	Br	R
2984	Same	419	C-N	R
2985	Same	617	C	Pl
2986				
2987				

Mechanicsburg

NUMBER	OBVERSE	REVERSE	METAL	EDGE
2988	Elliot & Swain Dry Goods Groceris Hardware Mechanicsburg Ind	446	C	Pl
2989				
2990				
2991	Ezra Swain/Dry Goods / Groceries / Hardware &c/Mechanicsburg/Indiana	470	C	Pl
2992	Same	621	C	Pl
2993				

Middlebury

NUMBER	OBVERSE	REVERSE	METAL	EDGE
2994	C Stutz / Dry / Goods / Clothing/Boots & Shoes/Middlebury Ind	416	C	R
2995				
2996	Same	419	C-N	R
2997				

INDIANA—Continued.

Middletown

NUMBER	OBVERSE	REVERSE	METAL	EDGE
2998	Large square and compasses in centre 'W W Cotteral P M' above—'Middletown Ind' below	419	C	R
2999	Same	Same	Br	R
3000	Same	Blank Reverse	C	R
3001				

Mishawaka

3002	H D Higgins / Jeweler/Optician/ & Mfn of/ Barometers/Mishawaka	6	C	Pl
3003	Same	626	C	Pl
3004				
3005	H D Higgins/Jeweler / Optician/ Mfr of/ Barometers/Mishawaka Ind	6	C	Pl
3006				
3007	H D Higgins/Jeweler / Optician/ &/Mfr of/Barometers/Mishawaka	544	C	Pl
3008				
3009	H D Higgins/Jeweler/&/Optician/Mishawaka Ind	69	C	Pl
3010	Same	Same	Br	Pl
3011				
3012	H D Higgins/Jeweler/&/Optician/Mishawaka Ind—no period after 'Ind'	436	C	Pl
3013	Same	588	C	Pl
3014	H D Higgins/Jeweler/&/Optician/ Mishawaka Ind The 'N' on line with 'D'	625	C	Pl
3015	Same	Same	Br	Pl
3016				
3017				
3018	B Holcomb/Dealer/in/Groceries/ Stone Ware/Oils &c/Mishawaka	69	C	Pl
3019				
3020	S H Judkins/Groceries/&/Provisions/Mishawaka Ind	438	C	Pl
3021				

Mooresville

3022	W H P Woodward/Dry/Goods/&c/ Mooresville Ind	419	C	R
3023				

New Castle

3024	M L Powell/Dealer in/Stoves/&/ Tin ware/New Castle Ind	444	C	Pl
3025	Same	470	C	Pl
3026	Same	524	C	Pl
3027	Same	521	C	Pl
3028				

INDIANA—Continued

New Paris

3029	A M Davis Dry Goods Groceries Crockery Drugs &c New Paris Ind	Variation of 150	C	Pl
3030				

North Vernon

3031	John Wentzel/Dealer /in/Stoves/ &/Tin Ware/North Vernon Ind	521	C	Pl

Oldenburg

3032	J Holker / good for / 1—drink / at the/bar/Oldenburg Ind	664	Br	R

Peru

3033	J Kreutzer / Dealer / in / Glass / Queensware/&/Crockery/Peru Ind	560	C	Pl
3034				
3035	J S Queeby/Dealer/in/Dry Goods/ &/Notions/Peru Ind	467	C	Pl
3036	Same	509	C	Pl
3037	Same	518	C	Pl
3038	Same	546	C	Pl
3039	Same	565	C	Pl
3040	Same	589	C	Pl
3041				
3042	Saine & Miller/Groceries/Notions/ Boots & shoes/Peru Ind	534	C	Pl
3043				

Pierceton

3044	Murray & Bro/Dry Goods / &/ Groceries/Pierceton/Ind	425	C	Pl
3045				
3046	Reed & Spayde/Dealers in/Dry Goods/&/Groceries / Pierceton Ind	472	C	Pl

Plainfield

3047	DRY Goods/&/Clothing/Johnson/ &/Oursler/Plainfield	416	C	R
3048				
3049				
3050	Same	420	C-N	R
3051				
3052	Johnson & Oursler/Dealer/in/ Dry/Goods/Boots & Shoes/Plain- fiield Ind	420	C-N	R
3053	Same	622	C	R
3054	Same	Same	Br	R
3055	Same	Same thr as 3047		

INDIANA—Continued

Plainfield—Continued

NUMBER	OBVERSE	REVERSE	METAL	EDGE
3056	M Osborn / Groceries / Notions/ Toys/&/Fancy Articles/Plainfield Ind	Queensware/Willow / & / Wooden/Ware/at / M. Osorn's.	C	R
3057	Same	Same	Br	R
3058	Same	Same	Z	R
3059	Same	Same as Die No 453-dated '1863'	C-N	R
3060				
3061	Queensware/ Willow/& / Woodenware/at/M Osborn's	419	C-N	R
3062	Same	420	C	R
3063				
3064	Dry Goods/&/Clothing / at/I M Shidlers / Post Office / Building/ Plainfield Ind	Hat and cap in centre— 'Isaac M. Shidler/Dealer/ in' above—'Boots & Shoes/ and/Notions' below	C	R
3065	Same	Same	Br	R
3066				
3067	Same	419	C-N	R
3068	Same	453 dated '1863'	C	Pl
3069				
3070	Tamsey & Ballard / Dealers / in/ Drugs/&/Medicines/Plainfield Ind	Motar and pestle in centre—' 'Perfumery, notions/and' above—'fancy/ articles' below	C	R
3071	Same	Same	Br	R
3072	Same	Same	Z	R
3073	Same	453 dated '1863'	C	Pl

Plymouth

3074	J M Dale/Dry Goods/Groceries/ Crockery/Boots shoes &c/Plymouth/Ind	556	C	Pl
3075				
3076				
3077	H B Dickson & Co / Hardware/ Stoves/and/Tinware/Plymouth/Ind	521	C	Pl
3078				
3079				
3080	H Humrichouser / Grain / &/ Produce/Dealer/Plymouth/Ind	459	C	Pl
3081				

Richmond

3082	C C Buhl/Dealer/in/Stoves and/ Tinware/51/Main St/Richmond Ind	478	C	Pl
3083	Same	521	C	Pl

INDIANA—Continued
Richmond—Continued

NUMBER	OBVERSE	REVERSE	METAL	EDGE
3084				
3085	G C Emswiler & Co/Fancy Goods/ &/Toys/49 Main St/Richmond Ind	418	C	Pl
3086	Same	Same	C	R
3087	Same	Same	Br	R
3088				
3089	Same	419	C-N	R
3090				
3091	E F Hirst / Watch / Maker / & / Jeweler/38 Main St/Richmond Ind	401	C	Pl
3092	Same	418	C	R
3093	Same	Same	Br	R
3094	Same	Same	Z	R
3095	Same	419	C-N	R
3096				

Rochester

3097	D S Gould/Dry/Goods/&/Groceries/opp/Court House/Sqr/Rochester Ind	419	C	R
3098	Same	Same	Br	R
3099	Same	Same	C-N	R
3100	Same	Same	Z	R
3101				

Seymour

3102	J F Johnson/News/Dealer/Seymour Ind	428	C	Pl
3103	Same	460	C	Pl
3104	Same	Same	Br	Pl

South Bend

3105	W W Bement/Edge/Tool/Manf'r/ South Bend Ind	H. D. Higgins/Jeweler/&/ Optician/Mishawaka. Ind.	C	Pl
3106	Blowney & Johns/Mfr's/composition/roofing/South Bend Ind	121	C	Pl
✕ 3107	S M Chord/Dealer in/Dry Goods/ Groceries/Crockery / Carpets &c/ South Bend Ind	152	Bronze	Pl
3108				
3109	Hammonds / Shoe / Store / South Bend Ind	26	C	Pl
3110				
3111	J C Knoblock/Baker/&/Grocer/ South Bend Ind	434	C	Pl
3112	Same	438	C	Pl
3113	Same	485	C	Pl
3114				
3115	A M Purdy/Nurseryman/&/Fruit/ Grower/South Bend Ind	206	C	Pl

INDIANA—Continued

Southbend—Continued

NUMBER	OBVERSE	REVERSE	METAL	EDGE
3116	Same	627	C	Pl
3117				
3118	George Wyman / Fancy / Dry Goods/South Bend/Ind	209	C	Pl
3119	Same	628	C	Pl
3120				
3121				

Sullivan

3122	Price Brothers/Dry/Goods/Clothing/Boots & Shoes/&c/Sullivan Ind	418	C	R
3123	Same	Same	Br	R
3124	Same	Same	Z	R
3125				
3126	Same	Same as Die No 453—dated '1863'	C-N	R
3127				
3128				

Swan

3129	D H Haines & Bro/Dealers/in/Dry Goods/Groceries/&c/Swan Ind	460	C	Pl
3130	Same	Same	Br	Pl
3131				
3132				

Valparaiso

3133	'Bartholomew & McClelland' around edge-'Dry Goods / Boots Shoes/&c/Ind/Valparaiso' in centre	152	C	Pl
3134	Same	169	C	Pl

Vincennes

3135	Chas F Raker/dealer/in/dry/goods/&/groceries Ind	598	Br	R

Wabash

3136	Gordon & Thurston / Dealers / in/ Drugs/Books/&/ Jewelry/Wabash Ind	'Drugs & medicines 1863' around edge—motar and pestle in a circles of 13 stars in centre.	C	Pl
3137				
3138				

INDIANA—Continued

Warsaw

NUMBER	OBVERSE	REVERSE	METAL	EDGE
3139	D Carlile/Dealer/in/oysters/Confectionery/cigars/&/ Warsaw Ind	Good for/25 / cents / payable in bank bills	Br	Pl
3140	Same	419	C-N	R
3141	John Lane / watchmaker/&/jeweler/Warsaw/Ind	Blank	C	Pl

Wheeling

3142
3143

Wolf Creek

| 3144 | WOLF/Creek/Pike/G Haines | 419 | C | R |
| 3145 | Same | Same | C-N | R |

IOWA

Cedar Rapids

3146	You can buy/Goods cheap/at/the/ New York / Store / Cedar Rapids Iowa	Female head to left—'Reynolds & Co' above—'New York Store' below.	C	Pl
3147	Same	25	C	Pl
3148	Same as reverse of No 3146	209	C	Pl

Lansing

3149	Wm Flemming & Bro/Lumber/ Lath/&/ Shingles / Lansing Iowa	416	C	R
3150	Same	Same	Br	R
3151				
3152	Same	420	C-N	R
3153				
3154				

Lyons

| 3155 | Gage Lyall & Keeler/Grocer/Main St/Lyons/Iowa | 575 | C | Pl |
| 3156 | | | | |

Waterloo

3157	H & G Goodhue/Lath shingles/&/ Lumber/Sash/Blind/&/Door/Factory/Waterloo Iowa	419	C	R
3158	Same	Same	Br	R
3159	Same	Same	C-N	R
3160				

KANSAS

Leavenworth

NUMBER	OBVERSE	REVERSE	METAL	EDGE
3165	A Cohen/clothing/and gents/furnishing goods/21 Delaware St/Leavenworth/Kansas	423	C	Pl
3166	Same	Same	Br	Pl

KENTUCKY

Covington

3175	Arbeiter/Halle/Pike/St/Covington Ky	412	C	R
3176	Same	Same	Br	R
3177				
3178	Same	418	C	R
3179	Same	Same	Br	R
3180				
3181	Same	629	C	Pl
3182				
3183				
3184	Cov & Cin/Ferry/Company	418	C	R
3185	Same	Same	Br	R
3186				
3187	Same	419	C-N	R
3188				
3189	J Dolman/Stocking / Manufacturer/Cov Ky	339	C	Pl
3190				
3191	V C Engert / Germania / Saloon/6' St/Covington Ky	412	C	Pl
3192	Same	617	C	Pl
3193				
3194				
3195	Same	405	C	R
3196				
3197	Same	418	C	R
3198	Same	Same	Br	R
3199				
3200	Same	419	C-N	R

Henderson

3201	S Johnson & Bro/druggists/Henderson/Ky	Soda check/1/glass	W-M	Pl

Lexington

3202	John W Lee/Baker/&/Confectioner/10 Main St/Lexington Ky	420	C	R
3203				
3204	Same	453	C	R

KENTUCKY—Continued

Lexington—Continued

NUMBER	OBVERSE	REVERSE	METAL	EDGE
3205	Same	Same	Br	R
3206	Same	Same	C-N	R
3207				
3208	Same	One/half/pint/of/milk	C	R
3209	Same	Same	Br	R
3210	Same	Same	Z	R
3211	Same	1/pint/of/milk	C	R
3212	Same	Same	Br	R
3213	Same	Same	Z	R
3214	Same	One/quart/of/milk	C	R
3215	Same	Same	Br	R
3216	Same	Same	Z	R
3217	Same	One/half/gal/of/milk	C	R
3218	Same	Same	Br	R
3219	Same .	Same	Z	R
3220	Same	One/gall/of/milk	C	R
3221	Same	Same	Br	R
3222	Same	Same	Z	R
3223				

Louisville

3224	Made by H Miller & Co/1/pint/ Louisville	'A/Weber'	Br	Pl
3225	Same	Same	S	Pl
3226				
3227	Hand holding a beer mug with '5' inclosed by capital 'C' in centre— 'H Miller & Co' to left—'Louisville' to right	Same	C	Pl
3228				
3229				
3230	Same	'Garrett Townsend' in a circle of stars	S	Pl
3231				
3232				
3233	Same	'George/Brucklacher'	C	Pl
3234	Same	Same	Br	Pl
3235	Same	Same	S	Pl
3236				
3237	Same	'J/Kuntz'	Br	Pl
3238				

Newport

3239	J Butcher's/Dry/Goods/Store/ Newport Ky	414	C	Pl
3240	Same	617	C	Pl
3241				
3242	Same	418	C	R
3243	Same	Same	Br	R
3244				

KENTUCKY—Continued

Newport—Continued

NUMBER	OBVERSE	REVERSE	METAL	EDGE
3245	N'Pt & Cov/Bridge/Company	415	C	Pl
3246				
3247	Same	418	C	R
3248	Same	Same	Br	R
3249				
3250	Same	420	C-N	R
3251				

MAINE

Bangor

3255	R S Torrey/inventor/of the/ Maine State/Bee Hive/5th St/ Bangor Me	25	C	Pl
3256				
3257	'Inventor / of the / Maine State/ Bee hive/1864' in centre—' 'R S Torrey' above—'Bangor Me' below	121	C	Pl
3258				

MARYLAND

3259	G R Brown/confectioner / 1862 / Hagerstown Md	'To observatory' above— telescope in centre—'and/ telescope' below	Br	Pl

MASSACHUSETTS

Boston

3260	'Dunn & Co's' above — 'Oyster House' below — '1864' within wreath of 24 leaves	630	Br	Pl
3261				
3262	Same	631	C	Pl
3263				
3264	Same, but wreath contains only 22 leaves	631	C	Pl
3265				
3266	Dunn & Co/Oyster/House/1864	Similar to 631—wreath has only 28 leaves with 13 berries added to the wreath	C	Pl
3267				

Nantucket, Mass

12556a Great Seal - U.S. Country Commission - 18
·189 Reverse

MASSACHUSETTS—Continued

Boston—Continued

NUMBER	OBVERSE	REVERSE	METAL	EDGE
3268	Jos H Merriam/Medalist/DieSinker/and / letter cutter / established 1850/No 18/Brattle Square Boston	503	C	Pl
3269	Same	'not one cent' in centre—' 'Jos H Merriam Boston' above—'1863' below.	C	Pl
3270	Same	Same	Br	Pl
3271	Design of a frog in centre—'Merrian & Co / Boston' above—'18 Brattle/Sqr' below	503	C	Pl
3272	Same	Same	Br	Pl
3273				
3274				
3275	Steer's head in centre—'G F Tuttle's above—'Restaurant' below	130 Washington street/ good for / 5 / cents in / refreshments.	C	Pl
3276	Same	Same but '10' cents	C	Pl
3277	Same	Same but '25' cents	C	Pl
3278	Same	Same but '50' cents	C	Pl
3279				
3280				

Fall River

3281	E P Francis/City/Hotel/Fall River/Mass/1864	'No / 27-31 / Pleasaant / Street' in centre—'Billiard Room & Restaurant' around border	C	Pl
3282	Same	Same	Br	Pl
3283	Same	Same	N	Pl
3284	Same	Same	W-M	Pl
3285				

Harvard

3286	Bay State/Horse Power/send for/ circular/A & C F Wright/Harvard/Mass	Female head to left—'shop rights for sale in West'n Sts.' above	C	Pl

Worcester

3287	Male head to left—'Charles Lang' above—'1863' below	Die sinker/&/Gen'l / Engraver/Worcester, Ms.	C	Pl
3288	Same	Same	Br	Pl

MICHIGAN

Addison

NUMBER	OBVERSE	REVERSE	METAL	EDGE
3300	Sheaf of wheat in center—'Smith Brothers' above—'Addison, Mich' below	Dealers in/Dry Goods/ Groceries/Hardware/1868		
— 3301	Same	Same	Br	Pl
3302				

Adrian

3303	Blackman & Dibble / druggists/ Adrian Mich	472	C	Pl
3304	Buck & Farrar/Dealers/in/Hardware/Stoves/& tin/Adrian Mich	434	C	Pl
3305	Same	594	C	Pl
3306				
3307	J A Castle/Grocer/Maumee/St/ Adrian Mich	209	C	Pl
3308	Same	432	C	Pl
3309	Same	434	C	Pl
3310				
3311	Remington & Bennett/Druggists/ &/Grocers/Maumee St/Adrian	25	C	Pl
— 3312	Same	432	C	Pl
3313	Same	433	C	Pl
3314	Similar inscription—different die	432	C	Pl
3315				
3316	S Sammons/Inn/Keeper/Mansion/ House/Maumee ST Adrian	433	C	Pl
3317	Same	434	C	Pl
3318	Same	594	C	Pl
3319				

Albion

— 3320	Albion Commercial College/Ira Mayhew/Pres't/Albion/Mich	Mayhew's Practical Bookkeeping/the/greatest / and the/best/1863.	C	Pl
3321	Same	Same	Br	Pl
3322				
3323	Comstock & Bro/Druggists/Albion/Mich	209	C	Pl
3324	Same	611	C	Pl
3325	Same	632	C	Pl
3326				

Almont

3327	D W Richardson / Drugs / and/ Books/Almont Mich	209	C	Pl
3328	Same	434	C	Pl
3329				

Ann Harbor

— 3330	Philip Bach/Dry/Goods/1863	49	C	Pl

MICHIGAN—Continued

Ann Harbor—Continued

NUMBER	OBVERSE	REVERSE	METAL	EDGE
3331	Same	Same	Br	Pl
3332	Same	Same	N	Pl
3333	Same	Same	C-N	Pl
3334	Same	Same	W-M	Pl
3335	Same	Same	S	Pl
3336	Same	451	C	Pl
3337	Same	Same	Br	Pl
3338	Same	Same	N	Pl
3339	Same	Same	C-N	Pl
3340	Same	Same	W-M	Pl
3341	Same	Same	S	Pl
3342				
3343	Dean & Co/House/Furnishing/Goods/1863	49	C	Pl
3344	Same	Same	Br	Pl
3345	Same	Same	N	Pl
3346	Same	Same	C-N	Pl
3347	Same	Same	W-M	Pl
3348	Same	Same	S	Pl
3349	Same	451	C	Pl
3350	Same	Same	Br	Pl
3351	Same	Same	N	Pl
3352	Same	Same	C-N	Pl
3353	Same	Same	W-M	Pl
3354	Same	Same	S	Pl
3355	G H Millen/Dealer/in/Dry Goods/& Groceries/Ann Arbor/Mich	209	C	Pl
3356	Same	633	C	Pl
3357				
3358	Stebbins & Wilson/Dry Goods/and/Groceries/Business Card 'D' between 'S' and 'D'	Mortar and pestle in centre—'Druggist' above—'Ann Arbor Mich' below.	Bronze	Pl
3359	Same but 'D' opposite 'S'	Same	Bronze	Pl
3360				
3361	Wm Wagner / Merchant / Tailor/ Dealer in / Clothing / Ann Arbor Mich	594	C	Pl
3362	Same	633	C	Pl
3363				
3364				

Atlas

3365	F J & F Palmer's/Woolen/Factory/Atlas/Genesee Co Mich	418	C	R
3366	Same	Same	Br	R
3367	Same	634	C	R
3368				
3369	Same	420	C-N	R
3370				

MICHIGAN—Continued

Battle Creek

NUMBER	OBVERSE	REVERSE	METAL	EDGE
	For the Wm. Brooks cards see under Elkhart, Indiana			
3371				
3372	J B Leonard/Boot/&/shoe/maker/ Battle Creek Mic	474	C	Pl
3373				
3374	Stuart & Son/Stoves / Hardware/ Iron &/nails/Battle Creek	433	C	Pl
3375	Same	594	C	Pl
3376				

Bay City

3377	Binder & Co/in/Dry Goods/Groceries/Hardware/&c/Bay City Mich	206	C	Pl
3378	Same	633	C	Pl
3379				

Brighton

3380	Roswell Barnes/Maker & Dealer/ in/Boots/&/shoes / Brighton Mich	416	C	R
3381	Same	Same	Br	R
3382	Same	Same	Z	R
3383	Same	420	C-N	R
3384				
3385	Wm R Cobb/Dry/Goods/&/Groceries/Brighton Mich	416	C	R
3386				
3387	Same	418	C	R
3388	Same	Same	Br	R
3389				
3390	Same	420	C-N	R
3391				
3392	W H Naylor/Dealer in/Harware/ &/cutlery/Brighton Mich	416	C	R
3393				
3394	Same	418	C	R
3395	Same	Same	Br	R
3396				
3397	Same	420	C-N	R
3398				

Buchanan

3399	Weaver & Fox/Stoves/Tin/ Hardware/&c/Buchanan/Mich	25	C	Pl
3400	Same	627	C	Pl
3401				
3402				
3403				

MICHIGAN—Continued

Charlotte

NUMBER	OBVERSE	REVERSE	METAL	EDGE
3404	C Cummings/dry goods/groceries/boots shoes &c/Charlotte/Mich	462	C	Pl
3405	Same	Same	Br	Pl
3406				
3407	Same	478	C	Pl
3408	Same	Same	Br	Pl
3409				
3410	Higby & Brother / General / Merchants/Charlotte/Mich	462	C	Pl
3411	Same	Same	Br	Pl
3412				
3413	J Mikesell & Bro/dealers/in/Groceries/and/provisions/Charlotte Mich	462	C	Pl
3414	Same	Same	Br	Pl
3415				
3416	C J Piper/groceries/boots shoes &c/ Charlotte/Mich	533	C	Pl
3417	Same	Same	Br	Pl
3418				

Chelsea

3419	Congdon Brothers / dry goods/ groceries / & Hardware / Chelsea Mich	474	C	Pl
3420				

Clarkeston

3421	M H Clark/dry/goods/hardware/boots/&/shoes/Clarkston Mich	416	C	R
3422				
3423	Same	418	C	R
3424				
3425	Same	420	C-N	R
3426				
3427	H & J T Peter/druggists/Clarkston	418	C	R
3428	Same	Same	Br	R
3429				

Coldwater

3430
3431

Constantine

3432	Buy your hardware/at/E H Sheldon/Constantine/Mich	U. S. shield in cenre—'E. H. Sheldon' above—'1863' below	C	Pl
3433	ʻʼ	ʻʼ	Br	

MICHIGAN—Continued

Corunna

NUMBER	OBVERSE	REVERSE	METAL	EDGE
3434	H A Crane/Stoves/&/Hardware/ Corunna Mich	20	C	Pl
3435	Same	209	C	Pl
3436	Same	434	C	Pl
3437				
3438	G W Goodell/Drugs/Medicines/ &c/ Corunna Mich	20	C	Pl
3439	Same	206	C	Pl
3440	Same	432	C	Pl
3441	Same	434	C	Pl
3442				

Detroit

NUMBER	OBVERSE	REVERSE	METAL	EDGE
3443	W J Adderley/Grocer/157/Gratoit/St/Detroit—star at sides	Same as No 453—dated '1863'	C	R
3444	Same	453	C	R
3445	Same	419	C-N	R
3446				
3447	Same as preceeding—no star at side	412	C	Pl
3448	Same	416	C	R
3449	Same	418	C	R
3450	Same	Same	Br	R
3451	Same	Same	Z	R
3452	Same	420	C-N	R
3453				
3454	American/Coffee/Mills/25 Jeff Ave/Detroit	418	C	R
3455	Same	Same	Br	R
3456	Same	Same	Z	R
3457	Same	416	C	R
3458	Same	420	C-N	R
3459				
3460	T H Armstrong/dealer/in/hats/ caps and furs/Detroit	410	C-N	R
3461	Same	418	C	R
3462	Same	Same	Br	R
3463	Same	Same	Z	R
3464	Same	420	C-N	R
3465				
3466	Blinbury's / hotel / Antisdel / & / Hills/Detroit Mich	404	C	R
3467	Same	418	C	R
3468	Same	Same	Br	R
3469	Same	Same	Z	R
3470				
3471	Same	420	C	R
3472	G Bamlet / Grocer/&/Produce/ Dealer/17 Gr Riv St/Detroit	416	C	R
3473	Same	418	C	R

MICHIGAN—Continued

Detroit—Continued

NUMBER	OBVERSE	REVERSE	METAL	EDGE
3474	Same	Same	Br	R
3475				
3476	Same	420	C-N	R
3477				
3478				
3479	L W Barie/baker/114/Fort/ St/Detroit	405	C	R
3480				
3481	Same	418	C	R
3482	Same	Same	Br	R
3483	Same	Same	Z	R
3484				
3485	Same	Same	C-N	R
3486				
3487	Geo Beard & Son / oyster / fruit / fish & game/depot/Detroit	410	C	Pl
3488				
3489	Same	418	C	R
3490	Same	Same	Br	R
3491	Same	Same	Z	R
3492				
3493	Same	420	C-N	R
3494				
3495	H W Beeson/groceries / & / ship/ stores/22 Woodward Ave/Detroit	410	C	R
3496				
3497	Same	418	C	R
3498	Same	Same	Br	R
3499	Same	Same	Z	R
3500				
3501	Same	420	C-N	R
3502				
3503	Same	635	C	R
3504				
3505	Fred'r C Blome / dry / goods/61 Wood Ave/Detroit	418	C	R
3506	Same	Same	Br	R
3507	Same	Same	Z	R
3508				
3509	Same	420	C	R
3510				
3511	Same	577	C	R
3512				
3513	Broeg & Gerber / Butchers / 35/ Mich/Ave/Detroit	410	C	R
3514	Same	418	C	R
3515	Same	Same	Br	R
3516	Same	Same	Z	R
3517	Same	420	C	R
3518	F. A. Burkhart/butcher/cor/Hasting/& Gratiot/Sts/Detroit	416	C	R
3519				

MICHIGAN—Continued

Detroit. Continued

NUMBER	OBVERSE	REVERSE	METAL	EDGE
3520	Same	418	C	R
3521	Same	418	Br	R
3522	Same	418	Z	R
3523				
3524	Same	420	C-N	R
3525				
3526	Same	634	C	R
3527				
3528	Charles Bisch / Hardware/stoves/ &/ grates/ 201 Jeff Ave/ Detroit	404	C	R
3529				
3530	Same	411	C	R
3531				
3532	Same	418	C	R
3533	Same	Same	Br	R
3534	Same	Same	Z	R
3535				
3536				
3537	Same	420	C	R
3538				
3539	Campbell & Calnon/grocers/Mich/ Grand Ave/Detroit	418	C	R
3540	Same	Same	Br	R
3541	Same	Same	Z	R
3542				
3543	Same	420	C-N	R
3544				
3545	Same	635	C	R
3546				
3547	Narrow leaved thistle in centre— 'Campbell Linn & Co' above— 'Business Card' below	Scotch store/dry goods/ and / millinery / Detroit Mich	Bronze	Pl
3548	Same—broad leaved thistle	Same	same	Pl
3549	Same as No 3447	Same as No 3447—ornaments added	same	Pl
3550	Same as No 3448	Same as No 3449	same	Pl
3551				
3552	H. A. Christiansen / groceries/&/ Provisions/ 259 Jeff Ave/Detroit	404	C	R
3553				
3554	Same	416	C	R
3555				
3556	Same	418	C	R
3557	Same	Same	Br	R
3558	Same	Same	Z	R
3559				
3560	Same	420	C-N	R
3561				
3562	G & W Clark/Butchers/cor/ Larned & 1'st/Detroit	416	C	Pl
3563	Same	418	C	R

MICHIGAN—Continued

Detroit—Continued

NUMBER	OBVERSE	REVERSE	METAL	EDGE
3564	Same	Same	Br	R
3565	Same	Same	Z	R
3566				
3567	Same	420	C-N	R
3568				
3569	S Cohen / Clothing / Dealer/ 155 Jeff Ave/Detroit	411	C	R
3570				
3571	Same	418	C	R
3572	Same	Same	Br	R
3573	Same	Same	Z	R
3574				
3575	Same	420	C-N	R
3576				
3577	A W Copland's / steam / Bakery/ 20 Monroe Ave/Detroit	418	C	R
3578	Same	Same	Br	R
3579	Same	Same	Z	R
3580				
3581	Same	420	C-N	R
3582				
3583	Same	635	C	R
3584				
3585	C L Crosby / Fruit / & / Produce/ dealer/Detroit	418	C	R
3586	Same	Same	Br	R
3587				
3588	Same	420	C-N	R
3589				
3590	Same	635	C	R
3591	Geo E Curtis/leather/&/findings/ 215 Jeff Ave/Detroit	411	C	R
3592				
3593	Same	418	C	R
3594	Same	Same	Br	R
3595	Same	Same	Z	R
3596				
3597	Same	420	C	R
3598	Same	Same	C-N	R
3599	Godfrey Dean & Co/Painters/&/ picture frame/makers/Detroit	416	C	R
3600				
3601	Same	418	C	R
3602	Same	Same	Br	R
3603	Same	Same	Z	R
3604				
3605	Same	420	C	R ·
3606	Same	Same	C-N	R
3607	Detroit/City/Flour/Mills/Cor Larned & 2' Sts/	416	C	R
3608				

MICHIGAN—Continued

Detroit—Continued

NUMBER	OBVERSE	REVERSE	METAL	EDGE
3609	Same	418	C	R
3610	Same	Same	Br	R
3611	Same	Same	Z	R
3612				
3613	Same	420	C-N	R
3614				
3615	D Dickson/Grocer / &/Provision/ Dealer/1' & Larned, Sts/Detroit	416	C	R
3616				
3617	Same	418	C	R
3618	Same	Same	Br	R
3619	Same	Same	Z	R
3620				
3621	Same	420	C	R
3622	Same	Same	C-N	R
3623				
3624	E A Drury/grocer/150/Woodward/Avenue/Dertoit	410	C	R
3625				
3626	Same	418	C	R
3627	Same	Same	Br	R
3628	Same	Same	Z	R
3629				
3630	Same	420	C-N	R
3631				
3632	Francis Eccard/Tobacconist/ Detroit	409	C	R
3633				
3634	Same	416	C	R
3635				
3636	Same	418	C	R
3637	Same	Same	Br	R
3638	Same	Same	Z	R
3639				
3640	Same	420	C	R
3641	Same	Same	C-N	R
3642				
3643	Peninsular/Hotel/Detroit/ Wm Eisenlord	416	C	R
3644				
3645	Same	418	C	R
3646	Same	Same	Br	R
3647				
3648	Same	420	C	R
3649	Same	Same	C-N	R
3650	Farmers / clothing / store / 251 & 253/Gratiot St/Detroit	418	C	R
3651	Same	Same	Br	R
3652	Same	Same	Z	R
3653	Same	420	C-N	R
3654				

MICHIGAN—Continued

Detroit—Continued

NUMBER	OBVERSE	REVERSE	METAL	EDGE
3655	C Fitzsimons & Co/grocer/7 & 9/ Woodward/Ave/Detroit	418	C	R
3656	Same	Same	Br	R
3657				
3658	Same	420	C-N	R
3659				,
3660	Same	635	C	R
3661				
3662	L S Freeman / news / dealer/opposite/Biddle/house/Detroit Mich	418	C	R
3663	Same	Same	Br	R
3664	Same	Same	Z	R
3665				
3666	Same	420	C-N	R
3667				
3668	Same	615	C	R
3669				
3670	'Frisbie's / card ' within wreath	'55 Woodward & 167 Jefferson Ave' above—'wholesale / & retail / dry goods' in centre—'Detroit Mich' below	Bronze	Pl
3671				
3672	F Geis & Bro's/fire & / water/proof/roofing/cor/Cong & Brush/sts/Detroit	416	C	R
3673				
3674	Same	418	C	R
3675	Same	Same	Br	R
3676				
3677	Same	420	C-N	R
3678				
3679	Same as No 3672—name spelled 'Geiss'	418	C	R
3680	Same	Same	Br	R
3681				
3682	Same	F. Geiss / dealer in / groceries/& / provisions / hay &/straw/boots &/shoes	C	R
3683	Same	Same	Br	R
3684	Same as No 3672—name spelled 'Gies'	416	C	R
3685	Same as reverse of No 3682	418	C	R
3686	Same	418	Br	R
3687	Same	418	Z	R
3688				
3689	Same	420	C-N	R
3690				
3691	Same—name spelled with larger letters	404	C	R
3692	Same	418	C	R

MICHIGAN—Continued

Detroit—Continued

NUMBER	OBVERSE	REVERSE	METAL	EDGE
3693	Same	Same	Br	R
3694				
3695	C B Goodrich/dealer in/boots & shoes/opp/Perkins/Hotel/Detroit	416	C	R
3696				
3697	Same	418	C	R
3698	Same	Same	Br	R
3699	Same	Same	Z	R
3700				
3701	Same	420	C-N	R
3702				
3703	F Hamman & Co/liquor/store/cor Macomb Ave/& Gr Riv st/Detroit	418	C	R
3704	Same	Same	Br	R
3705				
3706	Same	420	C-N	R
3707				
3708	Same	635	C	R
3709				
3710	Hanna & Co/wholesale/tobacconists/112/Woodward/Ave/Detroit	416	C	R
3711				
3712	Same	418	C	R
3713	Same	Same	Br	R
3714				
3715	Same	420	C-N	R
3716				
— 3717	Herintons/double thread/15/Sewing/machine/Detroit Mich	26	C	Pl
3718				
3719	Higby & Stearns/Druggists/Detroit	410	C	R
3720				
3721	Same	418	C	R
3722	Same	Same	Br	R
3723	Same	Same	Z	R
3724				
3725	Same	420	C-N	R
3726				
3727	Hilterscheid Bro's/Meat/Market/ Cor Fort &/Russell St/ Detroit	418	C	R
3728	Same	Same	Br	R
3729	Same	Same	Z	R
3730				
3731	Same	420	C-N	R
3732				
3733	Same	635	C	R
3734				
3735	Jacob Hochstandt/Butcher/cor/2nd &/Mich Ave/Detroit	416	C	R
3736				

MICHIGAN—Continued

Detroit—Continued

NUMBER	OBVERSE	REVERSE	METAL	EDGE
3737	Same	418	C	R
3738	Same	Same	Br	R
3739	Same	Same	Z	R
3740				
3741	Same	420	C-N	R
3742				
3743	C J Holthofer/Dealer in/dry/goods/Detroit	409	C	R
3744				
3745	Same	416	C	R
3746				
3747	Same	418	C	R
3748	Same	Same	Br	R
3749	Same	Same	Z	R
3750				
3751	Same	420	C-N	R
3752				
3753	Wm B Howe/Book/Seller/192 Jeff Ave/Detroit	411	C	R
3754				
3755	Same	418	C	R
3756	Same	Same	Br	R
3757	Same	Same	Z	R
3758				
3759	Same	420	C-N	R
3760				
3761	Edward Kanter/groceries/produce/&/ship/chandlery/Detroit	418	C	R
3762	Same	Same	Br	R
3763	Same	Same	Z	R
3764				
3765	Same	420	C-N	R
3766				
3767	P N Kneeland/dealer/in/stoves/&/tinware/cor Grand River/& Griswold St/Detroit	418	C	R
3768	Same	Same	Br	R
3769	Same	Same	Z	R
3770				
3771	Same	420	C-N	R
3772				
3773	Same	635	C	R
3774				
3775	Lapham & Thayer/new/&/second hand/furniture/14/Mich Ave/Detroit	418	C	R
3776	Same	Same	Br	R
3777	Same	Same	Z	R
3778				
3779	Same	420	C-N	R
3780				

MICHIGAN—Continued

Detroit—Continued

NUMBER	OBVERSE	REVERSE	METAL	EDGE
3781	Lewis & Moses/dealers/in/crockery/&/glassware/221 Jeff Ave/Detroit	410	C	R
3782				
3783				
3784	Same	418	C	R
3785	Same	Same	Br	R
3786	Same	Same	Z	R
3787				
3788	Same	420	C	R
3789				
3790	C Lotz/grocer/cor/Hastings/ & /Catherine Sts/Detroit	416	C	R
3791	Same	Same	Br	R
3792				
3793	Same	418	C	R
3794				
3795	Same	Same	Z	R
3796				
3797	Same	420	C-N	R
3798				
3799	Martin's/cheap/boot/&/shoe/store/154 Woodward Ave	418	C	R
3800	Same	Same	Br	R
3801				
3802	Same	420	C-N	R
3803				
3804	M Marx/grocer/&/liquor/dealer/94 Gratoit St/Detroit	416	C	R
3805				
3806	Same	418	C	R
3807	Same	Same	Br	R
3808	Same	Same	Z	R
3809				
3810	Same	420	C-N	R
3811				
3812	Mather & Shefferly/crockery/store/138 & 140/Woodward / Ave/Detroit	410'	C	R
3813				
3814	Same	416	C	R
3815				
3816	Same	418	C	R
3817	Same	Same	Br	R
3818	Same	Same	Z	R
3819				
3820	Same	420	C-N	R
3821				
3822	Messmore & Lucking / butchers/209/Woodward/Ave/Detroit	418	C	R
3823	Same	Same	Br	R

MICHIGAN—Continued
Detroit—Continued

NUMBER	OBVERSE	REVERSE	METAL	EDGE
3824	Same	Same	Z	R
3825				
3826	Same	420	C-N	R
3827				
3828	Same	635	C	R
3829				
3830	Robt Millar/grocer/&/liquor/dealer/200 Woodward Ave/Detroit	410	C	R
3831				
3832	Same	418	C	R
3833	Same	Same	Br	R
3834	Same	Same	Z	R
3835				
3836	Same	420	C-N	R
3837				
3838	Geo Moe/grocer/&/liquor/dealer/Detroit	416	C	R
3839				
3840	Same	418	C	R
3841	Same	Same	Br	R
3842	Same	Same	Z	R
3843				
3844	Same	420	C-N	R
3845				
3846	Geo H Parker/dealer in/hides,'/leather/&/wool/cor Gr State &/Farmer Sts/Detroit	416	C	R
3847				
3848	Same	418	C	R
3849	Same	Same	Br	R
3850	Same	Same	Z	R
3851				
3852	Same	420	C-N	R
3853				
3854	Perkins/Hotel/cor Gr River &/Middle/Sts/Detroit	418	C	R
3855	Same	Same	Br	R
3856	Same	Same	Z	R
3857				
3858	Same	420	C-N	R
3859				
3860	Same	Same as No 453—dated '1863'	C	R
3861				
3862	W. Perkins Jr/grocer/&/provision/dealer/Detroit	416	C	R
3863				
3864	Same	418	C	R
3865	Same	Same	Br	R
3866	Same	Same	Z	R
3867				

MICHIGAN—Continued

Detroit—Continued

NUMBER	OBVERSE	REVERSE	METAL	EDGE
3868	Same	420	C-N	R
3869				
3870	Same	Same as obverse of No 3654	C	R
3871	Same	Same	C	Pl
3872				
3873				
3874	G C Pond/grocer/&/ Provision / dealer/Detroit	416	C	R
3875				
3876	Same	418	C	R
3877	Same	Same	Br	R
3878				
3879	Same	420	C-N	R
3880				
3881	F Prouty/grocer/&/provision/dealer/Gr River St/Detroit	416	C	R
3882				
3883	Same	418	C	R
3884	Same	Same	Br	R
3885	Same	Same	Z	R
3886				
3887	Same	420	C-N	R
3888				
3889	Randal's / photographic / gallery/ Fishers/Block/Detroit	416	C	R
3890				
3891	Same	418	C	R
3892	Same	Same	Br	R
3893	Same	Same	Z	R
3894				
3895	Same	420	C-N	R
3896				
3897	Raymond's/photographic/gallery/ 205/Jeff Ave/Detroit	418	C	R
3898	Same	Same	Br	R
3899	Same	Same	Z	R
3900				
3901	Same	420	C-N	R
3902				
3903	Joseph Riggs/Groceries/Provi/sions/&/flour/Detroit	418	C	R
3904	Same	Same	Br	R
3905	Same	Same	Z	R
3906				
3907	Same	420	C-N	R
3908				
3909	Same	635	C	R
3910				
3911	J A Rodier/boot/&/shoe / dealer / Detroit	416	C	R

MICHIGAN—Continued

Detroit—Continued

NUMBER	OBVERSE	REVERSE	METAL	EDGE
3912				
3913	Same	418	C	R
3914	Same	Same	Br	R
3915	Same	Same	Z	R
3916				
3917	Same	420	C-N	R
3918				
3919	Alonzo Rolfe/produce/fruit/&/commission/merchant/Detroit	418	C	R
3920	Same	Same	Br	R
3921	Same	Same	Z	R
3922				
3923	Same	420	C-N	R
3924				
3925	Dr L C Rose/treats all/chronic/female/& venereal/diseases/Detroit	416	C	R
3926				
3927	Same	418	C	R
3928	Same	Same	Br	R
3929				
3930	Same	420	C-N	R
3931				
3932	M Rosenberger/dealer in/ready made/clothing/140 Gr Riv St/Detroit	416	C	R
3933				
3934	Same	418	C	R
3935	Same	Same	Br	R
3936	Same	Same	Z	R
3937				
3938	Same	420	C-N	R
3939				
3940	J Schmidt/grocer/cor Mich Ave/&/Bates Sts/Detroit	410	C	R
3941				
3942	Same	418	C	R
3943	Same	Same	Br	R
3944	Same	Same	Z	R
3945				
3946	Same	420	C-N	R
3947				
3948	John Schroder & Co/clothing/hats/&/caps/boots & shoes	418	C	R
3949				
3950				
3951	Same	Same as No 453—dated '1863'	C-N	R
3952				

MICHIGAN—Continued

Detroit—Continued

NUMBER	OBVERSE	REVERSE	METAL	EDGE
3953	Same	Farmers/clothing/ store / 251 & 253/Gratoit St/Detroit	C	R
3954				
3955	H A Sealy/Rutcher/65/Gr River St/Detroit	416	C	R
3956				
3957	Same	418	C	R
3958				
3959	Same	Same	Z	R
3960				
3961	Same	420	C	R
3962				
3963	Cheap/John/Seeley/Detroit	416	C	h
3964				
3965	Same	418	C	R
3966	Same	Same	Br	R
3967	Same	Same	Z	R
3968				
3969	Same	420	C-N	R
3970				
3971	J B Shagnon/grocer/&/provision/dealer/Detroit	418	C	R
3872	Same	Same	Br	R
3973	Same	Same	Z	R
3974	Same	Same	C	Pl
3975	Same	Same	Br	Pl
3976				
3977	Same	420	C-N	R
3978				
3979	E B Smith/book seller/&/stationer/116/Woodward/Ave/Detroit	416	C	R
3980				
3981	Same	418	C	R
3982	Same	Same	Br	R
3983	Same	Same	Z	R
3984				
3985	Same	420	C-N	R
3986				
3987	Wm B Smith/butcher/129 & 131/Woodbridge/St/Detroit	418	C	R
3988	Same	Same	Br	R
3989	Same	Same	Z	R
3990		419		
3991	Same	420	C-N	R
3992				
3993	Yankee/Smith's/Saloon/No 1 Mich Ave/Detroit	410	C	R
3994				
3995	Same	418	C	R
3996				

MICHIGAN—Continued

Detroit—Continued

NUMBER	OBVERSE	REVERSE	METAL	EDGE
3997	Same	Same	Z	R
3998				
3999	Same	420	C-N	R
4000				
4001	Same	635	C	R
4002				
4003	Geo Snooks/fish/depot/cor/ 1' & Larned sts/Detroit	416	C	R
4004				
4005	Same	418	C	R
4006	Same	Same	Br	R
4007				
4008	Same	420	C-N	R
4009	Wm Snow/wire/cloth/hardware/&/ cutlery/Detroit	418	C	R
4010	Same	Same	Br	R
4011				
4012	Same	420	C-N	R
4013				
4014	Same	635	C	R
4015				
4016	J D & C B Standish's/pork/&/ wool/dealers/Detroit/Mich	U. S. shield within a circle of 24 stars	C	Pl
4017				
4018	L J Staples/wholesale/grocer/&/ confectioner/185/Woodward/Ave/ Detroit	410	C	R
4019				
4020	Same	416	C	R
4021				
4022	Same	418	C	R
4023	Same	Same	Br	R
4024				
4025	Same	420	C-N	R
4026				
4027	Goff Stenton/meat/market/cor/ Rivard & Jeff/Ave/Detroit	418	C	R
4028	Same	Same	Br	R
4029				
4030	Same	420	C-N	R
4031				
4032	Same	635	C	R
4033				
4034	Mrs A Stringer/dry/goods/milli- nery/&/dress making/Mich Ave/ Detroit	418	C	R
4035	Same	Same	Br	R
4036	Same	Same	Z	R
4037	Same	420	C-N	R
4038				
4039	Same	635	C	R

MICHIGAN—Continued

Detroit—Continued

NUMBER	OBVERSE	REVERSE	METAL	EDGE
4040				
4041	G W Cutherland/grocer/Market/ square/Detroit	409	C	R
4042				
4043	Same	410	C	R
4044				
4045	Same	418	C	R
4046	Same	Same	Br	R
4047	Same	Same	Z	R
4048				
4049	Same	420	C-N	R
4050				
4051				
4052	I & C Taylor/grocers/&/provisions/dealers/Detroit	418	C	R
4053	Same	Same	Br	R
4054	Same	Same	Z	R
4055				
4056	Same	420	C	R
4057				
4058	Same	635	C	R
4059				
4060	The/Tea/store/140/Woodward/ Ave/Detroit	416	C	R
4061				
4062	Same	418	C	R
4063	Same	Same	Br	R
4064	Same	Same	Z	R
4065				
4066	Same	420	C	R
4067				
4068	W E Tunis/general/news/dealer/ Detroit/Clifton C W/& Milwaukee	416	C	R
4069				
4070	Same	418	C	R
4071	Same	Same	Br	R
4072	Same	Same	Z	R
4073				
4074	Same	420	C	R
4075				
4076	Turner Hubbell Co/Wholesale/ boot & shoe/manufacturer/195 Jeff Ave/Detroit	411	C	R
4077				
4078	Same	418	C	R
4079	Same	Same	Br	R
4080	Same	Same	Z	R
4081				
4082	Same	420	C	R
4083				

MICHIGAN—Continued

Detroit—Continued

NUMBER	OBVERSE	REVERSE	METAL	EDGE
4084	R G Tyler/wholesale/grocer/Detroit Mich	Same at 569—not dated	Bronze	Pl
4085				
4086	Same as No 4084—no period after 'Mich'	Same	Bronze	Pl
4087				
4088	Venn & Wreford/Butchers/271/Jeff/Ave/ Detroit	418	C	R
4089				
4090	Same	Same	Z	R
4091				
4092	Same	420	C	R
4093				
4094	Same	635	C	R
4095				
4096	'Wards / Lake / Superior / Line/ Steamer/Planet' in centre—'Cleveland Detroit & Lake Superior' around edge	409	C	R
4097				
4098	Same	418	C	R
4099	Same	Same	Br	R
4100	Same	Same	Z	R
4101				
4102	Same	420	C	R
4103				
4104	Henry Weber/furniture/dealer/129/Woodward A/Detroit	418	C	R
4105	Same	Same	Br	R
4106	Same	Same	Z	R
4107				
4108	Same	420	C	R
4109				
4110	Same as No. 4104—address altered to '140'	418	C	R
4111	Same	Same	Br	R
4112				
4113	Same	420	C	R
4114				
4115	B Webster/wholesale/& retail/fish/dealer/Detroit	418	C	R
4116	Same	Same	Br	R
4117	Same	Same	Z	R
4118				
4119	Same	420	C	R
4120				
4121	Same	635	C	R
4122				
4123	W W Whitlark/with/Grover/& Baker/S M Co/Fishers Block/Detroit	418	C	R

MICHIGAN—Continued

Detroit—Continued

NUMBER	OBVERSE	REVERSE	METAL	EDGE
4124	Same	Same	Br	R
4125	Same	Same	Z	R
4126				
4127	Same	420	C	R
4128				
4129	Wilkins & Martins/celebrated/ink/&/blacking/depot/Detroit	Martin Bro's/cheap/boot/&/shoe/store/154 Woodward Ave		
4130			C	R
4131	Same	418	C	R
4132	Same	Same	Br	R
4133	Same	Same	Z	R
4134	Same	420	C	R
4135				
4136	J W Winckler/Baker/81/Larned/St/Detroit	416	C	R
4137				
4138	Same	418	C	R
4139	F M Wing/grocer/&/commission/merchant/83 Cong St/Detroit	416		
4140				
4141	Same	418	C	R
4142	Same	Same	Br	R
4143	Same	Same	Z	R
4144				
4145	Same	420	C	R
4146				
4147	G Winter/Hatter/250/Biddle House/Detroit	418	C	R
4148	Same	Same	Br	R
4149	Same	Same	Z	R
4150				
4151	Same	420	C	R
4152				
4153	A Witgen/Groceries/&/Meat/market/Detroit	418	C	R
4154	Same	Same	Br	R
4155	Same	Same	Z	R
4156				
4157	Same	420	C	R
4158				
4159	Same	635	C	R
4160				
4161	Henry Wolff/trunk/manufactory/211/Jeff Ave/Detroit Mich	404	C	R
4162	Same	405	C	R
4163	Same	411	C	R
4164	Same	418	C	R
4165	Same	Same	Br	R
4166	Same	Same	Z	R
4167	Same	420	C	R

MICHIGAN—Continued

Detroit—Continued

NUMBER	OBVERSE	REVERSE	METAL	EDGE
4168				
4169	Same	Same as No. 453—dated '1863'	C	R
4170				
4171				

Dowagiac

NUMBER	OBVERSE	REVERSE	METAL	EDGE
4172	A N Alward/books/stationery/ & wall/papers/Dowagiac Mich	20	C	Pl
4173				
4174	Same	206	C	Pl
4175				
4176	Andrews & Cooper/groceries/&/ provisions/Front/St/Dowagiac Mich	25	C	Pl
4177	Same	26	C	Pl
4178	Same	27	C	Pl
4179				
4180	Same	209	C	Pl
4181				
4182	A M Dickson & Co/dry/goods/ boots/& shoes/Dowagiac Mich	27	C	Pl
4183	Same	209	C	Pl
4184	Same	484	C	Pl
4185				
4186	D Larzelere & Co/dry/goods/groceries/&/clothing/Dowagiac Mich	20	C	Pl
4187	Same	25	C	Pl
4188				
4189	D Pond/grocer/and/confectioner/ Dowagiac/Mich	20	C	Pl
4190	Same	25	C	Pl
4191				
4192	G A Wheelock/dealer/in/groceries/& provisions/Dowagiac/Mich	209	C	Pl
4193				
4194				

East Saginaw

NUMBER	OBVERSE	REVERSE	METAL	EDGE
4195	Charles W. Bernacki/druggist/ East/Saginaw/Mich	594	C	Pl
4196	Same	628	C	Pl
4197				
4198	N W Clark & Co/merchants/commercial/block/East Saginaw Mich	418	C	R
4199	Same	Same	Br	R
4200				
4201	Same	420	C	R
4202				
4203	Same	635	C	R
4204				

MICHIGAN—Continued

East Saginaw—Continued

NUMBER	OBVERSE	REVERSE	METAL	EDGE
4205	S T Leggett/practical/watch maker/&/jeweler/East Saginaw/Mich	Same as No. 209—'Union' spelled in larger letters	C	R
4206				
4207	John McKay/oyster/fruit/&/fish/depot/East Saginaw	418	C	R
4208	Same	Same	Br	R
4209				
4210				
4211	Same	420	C	R
4212				
4213	Same	635	C	R
4214				
4215	A Schmitz/East/Saginaw/Mich Plow in centre	Dealer in/iron/nails/stoves/crockery/&/paints	C	Pl
4216	Same	594	C	Pl
4217				
4218				

Eaton Rapids

NUMBER	OBVERSE	REVERSE	METAL	EDGE
4219	A C Dutton M D/books/stationary/Groceries &c/Eaton Rapids/Mich	528	C	Pl
4220	Same	Same	Br	Pl
4221				
4222	H M Frost/druggist/and/grocer/Eaton Rapids/Mich	528	C	Pl
4223	Same	Same	Br	Pl
4224				
4225	Frost & Daniels/dry goods/groceries/boots shoes &c/Eaton Rapids/Mich	462	C	Pl
4226	Same	Same	Br	Pl
4227				
— 4228	P Leonard/dry goods/groceries/boots shoes &c/Eaton Rapids/Mich	478	C	Pl
4229	Same	Same	Br	Pl
4230				
4231	A Mester & Co/Marble/Works Eaton Rapids/Mich	554	C	Pl
4232	Same	Same	Br	Pl
4233				
4234	Wm F Stirling/dry goods/Union Block/Eaton Rapids/Mich	The celebrated/Tea/establishment	C	Pl
4235	Same	Same	Br	Pl
4236				
4237				

Flint

NUMBER	OBVERSE	REVERSE	METAL	EDGE
— 4238	Giles Bishop/groceries/and/liquors/Business card	Mortar and pestle in centre —'Druggist' above—'Flint Mich' below	Bronze	Pl
— 4239				

MICHIGAN—Continued

Flint—Continued

NUMBER	OBVERSE	REVERSE	METAL	EDGE
4240	Clark's/drugs/medicines/groceries/&c/Flint Mich	209	C	Pl
4241				
4242	Same	628	C	Pl
4243				

Grand Haven

4244	H Brower/& Bro/dry goods/groceries/boots &/shoes/Grand Haven Mich	20	C	Pl
4245	Same	209	C	Pl
4246				
4247	Geo E Hubbard/dealer/in/stoves/and/hardware/Grand Haven/Mich	463	C	Pl
4248				
4249	Schelven			
4250				
4251				

Grand Rapids

4252	Geo P Barnard/book/seller/&/stationer/Grand/Rapids/Mich	594	C	Pl
4253	Same	628	C	Pl
4254				
4255	Russian Clothing/store/Courlander/&/Pressgood/Grand Rapids/Mich	552	C	Pl
4256	Same	Same	Br	R
4257	Same—'O' omitted from 'clothing'	Same	C	Pl
4258	Same	Same	Br	Pl
4259				
4260	'Foster & Metcalf' above—cook stove in centre—'Grand Rapids Mich' below	1861/workers in/copper tin brass/and/heavy sheet iron/plumbing/gas fittings/ etc etc etc	Brass Bronze	Pl
4261	Same	Same	W-M	Pl
4262				
4263	Goodrich & Gay/dealers/in/hardware/iron steel/nails & glass/Grand Rapids Mich 'N' of 'nails' above 'A' of 'grand'	525	Br	Pl
4264	Same—'N' of 'nails' above 'N' of 'grand'	636	C	Pl
4265	Same	Same	Br	Pl
4266				
4267	Kruger & Booth/dealers in/saddles/harness/trunks/Grand Rapids/Mich	206	C	Pl
4268	Same	628	C	Pl
4269				

MICHIGAN—Continued

Grand Rapids Continued

NUMBER	OBVERSE	REVERSE	METAL	EDGE
4270	Horse and wagon in centre—'C. Kusterer' above—'Grand Rapids/ Mich' below	City Brewery/Manf'r/of/ lager beer/stock/& cream/ ale	C	Pl
4271	Same	209	C	Pl
4272				
4273	L A Merrill/photographic/artist/ Grand/Rapids/Mich	25	C	Pl
4274	Same	628	C	Pl
4275				
4276	J W Peirce/dry goods/and/groceries/Grand Rapids Mich. 'G' of groceries below 'A' in grand	569	Bronze	Pl
4277	Same	570	Bronze	Pl
4278	Same, but 'G' even with 'A'	571	C	Pl
4279	Same	Same	Bronze	Pl
4280	Same	572	C	Pl
— 4281	Same	Same	Br	Pl
4282	Same	573	C	Pl
— 4283	Same	Same	Br	Pl
4284	Same	637	Br	Pl
4285				
4286				
4287	E K Powers/confectioner/& dealer in/soda water/Grand/Rapids/Mich	209	C	Pl
4288	Same	628	C	Pl
4289				
4290	L H Randall/wholesale/&/retail/ grocer/Grand Rapids Mich	Tea chest in centre—13 stars and 'L H Randall' above—'1862' below	C	Pl
— 4291	Same	Same	Br	Pl
4292	A Roberts & Son/dry goods/groceries/crockery/&c/Grand Rapids	572	Br	Pl
4293	Same	637	Br	Pl
4294	Same	638	Br	Pl
4295				
4296	Tompkins/photograph/and/ambrotype/gallery/Grand/Rapids/Mich	25	C	Pl
4297	Same	209	C	Pl
5298				
4299				

Hastings

4300	D C Hawley/groceries/&/provisions/Hastings/Mich	20	C	Pl
4301	Same	25	C	Pl
4302	Same	27	C	Pl
4303	Same	209	C	Pl
4304	Same	628	C	Pl
4305				

Hillsdale

4306	J O Ames/books/&/stationery/ Hillsdale Mich	639	Br	Pl

MICHIGAN—Continued

Hillsdale Continued

NUMBER	OBVERSE	REVERSE	METAL	EDGE
4307				
4308	O S Betts/dealer in/watches jewelry/&/silverware/Hillsdale Mich	472	C	Pl
4309	Same	474	C	Pl
4310				
4311	Card Pearce & Co/engines/and/agricultural/implements/Hillsdale Mich	472	C	Pl
4312	Same	474	C	Pl
4313	Same	639	C	Pl
4314	Farnhams Bronchial tablets	473	C	Pl
4315	French & Parsons/druggists/&/grocers/Hillsdale Mich	436	C	Pl
4316	J Gottlieb Clothier Hillsdale Mich	473	C	Pl
4317				
4318	A Gleason/die sinker/&/engraver/Hillsdale Mich	128	C	Pl
4319	Same	472	C	Pl
4320	Same	474	C	Pl
4321	Same	639	C	Pl
4322	Same	640	C	Pl
4323				
4324	473	515	C	Pl
4325				
4326	474	515	C	Pl
4327	Same	Same	Br	Pl
4328	639	515	C	Pl
4329				
4330				
4331	E C Keating/Grocer/and/produce dealer/Hillsdale Mich	473	C	Pl
4332	Same	474	C	Pl
4333				
4334	D H Lord & Co/dealer in/boots/shoes &c/Hillsdale Mich	474	C	Pl
4335				
4336	C T Mitchell & Co/hardware/dealers/Hillsdale Mich	473	C	Pl
4337	Same	474	C	Pl
4338	C E Mott & Co/dry/goods/carpeting/&c/Hillsdale Mich	436	C	Pl
4339	Same	618	C	Pl
4340				
4341	Mott & Bro/druggists/and/grocers/Hillsdale Mich	473	C	Pl
4342	Same	618	C	Pl
4343				
4344	Samm & Kuhlke Groceries Hillsdale Mich	473	C	Pl
4345	Same	474	C	Pl

MICHIGAN—Continued

Hillsdale—Continued

NUMBER	OBVERSE	REVERSE	METAL	EDGE
4346	Union Planing & Stave Mills/ R Rowe/Hillsdale/Mich	472	C	Pl
4347	Same	474	C	Pl
4348				
4349	Geo W Underwood/druggist/&/ grocer/Hillsdale Mich	618	C	Pl
4350				

Hudson

4351	Baker & Brown/dry/goods/and/ groceries/Hudson Mich	474	C	Pl
4352				
4353	Gillett & Niles/druggists/Hudson/ Mich. Mortar and pestle	594	C	Pl
4354	Same	628	C	Pl
4355				
4356	Green & Wardsworth Hudson Mich Livery	640	C	Pl
4357	H Howe & Co/dealers in/general/ hardware/Hudson Mich	472	C	Pl
4358	Same	474	C	Pl
4359				
4360	Palmer & Goodsall/hardware/dealers/Hudson Mich	472	C	Pl
4361	Same	474	C	Pl
4362	Tubbs & Spear/grocers/Hudson Mich	474	C	Pl

Ionia

4363	'James Kennedy' above — Indian head to left in centre—'1863' below—star on sides	Exchange insurance/collection/& U. S./war claim/ office/Ionia Mich	C	Pl
4364	Same—U S shield instead of Indian head	Same	C	Pl
4365				
4366	F Sloan/stoves/hardware/iron steel/& nails/Ionia Mich	206	C	Pl
4367	Same	628	C	Pl
4368	Same	641	C	Pl
4369				

Jackson

4370	S Holland & Son/druggists/Jackson/Mich. Mortar and pestle	433	C	Pl
4371	Same	594	C	Pl
4372				
4373	H S Ismon/dealer/in/staple / & fancy/dry goods/Jackson Mich	433	C	Pl
4374				

MICHIGAN—Continued

Jackson—Continued

NUMBER	OBVERSE	REVERSE	METAL	EDGE
4375	Wm Jackson/X/clusive/trade/in/groceries. Star at sides	Jackson Hall/Block/Jackson/Mich	C	Pl
4376	Same	Jackson Hall/Jackson/Mich/1863 Ornaments below date	C	Pl
4377	Same	Same	Br	Pl
4378	Same as preceeding, but star omitted from side of 'clusive'	Same as preceding but no ornaments below date	C	Pl
4379	Same	Same	Br	Pl
4380	Same as No 4375	Same as No 4376	C	Pl
4381				
4382	Same as No 4378	Same as No 4376	C	Pl
4383				
4384	Same as No. 4375—larger letters	Jackson Hall/Eagle in glory/Jackson/Mich/1863. 3 stars at sides	C	Pl
4385				
4386	Same as reverse of No 4376	624	C	Pl
4387	Wm Jackson/dealer/in/groceries/Jackson/Mich	20	C	Pl
4388	Same	25	C	Pl
4389	Same	434	C	Pl
4390				
4391	W Jaxon/grocer/Jackson Hall/Jackson/Mich/1863	478	C	Pl
4392				
4393	Same	561	C	Pl
4394	Same	Same	Br	Pl
4395				
4396	Same	591	C	Pl
4397				
4398	W Jaxon/grocer/Jackson Hall/Jackson/Mich/1864	562	C	Pl
4399				

Jonesville

4400	C C Blakeslee/druggist/Jonesville/Mich. Mortar and pestle	639	C	Pl
4401				
4402	A & H Gale Manfrs Agricultural Implements Jonesville M	639	C	Pl
4403				
4404	H R Gardner & Co/woolen/Manuf'rs/Jonesville Mich	473	C	Pl
4405	Same	474	C	Pl
4406				
4407	J S Lewis Hardware Iron Nails Jonesville Mich	473	C	Pl
4408				
4409	Van Ness & Turner/dry goods/and/groceries/Jonesville Mich	473	C	Pl

MICHIGAN—Continued

Jonesville—Continued

NUMBER	OBVERSE	REVERSE	METAL	EDGE
4410				
4411	D A Wisner & Son/dry/goods/and/groceries/Jonesville Mich	473	C	Pl
4412				
4413				

Juneau

4414	S H Coleman/dealer/in/dry goods/Juneau/Mich	442	C	Pl
4415				

Kalamazoo

4416	Babcock & Cobb/dry/goods/carpets/&/clothing/Kalamazoo	206	C	Pl
4417	Same	435	C	Pl
4418	Same	611	C	Pl
4419	Cobb & Fisher/dealers/in/crockery/Kalamazoo	20	C	Pl
4420	Same—no period after Kalamazoo	20	C	Pl
4421	Same	209	C	Pl
4422				
4423	Davis & Bates/one/price/cash/store/Kalamazoo	20	C	Pl
4424	Same	594	C	Pl
4425	Same	633	C	Pl
4426	R R Howard/hardware/cutlery &c/Kalamazoo/Mich	20	C	Pl
4427	Same	206	C	Pl
4428				
4429	Kellogg & Co/Manfr's/of/lumber/doors/blinds & sash/Kalamazoo/Mich	20	C	Pl
4430	Same	21	C	Pl
4431	Same	25	C	Pl
4432	Same	206	C	Pl
4433				
4434	H S Parker & Co/hats/caps/boots/& shoes/Kalamazoo	20	C	Pl
4435	Same	435	C	Pl
4436	Same	594	C	Pl
4437				
4438	L W Perrin/dry/goods/groceries/&/carpets/Kalamazoo	416	C	R
4439				
4440	Same	420	C	R
4441				
4442	Roberts &/Hillhouse/Druggists/sign/of/eagle & mortar/Kalamazoo Mich	206	C	Pl
4443				

MICHIGAN—Continued

Kalamazoo—Continued

NUMBER	OBVERSE	REVERSE	METAL	EDGE
4444	Same	611	C	Pl
4445				
4446				

Lansing

NUMBER	OBVERSE	REVERSE	METAL	EDGE
4447	David Ekstein/dealer/in/groceries/ and/provisions/Lansing/Mich	117	C	Pl
4448	Same	445	C	Pl
4449	Same	"W K Lanphear' above— 'Manu'fr/of/metallic/cards' within a corn wreath— 'Cincinnati O' below	C	Pl
4450	A J Viele/books/stationery/pianos &/sewing/machines/Lansing/Mich	478	C	Pl
4451				
4452	Same	537	C	Pl
4453	Same	Same	Br	Pl
4454	Same	540	C	Pl
4455	Same	Same	Br	Pl
4456				

Lapeer

NUMBER	OBVERSE	REVERSE	METAL	EDGE
4457	H Griswold & Co/dealers/in/dry/ goods/groceries/&c/Lapeer Mich	409	C	R
4458				
4459	Same	418	C	R
4460				
4461	Same	420	C	R
4462				

Lawton

NUMBER	OBVERSE	REVERSE	METAL	EDGE
4463	Fairbank & Scriver/stoves/hard- ware/and/cutlery/Lawton Mich	209	C	Pl
4464				
4465	Same	434	C	Pl
4466				
4467	Same	632	C	Pl
4468				

Ligonier

NUMBER	OBVERSE	REVERSE	METAL	EDGE
← 4469	J Pearce/drugs/groceries/& no- tions/Ligonier/Mich	528	C	Pl
4470	Same	Same	Br	Pl
4471				

Litchfield

NUMBER	OBVERSE	REVERSE	METAL	EDGE
4472	A Burleson dry goods groceries boots & shoes Litchfield Mich	639	C	Pl
4473	Same	Same	Br	Pl
4474				

MICHIGAN—Continued

Lowell

NUMBER	OBVERSE	REVERSE	METAL	EDGE
4475	W R Blaisdell/stoves/tin/&/ hardware/Lowell/Mich	209	C	Pl
4476				
4477	Same	628	C	Pl
4478				
4479	Same as preceding, but no comma after 'Lowell'	25	C	Pl
4480				
4481	Hatch & Craw/manfr's/&/dealers in/flour &/grain/Lowell/Mich	25	C	Pl
4482	Same	435	C	Pl
4483	Same	628	C	Pl
4484				

Lyons

4485	Bauder & Button/war/claim/ agents/attorneys/at law/Lyons Mich	25	C	Pl
4486				
4487				
4488	A Button/war/claim attorney/and general/general/collecting/agent/ Lyons Mich	479	C	Pl
4489	Same	Same	Br	Pl
4490	A Button/war/claim attorney/general/collecting/and/insurance/ agent/Lyons Mich. 2 stars at sides	481	C	Pl
4491	Same	Same	Br	Pl
4492				
4493	L F Heath/watch/maker/and/ photographer/Lyons/Mich	537	C	Pl
4494	Same	Same	Br	Pl
4495				

Manchester

4496	Van Duyn & Lynch/druggists/and/ grocers/Manchester/Mich	528	C	Pl
4497	Same	Same	Br	Pl
4498	Same	532	C	Pl
4499	Same	Same	Br	Pl
4500				

Maple Rapids

4501	Isaac Hewitt/dry/goods/&/groceries/Maple/Rapids/Mich	25	C	Pl
4502	Same	628	C	Pl

Marshall

4503	Isaac Beers/stoves/hardware/ tools/&/tinware/Marshall Mich	.594	C	Pl

MICHIGAN—Continued

Marshall—Continued

NUMBER	OBVERSE	REVERSE	METAL	EDGE
4504	C M Brewer/dealer/in/dry/goods/ groceries &/hardware/Marshall/ Mich	21	C	Pl
4505	Same	209	C	Pl
4506	Same	433	C	Pl
4507				
4508	L H Robinson/dealer/in/groceries/ &/notions/Marshall Mich	410	C	R
4509	Same	415	C	R
4510	Same	418	C	R
4511	Same	Same	Br	R
4512				
4513	Same	Same as die No 453—dated '1863'	C-N	R
4514	Same	642	C	R
4515				

Mason

4516	J W Phelps & Co/hardware/tin & copper/ware/drugs/&/medicines / Mason Mich	409	C	R
4517				
4518	Same	418	C	R
4519	Same	Same	Br	R
4520	Same	420	C	R
4521				

Morenci

4522	J M Page & Co/dealers in/general/ hardware/Morenci Mich	474	C	Pl
4523				
4524	Richards & Co/dealers/in/dry/ goods/hardware/&c/Morenci/Mich	209	C	Pl
4525	Same	433	C	Pl
4526	Same	434	C	Pl
4527				

Niles

4528	G A Colby & Co/wholesale/gro- ceries/&/bakery/Niles Mich	611	C	Pl
4529	Same	643	C	Pl
4530				
4531	H Eastman/dealer/in/dry goods/ clothing/boots &/shoes/Niles Mich	434	C	Pl
4532	Same	594	C	Pl
4533				
4534	E S Parker/dealer/in/hats & Caps/ & Furs/Niles Mich	25	C	Pl
4535	Same	433	C	Pl

MICHIGAN—Continued

Niles—Continued

NUMBER	OBVERSE	REVERSE	METAL	EDGE
4536				
4537	E S Parker/dealer/in/hats caps/ &/furs/Niles Mich. Hat and cap in centre	419	C	R
4538	Same	Same	Br	R
4539	Same	Same	C-N	R
4540	Same	Same	Z	R
4541				
—4542	G W & H C Platt/stoves/and/ hardware/Niles/Mich	628	C	Pl
4543				
4544	H G Sleight/dealer/in/groceries/ seeds/&c/Niles Mich	206	C	Pl
4545	Same	433	C	Pl
4546	Same	628	C	Pl
—4547	Same	633	C	Pl
4548				

Owasso

4549	C E Shattuck/dealer in/brick/&/ drain tile/Owasso Mich	443	C	Pl
4550	Same	Same	Br	Pl
4551				

Owosso

4552	M L Stewart/wholesale/and/re- tail/grocer/Owosso/Mich	446	C	Pl
4553				
4554	Same	447	C	Pl
4555	Same	Same	Br	Pl
4556				

Parma

4557	Mortar and pestle in centre— 'Glazier's Pharmacy' above— 'Parma Mic' below	Buy your medicines paints/ and/oils/at	C	Pl
4558	Same	Same	Br	Pl
4559				

Paw Paw

4560	J R Foote/crockery/glassware/&/ groceries/Paw Paw/Mich	209	C	Pl
4561	Same	434	C	Pl
4562				
4563	G W Longwell/drugs/&/groceries/ Main St/Paw Paw/Mich	25	C	Pl
4564	Same	644	C	Pl
4565				

MICHIGAN—Continued

Paw Paw—Continued

NUMBER	OBVERSE	REVERSE	METAL	EDGE
4566	Ornaments in centre—'A Sherman & Co/ general merchants/&/ propr's of/Paw Paw' above— 'flouring mills/Paw Paw Mich' below	6	C	Pl
4567				
4568	J D Sherman/wholesale/groceries/ &/provisions/Paw Paw/Mich	25	C	Pl
4569	Same	611	C	Pl
4570				

Pontiac

4571	Fox & Smith/produce &/commission/merchants/& dealers in/ plaster/Pontiac Mich	25	C	Pl
4572	Same	Same as Die No 614— 'Union' in small letters— date close to eagle. Point below eagle points directly to '6' of date '1863'	C	Pl
4573	Same	641	C	Pl
4574				
4575	Morris & Messinger/dealers/in/ hardware/iron steel/nails & glass/ Pontiac	525	Br	Pl
4576				
4577	A Parker/dealer/in/drugs/medicines/groceries &/glass/Pontiac	'French's hair restorative/ for restoring gray hair' in semi-circle surrounding bottle on which is inscribed 'French'	Br	Pl
4578				

Saginaw City

4579	Wm Binder/dry goods/groceries/ Saginaw/City/Mich	209	C	Pl
4580	Same	628	C	Pl
4581				
4582	Epting & Eaton/dealers/in/drugs &/medicines/Saginaw City/Mich	21	C	Pl
4583	Same	206	C	Pl
4584				

Salina

4585	Small mortar and pestle in field— 'Gallagher & Hess' above—'Druggists/Salina/Mich' below	21	C	Pl
4586	Same	25	C	Pl
4587	Same	641	C	Pl
4588				

MICHIGAN—Continued

Saranac

NUMBER	OBVERSE	REVERSE	METAL	EDGE
4589	W Darling/Saranac/Mich/1864. Thirteen starts around border—ornaments in field	Boot and seven stars in field inclosed by wreath	C	Pl
4590				

Schoolcraft

4591	I Allen & Son/stoves/&/hardware/Schoolcraft/Mich	21	C	Pl
4592	Same	25	C	Pl
4593	Same	632	C	Pl
4594				
4595	I W Prusel & Co/dry/goods/groceries/boots/&/shoes/Schoolcraft. Dash above and below 'goods'	594	C	Pl
4596	Same	627	C	Pl
4597				
4598	Same as No. 4594—no dash above and below 'goods'	206	C	Pl
4599				

St. Johns

4600	G W Stephenson/general/merchant/St Johns/Mich	528	C	Pl
4601				
4602	G W Stephenson/& Son/dry goods/clothing/boots/shoes/St Johns Mich	628	C	Pl
4603				

Tecumseh

4604	Fisher & Hendryx/druggists/and/grocers/Chicago St/Tecumseh/Mich	528	C	Pl
4605	Same	Same	Br	Pl
4606				
4607	Dr E Hause/Dentist/Tecumseh/Mich	20	C	Pl
4608	Same	21	C	Pl
4609	Same	206	C	Pl
4610				
4611	G T Ketcham/newsdealers/&/book/seller/Tecumseh Mich	206	C	Pl
4612	Same	434	C	Pl
4613				
4614	C S Patterson/druggist/Tecumseh/Mich	25	C	Pl
4615	Same	434	C	Pl
4616				

MICHIGAN—Continued

Ypsilanti

NUMBER	OBVERSE	REVERSE	METAL	EDGE
4617	E Hewitt & Bro/dealers/in/dry goods/& Manfrs/of boots &/shoes/ Ypsilanti Mich	21	C	Pl
4618	Same	25	C	Pl
— 4619	Same	27	C	Pl
4620	E Hewitt & Bro/dealers/in/dry goods/& Manfrs/of boots/& shoes/ Ypsilanti Mich	594 27	C	Pl
— 4621				
4622	Showerman & Bro/dealers/in/dry goods/clothing/hats & caps/boots/ & shoes/Ypsilanti Mich	25	C	Pl
— 4623	Same	614	C	Pl
4624	Same	Similar to die No 614 but head of arrows points to '6' of date. Same as card No. 4571	.C	Pl
4625				
4626				

MINNESOTA

Red Wing

4650	A W E/Red Wing/Min	157	C	Pl
4651	Same	Same	Br	Pl
4652				
4653	Same	Same	C-N	Pl
4654	Same	Same	W-M	Pl
4655				
4656	Same	324	C	Pl
4657	Same	Same	Br	Pl
4658				
4659	Same	Same	C-N	Pl
4660	Same	Same	W-M	Pl
4661				
4662				

Rochester

4663	F W Andrews/dry goods/ &c/ Rochester/Minn eagle in glory	426	C	Pl
4664	Same	447	C	Pl
4665	Same	461	C	Pl
— 4666	Same	478	C	Pl
4667	Same	503	C	Pl
4668				

St. Paul

— 4669	D C Greenleaf/Watch/Maker/St Paul/Minn	Blank reverse	C	Pl

MINNESOTA

St. Paul—Continued

NUMBER	OBVERSE	REVERSE	METAL	EDGE

NOTE—These pieces were evidently intended for watch checks, and come with incused figures on the reverse from 1 to 100 The following numbers have been identified—2—4—5—6—7—8—1 3—17—18—19—25—32—37—38—41—44—45—48—51—58—63—64—70—74—79—80—84—85—92—95—97—

NUMBER	OBVERSE	REVERSE	METAL	EDGE
4670				
4671	Wheeler & Wilsons / sewing/machines/F M Johnson/Agt/3rd St/ St Paul Minn	520	C	Pl
4672				
4673				

Winona

NUMBER	OBVERSE	REVERSE	METAL	EDGE
4674	C Benson/Druggist/Winona/Minn	528	C	Pl
4675	Same	Same	Br	Pl
4676				
4677	Coe & Hayden / dry goods / &/ crockery/boots shoes/and/groceries/the regulator	The regulator/No 2/Simpson/block/Second St/Winona/Minn/1863	C	Pl
4678	Same	Same	Br	Pl
4679				

MISSOURI

Ironton

NUMBER	OBVERSE	REVERSE	METAL	EDGE
4700	D Peck & Co/dealers/in/groceries/drugs/&/ medicines / Ironton Mo	419	C	R
4701	Same	Same	Br	R
4702	Same	Same	Z	R
4703				

St. Louis

NUMBER	OBVERSE	REVERSE	METAL	EDGE
4704	Drovers/Hotel/125 North 4'st/ St Louis Mo	401	C	Pl
4705	Same	402	C	Pl
4706	Same	417	C	Pl
4707	Same	418	C	R
4708	Same	Same	Br	R
4709	Same	420	C	R
4710	Same	507	C	Pl
4711	Same	402 Tin Plated	C	Pl
4712	Henry Jenkins / wholesale / & /retail/clothier/St Louis Mo	582	C	Pl
4713	Same	Sames as obverse	C	Pl
4714	Same	Obverse incused	C	Pl
4715		Broken Die		
4716	Use/Lallemand's / specifiic / sold/ by/druggists/Jno H Blood Agt/ 24 Fifth St/ St Louis	Lallemand's/ rheumatism/ gout/&/neuralgia / specific	C	R
4717	Same	Same	Br	R
4718	Same as reverse of No 4716	Same as Die No 453—dated '1863'	C·N	R
4719				
4720		419	C	

NEW HAMPSHIRE

Concord

NUMBER	OBVERSE	REVERSE	METAL	EDGE
4721	A W Gale/restorator / at/depot/ Concord N H	Good for/one/cent/in goods	C	Pl

NEW JERSEY

Atlantic City

NUMBER	OBVERSE	REVERSE	METAL	EDGE
4725	'Neptune/House / Atlantic / City/ 1863' within a circle of thirteen large stars—thick planchet	'Smick's' within oak wreath	C	Pl
4726	Same—thin planchet	Same	C	Pl
4727	'Neptune/House/Atlantic/City' within a circle of thirteen small stars	'Smick's' within oak wreath small date '1863' below	C	Pl
4728				

Elizabethport

4729	John Engel/Merchant/Tailor/52/ First St/Elizabeth Pt N J	108	C	Pl
4730				
4731				
4732				
4733	Same	300	C	Pl
4734				
4735				
4736	Same	336	C	Pl
4737				
4738				
4739	Same	Same	W-M	Pl
4740				
4741				

Jersey City

4742	Terhune Brothers/71 & 73/Newark Ave/JerseyCity/N J/Hardware	645	C	Pl
4743				

Newark

4744	J L Agens & Co/NO 1/Commerce St/Newark N J/Newspapers	1	Br	Pl
4745				
4746				
4747				
4748				
4749	Same	29	Br	Pl
4750				
4751				
4752				
4753				
4754	Same	99	C	Pl
4755	Same	Same	Br	Pl
4756	Same	Same	C-N	Pl
4757	Same	Same	W-M	Pl
4758	Same	Same	S	Pl
4759				

NEW JERSEY—Continued

Newark—Continued

NUMBER	OBVERSE	REVERSE	METAL	EDGE
4760	Same	108	Br	Pl
4761				
4762				
4763				
4764	Same	300	C	Pl
4765				
4766				
4767				
4768				
4769	Same	Same	S	Pl
4770	Same	302	C	Pl
4771				
4772				
4773				
4774	Same	303	C	Pl
4775	Same	Same	Br	Pl
4776				
4777				
4778				
4779	Same	645	C	Pl
4780	Same	Same	Br	Pl
4781				
4782				
4783				
4784	Charles Kolb/102/Market St/ Restaurant	646	C	Pl
4785	Same	Same	Br	Pl
4786	Same	Same	N	Pl
4787	Same	Same	C-N	Pl
4788	Same	Same	W-M	Pl
4789				
4790	J Wightman/138/Washington/ St/Newark N J	1	C	Pl
4791	Same	Same	Br	Pl
4792	Same	Same	N	Pl
4793				
4794	Same	Same	W-M	Pl
4795				
4796	Same	50	C	Pl
4797				
4798	Same	56	C	Pl
4799	Same	Same	Br	Pl
4800	Same	Same	N	Pl
4801				
4802				
4803				
4804	Same	76	C	Pl
4805	Same	Same	Br	Pl
4806	Same	Same	N	Pl
4807				

NEW JERSEY—Continued

Newark—Continued

NUMBER	OBVERSE	REVERSE	METAL	EDGE
4808	Same	Same	W-M	Pl
4809				
4810	Same	87	C	Pl
4811	Same	Same	Br	Pl
4812	Same	Same	N	Pl
4813	Same	Same	C-N	Pl
4814	Same	Same	W-M	Pl
4815				
4816	Same	143	Br	Pl
4817	Same	Same	N	Pl
4818	Same	Same	C-N	Pl
4919	Same	Same	W-M	Pl
4820				
4821	Same	144	C	Pl
4822	Same	Same	Br	Pl
4823	Same	Same	C-N	Pl
4824	Same	Same	W-M	Pl
4825				
4826	Same	165	C	Pl
4827				
4828	Same	Same	N	Pl
4829				
4930	Same	Same	W-M	Pl
4831				
4832	Same	273	C	Pl
4933	Same	Same	Br	Pl
4834	Same	Same	N	Pl
4835	Same	Same	C-N	Pl
4836	Same	Same	W-M	Pl
4837				
4838	Same	274	C	Pl
4839	Same	Same	Br	Pl
4840	Same	Same	N	Pl
4841				
4842	Same	Same	W-M	Pl
4843				
4844	Same	301	C	Pl
4845				
4846	Same	Same	N	Pl
4847				
4848				
4849	Same	338	C	Pl
4850	Same	Same	Br	Pl
4851	Same	Same	N	Pl
4852				
4853	Same	Same	W-M	Pl
4854				

NEW JERSEY—Continued
Perth Amboy

NUMBER	OBVERSE	REVERSE	METAL	EDGE
4855	Coutts & Bro/dry goods/&/P Amboy N J	300	C	Pl
4856				
4857	Same	303	C	Pl
4858				

Trenton

4859	B W Titus/20/E State St/ Trenton N J	Dry Goods / oil cloths / carpets/&c	Bronze	Pl
4860	Same	Same	Nickle Plated	Pl
4861				
4862	Same	Similar inscription, but diff die. Ornaments farther away from 'carpets'	Bronze	Pl

NEW YORK

Albany

NUMBER	OBVERSE	REVERSE	METAL	EDGE
4900	Benjamin & Herrick / fruit/dealers/Albany N Y—'fruit' in large letters 'F' touches 'N'	Redeemed at/427/Broadway / 1863 — ornament shows mullet in centre	C	Pl
4901	Same inscription as forgoing—'F' does not touch 'N' but is opposite to left leg of 'A'	Same inscription as foregoing—star in centre of ornament—on each side of star a diamond	C	Pl
4902	Same as 4901—double strike	Same as 4901—double strike	C	Pl
4903				
4904	Same inscription—'Fruit' in smaller letters—'F' almost touches 'J'	Similar to foregoing—cross on each side of star—Die break at lower part of '2'	Br	Pl
4905		123		
4906	Similar inscription—'T' touches left leg of second 'R'	Same as foregoing	C	Pl
4907	Same	Same	Br	Pl
4908				
4909	Similar—but 'T' of 'fruit' between the two 'R R'	Same	C	Pl
4910				
4911	Similar to No 4900—'Fruit' in large letters—more space between 'B' and 'D'	similar — two diamond shaped ornaments on sides of star	Br	Pl
4912	Same as No 4901	109	C	Pl
4913				
4914				
4915	Same as 4904	337	C	Pl
4916	Same	Same	Br	Pl
4917	Same	Same	N	Pl
4918	Same	Same	C-N	Pl
4919	Same	Same	W-M	Pl
4920	Same	Same	Ger-S	Pl
4921				
4922	Similar—'F' close to 'J'	Same as 4901	Br	Pl
4923				
4924	P V Fort & Co/dealers/in/fruit/and/nuts/Albany N Y—ornament close to 'N' of nuts	Redeemed/at/No 427/Broadway/1864	Bronze	Pl
4925	Similar—'N' farther away	Same	Bronze	Pl
4926				
4927	Jos Mc Burney/Cigar box Manuf'r/26/Mulberry St/Albany N Y	Redeemed/at/26/Mulberry St/Albany N Y	Bronze	Pl
4928				
4929	N Y C R R Ex trains/leave/Albany/7.30 & 9/A M/12.20 & 6/P M	N Y C R R Ex trains/leave/Buffalo/5 & 8/A M/5.45 & 10.55/P M	Bronze	Pl
4930				
4931				
4932	Elephant in boots with rug on back marked '398'—'Straight's Elephantine/shoe store" above—'Broadway/1863' below	Redeemed at my shoe store/398/Broadway / Albany/N Y	Bronze	Pl

NEW YORK—Continued

Albany—Continued

NUMBER	OBVERSE	REVERSE	METAL	EDGE
4933				
4934	John Thomas/premium/mills/coffee & spices	Redeemed/Exchange/ & / Dean Sts/ 1863/Albany N Y	Bronze	Pl
4935				
4936	D L Wing & Co/318/Broadway/ Albany N Y Tiny stars used as periods after 'N' and 'Y'	'Union/Flour' within wreath	Bronze	Pl

Note—There are at least three different dies known to the compilers—the differences would be extremely difficult to describe

| 4937 | Redeemed/by/D L Wing & Co/ Albany N Y | 'Union/flour/'within wreath | Bronze | Pl |

Note—There are five different dies known to the compilers—we leave to the indivdual collector to number them under sub-divisions

| 4938 | | | | |
| 4939 | | | | |

Almond

| 4940 | H Dartt/Dry goods/groceries/&/ exchange/office/Almond N Y | 327 | C | Pl |
| 4941 | | | | |

Belmont

4942	Langdons Hardware Store/&/Exchange/office/Belmont/N Y	27	C	Pl
4943	Same	431	C	Pl
4944	Langdon's/Hardware/store/& Exchange/office/Belmont N Y	465	C	Pl
4945				

Binghampton

4946	Evans & Allen/watches/&/jewelry/Binghamton/N Y	575	C	Pl
4947	Same	Same	N	Pl
4948				
4949	Herschman Bros/Dry/Goods/20/ Court St/Binghamton/N Y	575	C	Pl
4950	Same	Same	N	Pl

Brooklyn

4951	Braun & Schellworth's / 132 134 136/Court St/Brooklyn / Pavilion	185	C	Pl
4952				
4953	Same	300	C	Pl
4954	C J Hauck / 108 / Leonard St/ Brooklyn E D/N Y	290	C	Pl
4955	M Ibert/cor/Montrose &/Graham/ Ave/Brooklyn E D	Good for /1/cent	L	Pl

NEW YORK—Continued

Brooklyn—Continued

NUMBER	OBVERSE	REVERSE	METAL	EDGE
4956	T Ivory/cor/Fulton & Orange/Sts/Brooklyn/Billard Saloon	29	C	Pl
4957	Same	Same	Br	Pl
4958	Same	Same	N	Pl
4959				
4960				
4961				
4962				
4963	Same	99	C	Pl
4964	Same	Same	Br	Pl
4965	Same	Same	N	Pl
4966	Same	Same	C-N	Pl
4967	Same	Same	W-M	Pl
4968				
4969	Same	108	C	Pl
4970	Same	Same	Br	Pl
4971	Same	Same	N	Pl
4972				
4973				
4974				
4975	Same	185	C	Pl
4976	Same	Same	Br	Pl
4977	Same	Same	N	Pl
4978				
4979				
4980				
4981	Same	300	C	Pl
4982				
4983				
4984				
4985				
4986	Same	302	C	Pl
4987	Same	Same	Br	Pl
4988	Same	Same	N	Pl
4989				
4990				
4991				
4992	Same	303	C	Pl
4993	Same	Same	Br	Pl
4994				
4995	Same	Same	C-N	Pl
4996				
4997				
4998	Same	336	C	Pl
4999	Same	Same	Br	Pl
5000	Same	Same	N	Pl
5001				
5002	John Joergers/North 2nd St/Brooklyn E D/L I	290	C	Pl
5003				

NEW YORK—Continued

Brooklyn—Continued

NUMBER	OBVERSE	REVERSE	METAL	EDGE
5004	Daniel Williams / grocer / corner/ Court & Warren/Sts/Brooklyn	29	C	Pl
5005				
5006	Same	Same	N	Pl
5007				
5008				
5009	Same	99	C	Pl
5010	Same	Same	Br	Pl
5011				
5012	Same	Same	C-N	Pl
5013	Same	Same	W-M	Pl
5014				
5015	Same	300	C	Pl
5016				
5017				
5018				
5019				
5020	Same	302	C	Pl
5021	Same	Same	Br	Pl
5022	Same	Same	N	Pl
5023				
5024				
5025	Same	303	C	Pl
5026				
5027				

Buffalo

5028	James Adams & Co/Tobacco/&/ Cigars/207/Washington/St/ Buffalo	454	C	Pl
5029				
5030	Alberger's/Meat/Store/Buffalo	418	C	R
5031	Same	Same	Br	R
5032				
5033	Same	635	C	R
5034	Same	Same	Br	R
5035	E G Barrows/Brandies/Wines & cigars/No 6/East Swan/St/ Buffalo	409	C	R
5036				
5037	Same	418	C	R
5038	Same	Same	Br	R
5039				
5040	Same	420	C	R
5041				
5042	F J Bieler/157/Main St/ Buffalo	454	C	Pl
5043	Same-overstrike	454-overstrike	C	Pl
5044	Same	456	C	Pl
5045	Same	458	C	Pl

NEW YORK—Continued

Buffalo—Continued

NUMBER	OBVERSE	REVERSE	METAL	EDGE
5046	T J Conry/Picture/Frames/ Newspapers &c/19/Seneca St/ Buffalo	454	C	Pl
5047	'19' in centre, surrounded by 'Picture Frames &c' in circle—'T J Conry' above 'Seneca St Buffalo' below	454	C	Pl
5048	Same	455	C	Pl
5049	Same	456	C	Pl
5050				
5051	A M Duburn/Canal/Tin Shop/No 29/Commercial/St/Buffalo	409	C	R
5052	Same	418	C	R
5053	Same	Same	Br	R
5054	Same	420	C	R
5055	Howes / Scales/L Danforth/Agt/ 93 Main St/Buffalo	416	C	R
5056	Same	418	C	R
5057	Same	Same	Br	R
5058	Same	420	C	R
5059				
5060	W G Fox/Oysters/Fruits/&/ Liquors/195 Main St/Buffalo	409	C	R
5061	Same	418	C	R
5062	Same	Same	Br	R
5063	Same	419	C-N	R
5064	Same	420	C	R
5065	Geo Gage/grocer / 334 / Main/St/ Buffalo	413	C	R
5066	Same	416	C	R
5067	Same	418	C	R
5068	Same	Same	Br	R
5069				
5070	Same	420	C	R
5071				
5072	Hochstetter & Strauss/Dry/ Goods/280/Main/St/Buffalo	409	C	R
5073	Same	418	C	R
5074	Same	Same	Br	R
5075	Same	419	C	R
5076				
5077	A M Johnston / Grocer/52/Main/ St/Buffalo	418	C	R
5078	Same	Same	Br	R
5079	Same	Same	Z	R
5080	Same	635	C	R
5081	Same	420	C	R
5082	John C Post/Paints/Oils/&/Glass/ No 8 Swan St/Buffalo	409	C	R
5083	Same	418	C	R
5084	Same	Same	Br	R

NEW YORK—Continued

Buffalo—Continued

NUMBER	OBVERSE	REVERSE	METAL	EDGE
5085				
5086	Reilly's/Bazaar/228/Main St/Buffalo N Y	575	C	Pl
5087				
5088	Robinson & Ball/Gents/Furnishing/Goods/275 Main St/Buffalo	416	C	R
5089				
5090	Same	418	C	R
5091	Same	Same	Br	R
5092				
5093	Same	419	C	R
5094	Rowe & Co/Oysters/& Foreign/Fruit/Depot/197 Main St/Buffalo	409	C	R
5095	Same	418	C	R
5096	Same	Same	Br	R
5097	Same	420	C	R
5098	Use/Seward's/Cough/Cure/S B Seward/Druggist/Buffalo	416	C	R
5099	Same	418	C	R
5100	Same	Same	Br	R
5101	Same	419	C	R
5102	Same	420	C	R
5103				
5104	Sohm & Rohmann/Butchers/Buffalo	418	C	R
5105	Same	Same	Br	R
5106				
5107	'Watsons Neuralgia King' around border—'C R Walker/225/Main St/Buffalo' in centre	454	C	Pl
5108				
5109	Webster & Co/Grocers/No 1/Seneca/St Buffalo N Y	454	C	Pl
5110				

Cohoes

5111	'Alden & Frink' above—Indian head to left in centre—'1863' below	Merchants/40/Mohawk St/Cohoes N Y	C	Pl
5112				
5113	'Alden & Frink' above—U S Shield in centre—'1863' below	Same	C	Pl
5114	Same	Same	Bronze	Pl
5115				

Cooperstown

5116	Bingham/&/Jarvis / Drugs/Medicines/Paints Oils &c Thick planchet	120	C	Pl
5117	Same-thin planchet	Same	C	Pl
5118	Same	Same	Br	Pl

NEW YORK—Continued

Cooperstown—Continued

NUMBER	OBVERSE	REVERSE	METAL	EDGE
5119	Same	Same	N	Pl
5120	Same	Same	C-N	Pl
5121	Same	Same	W-M	Pl
5122	Same	Same	S	Pl
5123	Same thick planchet	165	C	Pl
5124	Same thin planchet	Same	C	Pl
5125	Same	Same	Br	Pl
5126	Same	Same	N	Pl
5127	Same	Same	C-N	Pl
5128	Same	Same	W-M	Pl
5129	Same	Same	S	Pl
5130	Same—thick planchet	338	C	Pl
5131	Same—thin planchet	Same	C	Pl
5132	Same	Same	Br	Pl
5133	Same	Same	N	Pl
5134	Same	Same	C-N	Pl
5135	Same	Same	W-M	Pl
5136	Same	Same	S	Pl
5137	G L Bowne/will/redeem/at the/ Iron Clad/Cooperstown N Y	Same as the obverse of the Bingham & Jarvis series	C	Pl
5138	Same	Same	Br	Pl
5139	Same	Same	N	Pl
5140	Same	Same	C-N	Pl
5141	Same	Same	W-M	Pl
5142				
5143	Same thick planchet	46	C	Pl
5144	Same thin planchet	Same	C	Pl
5145	Same	Same	Br	Pl
5146	Same	Same	N	Pl
5147	Same	Same	C-N	Pl
5148	Same	Same	W-M	Pl
5149	Same	Same	S	Pl

Fort Edwards

5150	'Harvey & Co' above—Indian head to left in centre—'1863' below	General/Store/Fort Edwards N Y	C	Pl
5151	Same	Same	Br	Pl
5152				

Elmira

5153	Louis Strauss & Co/Dry/Goods/No 3/Union/Block/Elmira N Y	409	C	R
5154				
5155	Same	418	C	R
5156	Same	Same	Br	R
5157				

Greenpoint

5158	A Killeen/NO 1 & 16/Ferry/St/Greenpoint	29	C	Pl

NEW YORK—Continued

Greenpoint—Continued

NUMBER	OBVERSE	REVERSE	METAL	EDGE
5159				
5160	Same	99	C	Pl
5161				
5162	Same	108	C	Pl
5163				
5164	Same	147	C	Pl
5165				
5166	Same	Same	W-M	Pl
5167				
5168	Same	300	C	Pl
5169				
5170	Same	303	C	Pl
5171				
5172	Same	Same	N	Pl
5173	Same	Same	C-N	Pl
5174	Same	Same	W-M	Pl
5175				
5176	Same	336	C	Pl
5177				

New York City

5178	Atlantic Garden/50/Bowery/New York/1863 Thick planchet	Lyre with oak branches at sides — 'Grand Concert / every night' above 'Admission/free' below	C	Pl
5179	Same—thin planchet	Same	C	Pl
5180	Same	Same	Br	Pl
5181	Same	Same	N	Pl
5182	Same	Same	C-N	Pl
5183	Same	Same	W-M	Pl
5184				
5185	Cafe Autenrieth/85/Chatham St/ N Y/1863	85	C	Pl
5186	Same	290	C	Pl
5187	Same	291	C	Pl
5188	Same	293	C	Pl
5189	Same	513	C	Pl
5190	Same	514	C	Pl
5191				
5192	C Bahr/cor Cliff/and/Frankfort St/New York	85	C	Pl
5193	Same	142	C	Pl
5194	Same	178	C	Pl
5195	Same	290	C	Pl
5196	Same	291	C	Pl
5197	Same	293	C	Pl
5198	Same	514	C	Pl
5199	Same	Tom Cullen/liquors / 609/ Grand St N Y	C	Pl
5200	Same	Knoops Segar & Tobacco/ 131/Bowery/ N Y/1863	C	Pl

NEW YORK—Continued

New York City—Continued

NUMBER	OBVERSE	REVERSE	METAL	EDGE
5201	Same	H M Lane/lamps/kerosene oils/18/Spring St N Y	C	Pl
5202				
— 5203	H J Bang/Restaurant/231/ Broadway	Bunch of grapes on vine in centre—'Importer of' above— 'Rhine Wines' below	C	Pl
5204	Same	Same	Br	Pl
5205				
5206	Same	Same	W-M	Pl
5207				
— 5208	'Thos Bennett' above—'N Y' in wreath in centre—'213 Fulton St'/ 'A L Henning N Y' below	'J C Bailey' above—'Jersey /City' in wreath in centre —'City Hotel' below	C	Pl
5209				
— 5210	Indian head in centre—'V Benner & C H Bendinger' above—'L Roloff/ 1863' below Eighth feather below level of 'R'	Bottle in wreath in centre —'Importers of wines & Liquors' above—'1 Ave A' below	C	Pl
5211				
— 5212	Same-eighth feather on level of 'R'	Same	C	Pl
5213	Same	Same	Br	Pl
5214	Same—double strike	Same—double strike	Br	Pl
5215				
5216	Same	Same	W-M	Pl
5217	'I W Blain' above—'10cts/16 & 18' in centre—'Fulton Market N Y' below date '1862' to left	Blank planchet	Br	Pl
— 5218	Mounted Stag's head in centre— 'J LBode' to left—'Birdstuffer' to right '1863' below	Bohemian / fancy / glass-work/16/N Williams St N Y	C	Pl
5219	Same	Same	Br	Pl
5220	Same	Same	N	Pl
5221	Same	Same	C-N	Pl
5222	Same	Same	W-M	Pl
5223	Same	Same	S	Pl
5224				
5225	Same	47	C	Pl
5226	Same	Same	Br	Pl
5227				
5228				
5229	Same	647	C	Pl
5230				
5231				
— 5232	Jas Brennan/37/Nassau St/Foreign/&/U S Postage Stamps	108	C	Pl
5233	Same	Same	Br	Pl
5234				
5235				
5236	Same	185	C	Pl
5237	Same	Same	Br	Pl
5238				

NEW YORK—Continued

New York City—Continued

NUMBER	OBVERSE	REVERSE	METAL	EDGE
5239				
5240	Same	~~330~~ 645	C	Pl
5241	Same	Same	Br	Pl
5242	Same	Same	Nickeled	Pl
5243	Same	Same	W-M	Pl
5244				
5245				
5246	Bridgens/Metal token/&/Store Cards/189/William St N Y	29	C	Pl
5247	Same	Same	Br	Pl
5248				
5249				
5250	Same	99	C	Pl
5251	Same	Same	Br	Pl
5252	Same	Same	N	Pl
5253	Same	Same	C-N	Pl
5254	Same	Same	W-M	Pl
5255				
5256	Same	108	C	Pl
5257	Same	Same	Br	Pl
5258				
5259				
5260	Same	185	C	Pl
5261	Same	Same	Br	Pl
5262				
5263				
5264	Figure '1' mortar, pestle and '1863' in laurel wreath in centre 'T Brimelow Druggist' above— '432 Third Avenue N Y' below	489	C	Pl
5265	Same	Same	Br	Pl
5266	Same	Same	N	Pl
5267				
5268	Same	Same	W-M	Pl
5269	Same	Same	S	Pl
5270	Same	490	C	Pl
5271	Same	Same	Br	Pl
5272	Same	Same	N	Pl
5273	Same	Same	W-M	Pl
5274	Same	Same	S	Pl
5275	Same	'Good for/one glass/of so-da' within a circles of 31 stars	C	Pl
5276	Same	Same	Br	Pl
5277	Same	Same	N	Pl
5278	Same	Same	W-M	Pl
5279	Same	Same	S	Pl
5280	Bust of Franklin in laurel wreath Inscription same as above	489	C	Pl
5281	Same	Same	Br	Pl
5282	Same	Same	N	Pl

NEW YORK—Continued

New York City—Continued

NUMBER	OBVERSE	REVERSE	METAL	EDGE
5283	Same	Same	W-M	Pl
5284	Same	Same	S	Pl
5285	Same	Same as obverse of No 5264	C	Pl
5286	Same	Same	Br	Pl
5287	Same	Same	N	Pl
5288	Same	Same	W-M	Pl
5289	Same	Same	S	Pl
5290				
5291	Same	Same as reverse of No 5275	C	Pl
5292	Same	Same	Br	Pl
5293	Same	Same	N	Pl
5294	Same	Same	W-M	Pl
✚ 5295	Same	Same	S	Pl
5296				
5297	'2' within wreath—'T Brimelow Druggist' above—432 Third Avenue N Y' below	490	C	Pl
─ 5298	Same	Same	Br	Pl
5299	Same	Same	N	Pl
5300	Same	Same	W-M	Pl
5301	Same	Same	S	Pl
5302				
5303	Mortar and pestle and '1864' in closed wreath—inscription same as above	88	C	Pl
5304	Same	Same	Br	Pl
5305	Same	Same	N	Pl
5306	Same	Same	C-N	Pl
5307	Same	Same	W-M	Pl
5308	Same	Same	S	Pl
5309				
✚ 5310	'Broas Bros' above—'Army/and/Navy' in wreath in centre—'New York' below	11	C	Pl
5311	Same	Same	Br	Pl
5312	Same	Same	C-N	Pl
5313	Same	Same	W-M	Pl
5314	Same	Same	S	Pl
5315				
✚ 5316	Same—small planchet	38—not dated	C	Pl
5317	Same	Same — small planchet—cracked die	C	Pl
5318	Same—Large planchet	Same — large planchet—cracked die	C	Pl
5319	Same	Same—perfect die	Br	Pl
5320	Same	Same—cracked die	Br	Pl
5321	Same	Same—perfect die	C-N	Pl
5322	Same	Same—cracked die	C-N	Pl
5323	Same	Same—perfect die	W-M	Pl
5324	Same	Same—cracked die	W-M	Pl
5325	Same	Same—perfect die	S	Pl
5326	Same	Same—cracked die	S	Pl

NEW YORK—Continued

New York City—Continued

NUMBER	OBVERSE	REVERSE	METAL	EDGE
5327	Same—small planchet	114	C	Pl
5328	Same—large planchet	Same	C	Pl
5329	Same	Same	Br	Pl
5330	Same	Same	C-N	Pl
5331	Same	Same	W-M	Pl
5332	Same	Same—struck over U S dime S		Pl
5333	Same—'Army and Navy' in larger Letters	649	C	Pl
5334	Same	Same	Br	Pl
5335				
5336				
5337	Broas Pie Baker/one/country/H/ 131 41st St N Y 'H' under star— 'B' and 'R' close to 'C' and 'Y'	448	C	Pl
5338	Same	Same	Br	Pl
5339	Same	Same	W-M	Pl
5340	Same	Same	L	Pl
5341				
5342	Same	649	C	Pl
5343				
5344	Same	Same	L	Pl
5345				
5346	Same inscription—'B' and 'R' farther from'C' and 'Y'—overstrike onreverse	449	C	Pl
5347	Same	Same	Br	Pl
5348	Same	Same	W-M	Pl
5349	Same	Same	L	Pl
5350				
5351	Same	450	Br	Pl
5352				
5353				
5354	Same inscription and spacing—but no 'H' under star and no overstrike	449	C	Pl
5355	Same	Same	Br	Pl
5356	Same	Same	C-N	Pl
5357	Same	Same	W-M	Pl
5358	Same	Same	L	Pl
5359				
5360	Same as No 5346	650	C	Pl
5361	Same	Same	W-M	Pl
5362				
5363	Same as No 5346	Identical to obverse but no overstrike	C	Pl
5364	Same	Same	Br	Pl
5365	Same	Same	W-M	Pl
5366	Same	Same	L	Pl
5367				
5368	'Our/Country' in closed wreath— 'Broas Brothers' above—'Pie Bakers' below	648	C	Pl

NEW YORK—Continued

New York City—Continued

NUMBER	OBVERSE	REVERSE	METAL	EDGE
5369	Same	Same	Br	Pl
5370	Same	Same	N	Pl
5371				
5372				
5373	'M S Brown/1863' in double row of Stars and dots—'E Pluribus Unum' on band above	'Eureka' in German letters —2 Warren St New York	Br	Pl
5374				
5375	'M S Brown/1863' in open oak wreath name much curved	Eureka/2/Warren St New York	C	Pl
5376	Same—name not curved as much different oak wreath	Same	C	Pl
5377	Same—name spelled with large and small letters—different oak wreath	Same	C	Pl
5378				
5379	Same	Same	W-M	Pl
5380				
5381	W S Brown/1863 in open wreath— U S shield above—same oak wreath as in No 5377	Same	C	Pl
5382	Same	Same	Br	Pl
5383	Same	Same	C-N	Pl
5384	Carland's/95/Bowery/Cor of/Hester St N Y	Fine ale/drawn/from wood	C	Pl
5385	City of New York/I O U / one/cent/1863 25M M	647	C	Pl
5386	Same	Same—broken die	C	Pl
5387	Same	Same—perfect die	Br	Pl
5388	Same	Same	N-	Pl
5389	Same—small planchet	Same	N-	Pl
5390	Same—25 M M	Same	C-N	Pl
5391				
5392	Same—struck over U S quarter dollar	Same	S	Pl
5393	G A Cefandorf/233/E 77th St/dentist	Same as obverse	Ger-S	Pl
5394	Tom Cullen/Liquors / 609 / Grand St N Y	180	C	Pl
5395	Same	287	C	Pl
5396	Same	290	C	Pl
5397	Same	291	C	Pl
5398				
5399	Coffin in open wreath in centre— 'J J Diehl Undertaker/133' above' —'Essex St/ New York' below	647	C	Pl
5400	Same—struck over 1848 U S cent	Same—stuck over 1848 U S cent	C	Pl
5401	Same	Same	Br	Pl
5402	Same	Same	N-	Pl
5403	Same	Same	W-M	Pl

NEW YORK—Continued

New York City—Continued

NUMBER	OBVERSE	REVERSE	METAL	EDGE
5404	Same	Same	S	Pl
5405				
5406	Carl Diem/Constanzer/Brauerei/ 505 & 507/4th St/ New York—small planchet	651	C	Pl
5407	Same—large planchet	Same	C	Pl
5408	Same	Same	Br	Pl
5409	Same	Same	W-M	Pl
5410	Same	Same	G-S	Pl
5411				
5412				
5413	'Not/one/cent/H' in closed wreath —'C Doscher 'above—'241 Washington St N Y 'below	16	C	Pl
5414	Same—large planchet	70	C	Pl
5415	Same—small planchet	Same	C	Pl
5416	Same	72	C	Pl
5417	Same	652	C	Pl
5418	Same	Blank	C	Pl
5419				
5420	Bust of Washington to right—'C Doscher 241 Wash St N Y' above '1863' below in larger figures	275	C	Pl
5421	Same—date in smaller figures	Same	C	Pl
5422	Same—broken die	Same	C	Pl
5423	Same	Same	Lead	Pl
5424				
5425	Felix/Dining/ Saloon / 256/Broadway/New York	49	C	Pl
5426	Same	Same	Br	Pl
5427	Same	Same	N	Pl
5428	Same	Same	C-N	Pl
5429	Same	Same	W-M	Pl
5430	Same	Same	S	Pl
5431				
5432	Same	260	C	Pl
5433	Same	Same	Br	Pl
5434	Same	Same	N	Pl
5435	Same	Same	C-N	Pl
5436	Same	Same	W-M	Pl
5437	Same	Same	S	Pl
5438				
5439	J Fisher/25 / Seventh / Av/Segar Store	645	C	Pl
5440				
5441				
5442				
5443	Same	Same	W-M	Pl
5444				
5445	'Fr Freise Leichenbesorgner 'above—Indian head to left in centre '12 Ave A New York' below	Similar to No 5399 with the exception of the name and address— '1863' added	C	Pl

NEW YORK—Continued

New York City—Continued

NUMBER	OBVERSE	REVERSE	METAL	EDGE
5446				
5447	J F Gardner/55/Henry/St/N Y	49	C	Pl
5448	Same	Same	Br	Pl
5449				
5450	Same	Same	C-N	Pl
5451				
5452	Same	Same	S	Pl
5453				
5454				
5455				
5456	A Gavron/213/Bowery/&/102 Pitt St/N Y/Sausages	29	C	Pl
5457	Same	Same	Br	Pl
5458	Same	Same	N	Pl
5459	Same	Same	C-N	Pl
5460				
5461	Same	Same	S	Pl
5462				
5463	Same	99	C	Pl
5464	Same	Same	Br	Pl
5465	Same	Same	N	Pl
5466	Same	Same	C-N	Pl
5467	Same	Same	W-M	Pl
5468				
5469	Same	108	C	Pl
5470	Same	Same	Br	Pl
5471	Same	Same	N	Pl
5472	Same	Same	C-N	Pl
5473	Same	Same	W-M	Pl
5474	Same	Same	S	Pl
5475				
5476	Same	185	C	Pl
5477	Same	Same	Br	Pl
5478	Same	Same	N	Pl
5479	Same	Same	C-N	Pl
5480	Same	Same	W-M	Pl
5481	Same	Same	S	Pl
5482				
5483	Same	300	C	Pl
5484				
5485				
5486	Same	302	C	Pl
5487	Same	Same	Br	Pl
5488	Same	Same	N	Pl
5489	Same	Same	C-N	Pl
5490	Same	Same	W-M	Pl
5491				
— 5492	Same	303	C	Pl
5493	Same	Same	Br	Pl
5494				
5495				

NEW YORK—Continued

New York City—Continued

NUMBER	OBVERSE	REVERSE	METAL	EDGE
5496	Same	Same	W-M	Pl
5497				
5498	Same	336	C	Pl
5499	Same	Same	Br	Pl
5500	Same	Same	N	Pl
5501	Same	Same	C-N	Pl
5502				
5503	Same	Same	S	Pl
5504				
5505	'Charles Gentsch' above — Indian head to left in centre—'1863' below	Cafe/Restaurant/Du Commerce/No 426/Broadway N Y	C	Pl
5506	Same	Same	Nickled	Pl
5507				
5508	H D Gerdts/Broker/&/Coin Dealer/240/Greenwich St N Y	99	C	Pl
5509	Same	Same	Br	Pl
5510	Same	Same	N	Pl
5511				
5512	Same	Same	W-M	Pl
5513				
5514	Same	185	C	Pl
5515	Same	Same	Br	Pl
5516				
5517	G Graham/cor / Henry/& Montgomery St/Cor Bleecker &/Tenth/St/Liquors	653	C	Pl
5518	Same	Same	Br	Pl
5519	Same	Same	N	Pl
5520	Same	Same	C-N	Pl
5521	Same	Same	W-M	Pl
5522	Same	Same	S	Pl
5523				
5524	J A C Grube/Segars/and/tobacco/7/Bowery/7/New York	180	C	Pl
5525	Same	291	C	Pl
5526	Same	292	C	Pl
5527	Same	Knoops segars & Tobacco/131/Bowery/N Y/1863	C	Pl
5528				
5529	'John P Gruber' above—Pair of balances in centre—'New York' below	486	C	Pl
5530	Same	Same	Br	Pl
5531	Same	Same	N	Pl
5532	Same	Same	C-N	Pl
5533	Same	Same	W-M	Pl
5534	Same	Same	S	Pl
5535				
5536	Same	Two story house in centre —on which is inscribed 'Warmkessel' 'Established' above—'1850' below	C	Pl

NEW YORK—Continued

New York City—Continued

NUMBER	OBVERSE	REVERSE	METAL	EDGE
5537	Same	Same	Br	Pl
5538	Same	Same	N	Pl
5539				
5540	Same	Same	W-M	Pl
5541	Same	Same	S	Pl
5542				
5543	Same as reverse of No 5529	653	C	Pl
5544	Same	Same	Br	Pl
5545				
5546				
5547	'John P Gruber' above—smaller scales in centre—'178 Chatham Sq' below	49	C	Pl
5548	Same—struck over reverse	Same—struck over obverse	C	Pl
5549	Same	Same	Br	Pl
5550	Same	Same	N	Pl
5551	Same	Same	C-N	Pl
5552	Same	Same	W-M	Pl
5553				
5554	Same	145	C	Pl
5555				
5556	Same	Same	N	Pl
5557	Same	Same	C-N	Pl
5558	Same	Same	W-M	Pl
5559				
5560	Same	260	C	Pl
5561	Same	Same	Br	Pl
5562	Same	Same	N	Pl
5563	Same	Same	C-N	Pl
5564	Same	Same	W-M	Pl
5565	Same—struck over an English sixpence of 1834	Same—Struck over an English six pense of 1834	S	Pl
5566				
5567	Same	487	C	Pl
5568	Same	Same	Br	Pl
5569	Same	Same	N.	Pl
5570				
5571				
5572	Same	Same	S	Pl
5573				
5574	Same	488	C	Pl
5575	Same	Same	Br	Pl
5576	Same	Same	N	Pl
5577	Same	Same	C-N	Pl
5578				
5579	Same	Same	S	Pl
5580				
5581	Same as reverse of No 5529	Same as reverse of No 5536	C	Pl
5582	Same	Same	Br	Pl
5583				
5584				

NEW YORK—Continued

New York City—Continued

NUMBER	OBVERSE	REVERSE	METAL	EDGE
5585	Same as Reverse of No 5574	654	C	Pl
5586	Same	Same	Br	Pl
5587	Same	Same	N	Pl
5588	Same	Same	C-N	Pl
5589	Same	Same	W-M	Pl
5590				
5591				
5592	Same as reverse of No 5585	324	Br	Pl
5593				
5594				
5595	A J Henning/Die/Sinker / &/Engraver	87/Fulton St/N Y	C	Pl
5596	Same	Same	Br	Pl
5597	Same	Same	W-M	Pl
5598	Same	Same	S	Pl
5599				
5600				
5601	'William Hastings' above—Indian head in cenre—'1863' below	'Im/ported/liquors' in wreath	Bronze	Pl
5602	Same	Same	L	Pl
5603				
5604	Chr E Hetzel/Roofer/New York	545	C	Pl
5605				
5606	Hussey's Special Message Post/ 50/William St/New York	Post boy on horse to right —'Time is money' above —'1863/Exigency' below	C	Pl
5607	Same	Same	Bronze	Pl
5608	Locomotive in centre—'Hussey's' above '50 Wm St/N York/Special Message Post' below	Same	Bronze	Pl
5609				
5610	Same as reverse of No 5606	155	C	R
5611				
5612	George Hyenlein/23/Chrystie St/ N Y	50	C	Pl
5613	Same	56	C	Pl
5614	Same	87	C	Pl
5615	Same	274	C	Pl
5616	Same	291	C	Pl
5617	Same	293	C	Pl
5618				
5619	Lyre in wreath in centre—'Christoph Karl' above—'42 Avenue A New York' below	190	C	Pl
5620	Same—thick planchet	Same	C	Pl
5621	Same	Same	Br	Pl
5622	Same	Same	N	Pl
5623	Same	Same	C-N	Pl
5624	Same	Same	W-M	Pl
5625	Same—overstrike	Same	S	Pl

NEW YORK—Continued

New York City—Continued

NUMBER	OBVERSE	REVERSE	METAL	EDGE
5626				
— 5627	Silk hat dividing date '1863' in centre 'R T Kelly' above—'1319 Third Ave/New York' below	260	C	Pl
5628	Same	Same	Br	Pl
5629	Same	Same	N	Pl
5630	Same	Same	C-N	Pl
5631	Same	Same	W-M	Pl
5632	Same	Same	S	Pl
5633				
5634	Same	145	C	Pl
5635				
5636	Knoop's Segars & Tobacco/131/ Bowery/N Y/1863	85	C	Pl
5637	Same	180	C	Pl
5638	Same	291	C	Pl
5639	Same	292	C	Pl
— 5640	Same	514	C	Pl
5641				
5642	H M Lane/Lamps/kerosene oils/ 18/Spring St N Y	1	C	Pl
5643	Same	Same	Br	Pl
5644	Same	Same	N	Pl
5645				
5646	Same	Same	W-M	Pl
5647				
5648	Same	50	C	Pl
5649				
5650	Same	56	C	Pl
5651	Same	Same	Br	Pl
5652	Same	Same	N	Pl
5653				
5654				
5655	Same	76	C	Pl
5656	Same	Same	Br	Pl
5657	Same	Same	N	Pl
5658				
5659	Same	Same	W-M	Pl
5660				
5661	Same	87	C	Pl
5662	Same	Same	Br	Pl
5663	Same	Same	N	Pl
5664	Same	Same	C-N	Pl
5665	Same	Same	W-M	Pl
5666				
— 5667	Same	142	C	Pl
5668	Same	Same	Br	Pl
5669	Same	Same	N	Pl
5670	Same	Same	C-N	Pl
5671				
5672	Same	Same	Silvered	Pl

NEW YORK—Continued

New York City—Continued

NUMBER	OBVERSE	REVERSE	METAL	EDGE
5673				
5674	Same	143	C	Pl
5675	Same	Same	Br	Pl
5676	Same	Same	N	Pl
5677				
5678				
5679	Same	144	C	Pl
5680	Same	Same	Br	Pl
5681	Same	Same	N	Pl
5682				
5683	Same	Same	W-M	Pl
5684				
5685	Same	165	C	Pl
5686	Same	Same	Br	Pl
5687	Same	Same	N	Pl
5688				
5689	Same	Same	W-M	Pl
5690				
5691	Same	180	C	Pl
5692				
➤ 5693	Same	269	C	Pl
5694	Same	Same	Br	Pl
5695	Same	Same	N	Pl
5696	Same	Same	C-N	Pl
5697	Same	Same	W-M	Pl
5698				
5699	Same	273	C	Pl
5700	Same	Same	Br	Pl
5701	Same	Same	N	Pl
5702				
5703	Same	Same	W-M	Pl
5704				
5705	Same	274	C	Pl
5706	Same	Same	Br	Pl
5707	Same	Same	N	Pl
5708				
5709	Same	Same	W-M	Pl
5710				
5711	Same	291	C	Pl
5712				
5713	Same	292	C	Pl
5714				
5715	Same	293	C	Pl
5716				
5717	Same	338	C	Pl
5718	Same	Same	Br	Pl
5719	Same	Same	N	Pl
5720				
5721	Same	Same	W-M	Pl
5722				

NEW YORK—Continued

New York City—Continued

NUMBER	OBVERSE	REVERSE	METAL	EDGE
— 5723	'Gustavus Lindenmueller' above —mug in closed wreath in centre— 'New York' below Wide space between 'New' & 'York'	Bust to left in centre—13 stars above—'1863' below 'L Roloff' below bust	C	Pl
5724	Same	Same	Br	Pl
5725	Same	Same	N	Pl
5726	Same	Same	W-M	Pl
5627	Same	Same	Lead	Pl
5728				
— 5729	Same	Same but 'L Roloff' omitted	C	Pl
5730	Same	Same	Br	Pl
5731	Same	Same	N	Pl
5732	Same	Same	W-M	Pl
5733				
— 5734	Same — Narrow space between 'New' and 'York'	Same as reverse of No 5723	C	Pl
5735	Same	Same	Br	Pl
5736	Same	Same	N	Pl
5737	Same	Same	W-M	Pl
5738	Same	Same	S	Pl
5739				
5740				
5741	Same	Same as reverse of No 5729	Br	Pl
5742	Same	Same	N	Pl
5743	Same	Same	W-M	Pl
5744				
5745				
— 5746	'Gustavus Lindenmueller' above— 'Odeon' in wreath in centre—'New York' below	Similar to reverse of No 5729—date smaller figures	C	Pl
5847	Same	Same	Br	Pl
5748	Same	Same	N	Pl
5749	Same	Same	W-M	Pl
5750	Same	Same	S	Pl
5751				
5752	Same as reverse of No 5723	Same as reverse of No 5729	C	Pl
5753				
5754				
— 5755	Charles A Luhrs/Pike Slip/cor Water St/New York	Beer glass in vine wreath —'Pike Slip Shades' above —'1863' below	C	Pl
5756	Same	Same	Br	Pl.
5757	Same	Same	N	Pl
5758	Same	Same	C-N	Pl
5759	Same	Same	W-M	Pl
5760	Same	Same	Ger-S	Pl
5761	Same	Same	S	Pl
5762				
5763	Eagle with scroll on shield in centre—'New York' above—'C Magnus National Printing Establishment' around border	'100 entitles to a $2.00 view of New York City' around a beaded circle in which is small profile of Washington	C	Pl

NEW YORK—Continued

New York City—Continued

NUMBER	OBVERSE	REVERSE	METAL	EDGE
5764	Same	Same	Br	Pl
5765	Same	Same	W-M	Pl
5766				
5767				
5768	Same	Small profile of Washington on plain planchet	C	Pl
5769				
5770	J Mahnken/19 & 22/West St/N Y/Liquors & Segars	29	C	Pl
5771	Same	108	C	Pl
5772	Same	300	C	Pl
5773	Same	303	C	Pl
5774	Same	336	C	Pl
5775				
5776	'B Maloney' above—Indian head in centre—'Proprietor' below	National/499/Third Avenue/1863	C	Pl
5777	Same	Same	Bronze	Pl
5778				
5779	'H B Melville' above—profile of him to left in cenre—'Agt 1863' below	Jeweler/Goodfor/one/cent/76 Beecher St N Y	C	Pl
5780	Same	Same	Br	Pl
5781	Same	Same	N	Pl
5782	Same	Same	C-N	Pl
5783	Same	Same	W-M	Pl
5784	Same	Same	S	Pl
5785				
5786	Edward Miehling's / 85/Ave B/N Y/Meat Market	47	C	Pl
5787	Same	Similar toDie No 47-end of ribbon touches 'L' of 'Rolof'	C	Pl
5788	Same	Similar to Die No 47—diadem beaded instead of 'Liberty'	C	Pl
5789				
5790	Use Miller's/50/cents/N Y/Hair Dye	Use/ Miller's / 25 / cents / Hair/invigorator	C	Pl
5791	Use Miller's/50/cent/Hair Dye--Incused lettering	Same as obverse die	C	Pl
5792	Use/ L Miler's/Hair/Invigorator/N Y—Incused lettering	Same as obverse die	C	Pl
5793				
5794	'G M Mittnacht's Eagle Safe' around border—safe in centre	Meat chopper on block in centre—'23 Spring St' above —'New York' below	Bronze	Pl
5795	Same—three stars above safe	Same	Bronze	Pl
5796	Same	Same	Nickled	Pl
5797				
5798	'Monk's/Metal/Signs' in circle of 34 stars—small eagle below	1	C	Pl
5799	Same	Same	Br	Pl

NEW YORK—Continued

New York City—Continued

NUMBER	OBVERSE	REVERSE	METAL	EDGE
5800	Same	Same	N	Pl
5801	Same	Same	C-N	Pl
5802	Same	Same	W-M	Pl
5803	Same	Same	S	Pl
5804	Same	Same	Lead	Pl
5805				
5806				
5807				
5808	Same	165	N	Pl
5809				
5810	Same	Same	W-M	Pl
5811				
5812	Same	273	C	Pl
5813	Same	Same	Br	Pl
5814	Same	Same	N	Pl
5815				
5816				
5817	Same	274	C	Pl
5818	Same	Same	Br	Pl
5819	Same	Same	N	Pl
5820	Same	Same	C-N	Pl
5821	Same	Same	W-M	Pl
5822				
5823	Same	301	C	Pl
5824				
5825				
5826				
5827	Same	Small bust of Washington to right in wreath in centre—'339 B'way N Y' above —'1863' below	C	Pl
5828	Same	Same	Br	Pl
5829	Same	Same	N	Pl
5830	Same	Same	C-N	Pl
5831	Same	Same	W-M	Pl
5832	Same	Same	S	Pl
5833				
5834	Same as reverse of No 5827	1	C	Pl
5835	Same	Same	Br	Pl
5836	Same	Same	N	Pl
5837	Same	Same	C-N	Pl
5838	Same	Same	W-M	Pl
5839	Same	Same	S	Pl
5840				
5841	Same	165	C	Pl
5842	Same	Same	Br	Pl
5843	Same	Same	N	Pl
5844	Same	Same	C-N	Pl
5845	Same	Same	W-M	Pl
5846	Same	Same	S	Pl
5847				

NEW YORK—Continued

New York City—Continued

NUMBER	OBVERSE	REVERSE	METAL	EDGE
5848	Same	273	C	Pl
5849	Same	Same	Br	Pl
5850				
5851				
5852				
5853	Same	274	C	Pl
5854	Same	Same	Br	Pl
5855	Same	Same	N	Pl
5856				
5857				
5858	Same	301	C	Pl
5859	Same	Same	Br	Pl
5860	Same	Same	N	Pl
5861	Same	Same	C-N	Pl
5862	Same	Same	W-M	Pl
5863	Same	Same	S	Pl
5864				
5865	Same	338	C	Pl
5866	Same	Same	Br	Pl
5867	Same	Same	N	Pl
5868	Same	Same	C-N	Pl
5869	Same	Same	W-M	Pl
5870	Same	Same	S	Pl
5871				
5872	'Henry C Montz' above—His profile to left in beaded circle in centre—'Orpheus Hall' below	A Token/of/the war / for the/Union/1863	C	Pl
5873	Same—thin planchet	Same	C	Pl
5874	Same	Same	Br	Pl
5875	Same	Same	N	Pl
5876	Same	Same	W-M	Pl
5877	Same	Same	S	Pl
5878				
5879	'New York and Albany' around border—'Peoples /line / of / steamboats' in centre—3 stars below	Time table/leave N Y/6 P M/leave Albany/7 1/2 P M	C	Pl
5880				
5881	G Parsons/24/John St/N Y/Fireworks	1	C	Pl
5882	Same	Same	Br	Pl
5883	Same	Same	N	Pl
5884				
5885	Same	Same	W-M	Pl
5886				
5887	Same	56	C	Pl
5888	Same	Same	Br	Pl
5889	Same	Same	N	Pl
5890				
5891				
5892				
5893	Same	76	C	Pl

NEW YORK—Continued

New York City—Continued

NUMBER	OBVERSE	REVERSE	METAL	EDGE
5894	Same	Same	Br	Pl
5895	Same	Same	N	Pl
5896				
5897	Same	Same	W-M	Pl
5898				
5899	Same	87	C	Pl
5900	Same	Same	Br	Pl
5901	Same	Same	N	Pl
5902				
5903	Same	Same	W-M	Pl
5904				
5905	Same	99	C	Pl
5906				
5907				
5908				
5909				
5910				
5911	Same	143	C	Pl
5912	Same	Same	Br	Pl
5913	Same	Same	N	Pl
5914				
5915	Same	Same	W-M	Pl
5916				
5917	Same	144	C	Pl
5918	Same	Same	Br	Pl
5919	Same	Same	N	Pl
5920				
5921	Same	Same	W-M	Pl
5922				
5923	Same	165	C	Pl
5924	Same	Same	Br	Pl
5925	Same	Same	N	Pl
5926				
5927	Same	Same	W-M	Pl
5928				
5929	Same	273	C	Pl
5930	Same	Same	Br	Pl
5931				
5932				
5933				
5934				
5935	Same	274	C	Pl
5936	Same	Same	Br	Pl
5937	Same	Same	N	Pl
5938				
5939				
5940				
5941	Same	301	C	Pl
5942				
5943	Same	Same	N	Pl
5944				

NEW YORK—Continued

New York City—Continued

NUMBER	OBVERSE	REVERSE	METAL	EDGE
5945	Same	Same	W-M	Pl
5946				
5947	Same	338	C	Pl
5948	Same	Same	Br	Pl
5949	Same	Same	N	Pl
5950				
5951	Same	Same	W-M	Pl
5952				
5953	Chas Pfaff/restaurant/647/ Broadway N Y	Figure of Priest Full size	C	Pl
5954				
5955	Prescott's/11/Wall St/N Y/ Soda Water	Spread eagle supported by four darts and olive branch —'20 for a dollar' above Ger—	S	Pl
5956				
5957				
5958	John Quinn/Grocer/Cor 26 Sts/ Lexington Av	29	C	Pl
5959	Same	Same	Br	Pl
5960	Same	Same	N	Pl
5961				
5962	Same	Same	C-N	Pl
5963				
5964	Same	99	C	Pl
5965	Same	Same	Br	Pl
5966	Same—thin planchet	Same	Br	Pl
5967	Same	Same	N	Pl
5968	Same	Same	C-N	Pl
5969	Same	Same	W-M	Pl
5970	Same	Same	S	Pl
5971				
5972				
5973	Same	108	Br	Pl
5974	Same	Same	N	Pl
5975	Same	Same	C-N	Pl
5976	Same	Same	W-M	Pl
5977				
5978	Same	185	C	Pl
5979	Same	Same	Br	Pl
5980	Same	Same	N	Pl
5981	Same	Same	C-N	Pl
5982	Same	Same	W-M	Pl
5983	Same	300	C	Pl
5984				
5985				
5986				
5987	Same	302	Br	Pl
5988	Same	Same	N	Pl
5989	Same	Same	C-N	Pl

NEW YORK—Continued

New York City—Continued

NUMBER	OBVERSE	REVERSE	METAL	EDGE
5990	Same	Same	W-M	Pl
5991				
5992	Same	336	C	Pl
5993	Same	Same	Br	Pl
5994	Same	Same	N	Pl
5995	Same	Same	C-N	Pl
5996	Same	Same	W-M	Pl
5997				
5998	Large basket of flowers in centre—'Christian Rauh' above—'48 Ave A N Y/confectioner' belo w	512	C	Pl
5999	Same	Same	Br	Pl
6000				
6001	Same	Same	C-N	Pl
6002	Same	Same	W-M	Pl
6003				
6004	Small basket of flowers in closed wreath in centre—'Christian Rauh' above—'N Y/Confectioner' below	512	C	Pl
6005	Same	Same	Br	Pl
6006	Same	Same	N	Pl
6007	Same	Same	C-N	Pl
6008	Same	Same	W-M	Pl
6009				
6010	'Frederick Rollwagen Jr' above—'1863' below—point of bust between '1' and '8' of date Period after 'Jr'	587/Third Avenue/and/20 & 21/Centre Market/N Y	Bronze	Pl
6011	Same—point of bust extends beyond '1' of date—no period after 'Jr'	Same	Bronze	Pl
6012				
6013	Ed Schaaf/14 & 16/Division St—five stars above and five stars below '14 & 16'	145	C	Pl
6014	Same	Same	Br	Pl
6015	Same	Same	N	Pl
6016	Same	Same	C-N	Pl
6017	Same	Same	W-M	Pl
6018	Same	Same	S	Pl
6019				
6020	Same—no stars	Same	C	Pl
6021	Same	Same	Br	Pl
6022	Same	Same	N	Pl
6023	Same	Same	C-N	Pl
6024	Same	Same	W-M	Pl
6025	Same	Same	S	Pl
6026				
6027	Same	New/York/1863 in circle of thirteen stars	C	Pl
6028				

NEW YORK—Continued

New York City—Continued

NUMBER	OBVERSE	REVERSE	METAL	EDGE
6029	J Schork/1863	Clock dial showing 3 o'clock	Lead	Pl
6030				
6031	John Schuh's/88/First Ave/ N Y/ Saloon	47	C	Pl
6032	Same—small planchet	Same	C	Pl
6033				
6034				
6035	Same	Same as obverse of No 5385	C	Pl
6036				
6037				
6038	'96/between/5th & 6th/Sts' in beaded circles in centre—'First Ave Hall' above—'Geo D Schmidt' below	49	C	Pl
6039	Same	Same—double strike	C	Pl
6040	Same	Same	Br	Pl
6041				
6042	Same	Same	C-N	Pl
6043	Same	Same	W-M	Pl
6044	Same	Same	S	Pl
6045	Edwd Schultze's/24/William/ Street/Restaurant	Stag' shead and '1863' in centre—'26 & 28 Exchange Place' above—'N Y' below	C	Pl
6046	Same but ver ysmall planchet	Same (511)	C	Pl
6047	Same	Same	Br	Pl
6048	Same	Same	N	Pl
6049	Same	Same	C-N	Pl
6050	Same	Same	W-M	Pl
6051				
6052	Same	Similar — first prong of antlers point to '8' of '28'	C	Pl
6053	Same	Same (510).	Br	Pl
6054				
6055				
6056	'Ph J Seiter's' above—bull's head in centre—'Market' below	Redeemed/at/ my market/ 102 Third Ave/N Y	C	Pl
6057	Same	Same	Br	Pl
6058	Same	Same	N	Pl
6059	Same	Same	C-N	Pl
6060	Same	Same	W-M	Pl
6061	Same	Same	S	Pl
6062				
6063	Similar—ear more horizontal— stars smaller	Same	C	Pl
6064	Same	Same	Br	Pl
6065				
6066				
6067	Same	Same	W-M	Pl
6068				
6069	Same as obverse of No 6056	144	C	Pl
6070				

NEW YORK—Continued

New York City—Continued

NUMBER	OBVERSE	REVERSE	METAL	EDGE
6071				
6072	Same as reverse of No 6056	76	C	Pl
6073				
6074				
6075	Jones Wood/Hotel/N Y/I Sommers	587	C	Pl
6076	Same	Same	Br	Pl
6077	Same	Same	N	Pl
6078	Same	Same	W-M	Pl
6079	Same	Same	S	Pl
6080				
6081	Staudinger's/116/Broadway N Y	Large U S Shield 12 stars 'E Pluribus' on ribbon '1863' below and 'L Roloff'	C	Pl
6082	Similar but smaller planchet	Similar but smaller design—'L Roloff' above shield	C	Pl
6083	"		W-M	
6084				
6085	St Charles Billiard Rooms/584 & 586/8th Ave/N Y	85	C	Pl
6086	Same	291	C	Pl
6087	Same	292	C	Pl
6088				
6089	'S Steinfeld' above—'sole agent for the U S' below—French coat of Arms in centre right hand sceptre points to 'G' of 'Agent'	Principal Depot/1863/ of the French / Cognac / Bitters / 70/Nassau ST N Y	C	Pl
6090	Similar—sceptre points to 'E' of 'Agent'	Principal / Depot / of the/ French / Cognac / Bitters / 70/Nassau St	C	Pl
6091	Same	Same as reverse of No 6089	C	Pl
6092				
6093	Story & Southworth/grocers/53/ Vesey St/New York	Die press in centre dividing date '1863'—'B & K' below	C	Pl
6094				
6095	Story & Southworth / grocers/53/ Vesey/St/N Y Wide space on each side of 'N Y'	50	C	Pl
6096				
6097	Same	56	C	Pl
6098	Same	Same	Br	Pl
6099	Same	Same	N	Pl
6100				
6101	Same	Same	W-M	Pl
6102				
6103	Same	76	C	Pl
6104	Same	Same	Br	Pl
6105	Same	Same	N	Pl
6106	Same	Same	C-N	Pl
6107	Same	Same	W-M	Pl

NEW YORK—Continued

New York City—Continued

NUMBER	OBVERSE	REVERSE	METAL	EDGE
6108				
6109				
6110	Same	87	Br	Pl
6111				
6112	Same	Same	C-N	Pl
6113	Same	Same	W-M	Pl
6114				
— 6115	Same	142	C	Pl
6116	Same	Same	Br	Pl
6117	Same	Same	N	Pl
6118	Same	Same	C-N	Pl
6119	Same	Same	W-M	Pl
6120				
6121				
6122	Same	143	Br	Pl
6123				
6124	Same	Same	C-N	Pl
6125	Same	Same	W-M	Pl
6126				
6127	Same	144	C	Pl
6128	Same	Same	Br	Pl
6129	Same	Same	N	Pl
6130	Same	Same	C-N	Pl
6131	Same	Same	W-M	Pl
6132				
6133	Same	269	C	Pl
6134				
6135	Same	273	C	Pl
6136	Same	Same	Br	Pl
6137				
6138				
6139	Same	Same	W-M	Pl
6140				
6141	Same	274	C	Pl
6142	Same	Same	Br	Pl
6143	Same	Same	N	Pl
6144				
6145	Same	Same	W-M	Pl
6146				
6147	Same	301	C	Pl
6148				
6149	Same	Same	N	Pl
6150				
6151	Same	Same	W-M	Pl
6152				
6153	Same	338	C	Pl
6154	Same	Same	Br	Pl
6155	Same	Same	N	Pl
6156				
6157	Same	Same	W-M	Pl
6158				

NEW YORK—Continued

New York City—Continued

NUMBER	OBVERSE	REVERSE	METAL	EDGE
6159	Similar—narrow space on side of 'N Y'	1	C	Pl
6160	Same	Same	Br	Pl
6161	Same	Same	N	Pl
6162				
6163	Same	Same	W-M	Pl
6164				
6165	Same	56	C	Pl
6166	Same	Same	Br	Pl
6167	Same	Same	N	Pl
6168				
6169	Same	Same	W-M	Pl
6170				
6171	Same	76	C	Pl
6172	Same	Same	Br	Pl
6173				
6174	Same	Same	C-N	Pl
6175	Same	Same	W-M	Pl
6176				
6177	Same	87	C	Pl
6178	Same	Same	Br	Pl
6179				
6180	Same	Same	C-N	Pl
6181	Same	Same	W-M	Pl
6182				
6183				
6184	Same	143	Br	Pl
6185	Same	Same	N	Pl
6186				
6187	Same	Same	W-M	Pl
6188				
6189	Same	144	C	Pl
6190	Same	Same	Br	Pl
6191	Same	Same	N	Pl
6192				
6193	Same	Same	W-M	Pl
6194				
6195	Same	273	C	Pl
6196	Same	Same	Br	Pl
6197	Same	Same	N	Pl
6198				
6199	Same	Same	W-M	Pl
6200				
6201	Same	274	C	Pl
6202	Same	Same	Br	Pl
6203	Same	Same	N	Pl
6204				
6205	Same	Same	W-M	Pl
6206				
6207	Same	291	C	Pl
6208				

NEW YORK—Continued

New York City—Continued

NUMBER	OBVERSE	REVERSE	METAL	EDGE
6209	Same	293	C	Pl
6210				
6211	Same	301	C	Pl
6212				
6213				
6214				
6215	Same	Same	W-M	Pl
6216				
6217	Same	338	C	Pl
6218	Same	Same	Br	Pl
6219	Same	Same	N	Pl
6220				
6221	Same	Same	W-M	Pl
6222				
6223	Strasburger & Nuhn / Importers/ 65/Maiden Lane/New York	476	Br	Pl
6224				
6225				
6226	Indian head to left in centre—'Wm Thierbach' to left—'142 Elm St' to right—'1863' below	'Grocer' in one line within a laurel wreath—star above	Lead	Pl
6227				
6228	Similar—has 'N Y' added to address—'1863' farther from bust	'Grocer' in two lines within a laurel wreath—small star	Lead	Pl
6229	Same	Same	Br	Pl
6230	Same	Same	W-M	Pl
6231	C Tollner & Hammacher/Hardware/209/ Bowery/New York	290	C	Pl
6232	Same	Same	Nickled	Pl
6233				
6234	Peter Warmkessel/8/Duane St/ New York	House in centre bearing sign 'Warmkessel'—'A' toleft —'D' to right—'established' above—'1850' below	C	Pl
6235	Same	Same	Br	Pl
6236	Same	Same	N	Pl
6237	Same	Same	C-N	Pl
6238	Same	Same	W-M	Pl
6239				
6240	Same	486	C	Pl
6241	Same	Same	Br	Pl
6242				
6243				
6244	Same	516	C	Pl
6245				
6246	Same as reverse of No 6234	486	C	Pl
6247	Same	Same	Br	Pl
6248				
6249	Same	516	C	Pl
6250	Same	Same	Br	Pl

NEW YORK—Continued

New York City—Continued

NUMBER	OBVERSE	REVERSE	METAL	EDGE
6251				
6252	486	516	C	Pl
6253				
6254	J H Warner/104/Barclay/St/ New York	590	C	Pl
6255	Same	Same	Br	Pl
6256	Same	Same	N	Pl
6257	Same	Same	C-N	Pl
6258	Same	Same	W-M	Pl
6259	Same	Same	S	Pl
6260	Same	Same	Lead	Pl
6261				
6262	Wm F Warner/No 1/Catherine Market	29	C	Pl
6263	Same	Same	Br	Pl
6264	Same	Same	N	Pl
6265				
6266	Same	300	C	Pl
6267				
6268	Gobbler in centre—'Washington Market' above—'Exchange' below	566	C	Pl
6269				
6270				
6271				
6272	Same	Same	W-M	Pl
6273	Same	Same	S	Pl
6274				
6275	Same	218	S	Pl
6276				
6277	Washington/No 1/Broadway/N Y/Restaurant	300	C	Pl
6278				
6279				
6280	Indian head in centre—'John Watson' to left—'381 Bowery N Y' to right '1863' below	'Union/ Tea / Stores'within a closed laurel wreath	C	Pl
6281	Same	Same	Br	Pl
6282	Same	Same	N	Pl
6283	Same	Same	C-N	Pl
6284	Same	Same	W-M	Pl
6285	Same	Same	S	Pl
6286				
6287	Same	144	C	Pl
6288	Same	Same	Br	Pl
6289	Same	Same	N	Pl
6290	Same	Same	C-N	Pl
6291	Same	Same	W-M	Pl
6292	Same	Same	S	Pl
6293				
6294	White/Hatter/216/Broadway	62	C	Pl

NEW YORK—Continued

New York City—Continued

NUMBER	OBVERSE	REVERSE	METAL	EDGE
6295				
6296	'Thomas White' above—Indian head in centre—'1863' below—ornaments at side of date	Butcher/No/13 & 14/Abattoir/Place—West 39th St N Y	C	Pl
6297				
6298	Same	'Butcher' above—'West 39th St N Y'—below blank centre	C	Pl
6299				
6300	Similar to above—pig instead of Indian head in centre	Same as reverse of No 6296	C	Pl
6301				
6302	Same	Fish in centre—'M L Marshall above—'1863/Oswego/ N Y' below		
6303				
6304	'Willard & Jackson' above—eagle on shield in centre—'Oyster House /532 Broadway N Y' below	Flag and staff on building in open wreath in centre—'1863' on small shield below	C	Pl
6305	Same	Similar—no flag nor staff on building	C	Pl
6306	Ornament above eagle	Flag + staff	C	Pl

Niagara Falls

6307	M Walsh & Sons/Staple & Fancy /Dry/Goods/Niagara Falls N Y	416	C	R
6308				
6309	Same	418	C	R
6310	Same	Same	Br	R
6511				
6312	Same	419	C	R
6313				
6314				

Ogdensburgh

6315	G Idler's/Meat/ Market/Odgensburgh N Y	416	C	R
6316				
6317	Same	418	C	R
6318	Same	Same	Br	R
6319				
6320	Same	419	C	R
6321				
6322	Johnson/House/A M Sherman/ Pro/ Odgensburgh N Y	416	C	R
6323				
6324	Same	418	C	R
6325	Same	Same	Br	R
6326				
6327	Same	419	C	R
6328				
6329				

NEW YORK—Continued

Oswego

NUMBER	OBVERSE	REVERSE	METAL	EDGE
6330	'M L Marshall's Variety Store' above—'1862' and man fishing in circle in centre—'Oswego N Y' below	Dealer / in / Berlin Wools/ embroidery Goods / fishing tackle/ & fancy goods/ generally Large planchet	C	Pl
6331				
6332	'M L Marshall' above—fish and '1863' in centre—'Oswego N Y' below	Boys fancy goods/fishing/ tackle/and/rare coin Small planchet	C	Pl
6333				
6334				

Poughkeepsie

6335	Eastman/National / Business/College/Pouhkeepsie N Y	'1' and 'C' divided by open book in centre—'Actual Business' above—'Department' below	C-'N	Pl
6336				
6337				

Seneca Falls

6338	'D Skidmore/Good for one' above—spread eagle with cigar in beak in centre—'Seneca Falls N Y' below	Skidmore's/head / quarters /95/Fall St/Hotel	C	Pl
6339	Same	Same	Br	Pl
6340				
6341				
6342	Same	Same	W-M	Pl
6343	Same	Same	S	Pl
6344				

Troy

6345	'Charles Babcock Jeweler Troy N Y' around border—'72/Cong/St' in closed laurel wreath in centre	403	C	Pl
6346	Same—double strike	Same—double strike	C	Pl
6347	Charles Babcock/Jeweler/Troy N Y	Redeemed at my store/72/ Cong St/ 1863	C	Pl
6348				
6349	C Babcock/Jeweler/Troy N Y Inverted arm and hammer below	One cent token/1/1863	W-M	Pl
6350				
6351	Oliver Boutwell/Miller/Troy N Y	Redeemed/at/my office/1863	Br	Pl

NOTE. There are at least 20 different combinations of the above obverse and reverse dies, known to the compilers. The differences consist in the scroll work, and it would be most difficult to describe them. The compilers have decided to let every collector to compile them as sub-divisions of No 6351.

NEW YORK—Continued

Troy—Continued

NUMBER	OBVERSE	REVERSE	METAL	EDGE
⊸ 6352	Oliver Boutwell/Miller/Troy N Y	Redeemed/in/bills/at/my office	Br	Pl

NOTE—There are four different combinations of the Boutwell card with this reverse. The compilers suggest that the collectors compile these varities as sub-divisions of No 6352.

6353				
—6354	Robinson & Ballou/Grocers/Troy N Y	Redeemed/at/ourstore/1863	Br	Pl

NOTE. The same suggestion applies to the cards of this firm. There are 12 different combinations known, and they are all found in brass, except one, which is in German silver.

6355

Utica

6356	Dickinson Comstock & Co/Druggists/&/Grocers/Utica N Y	610	C	Pl
6357				
6358	I J Knapp/No 8/Liberty St/Utica /N Y/Wines & Liquors	300	C	Pl
— 6359	Same	610	C	Pl
⟶ 6360		610	C	Pl *Silvered*
⟶ 6361	Sherwood & Hopson / China/Emporium/ Utica N Y	150	C	Pl
6362	Same	Same	Br	Pl
6363				

Waterloo

6364	Henry C. Welles/Druggist/&/Book/Seller/Waterloo N Y	569	C	Pl
— 6365	Same	Same	Bronze	Pl
⟶ 6366	Same	655	Bronze	Pl
6367	Similar—narrow space between 'Druggist' and 'Book'	Same	Bronze	Pl
6368				

Watertown

⟶ 6369	'Hart's/Arcade/Gallery' in centre—'Watertown N Y' above—'For best pictures" below	602	Bronze	Pl
6370	Same	603	Bronze	Pl
6371				

Whitehall

— 6372	' E W Hall/Whitehall/N Y 'in circle in centre—'To purify the blood' above' 'Use Atherton's Pills' below	Try Atherton's/Wild/Cherry/Syrup/for/coughs & colds	C	Pl
6373	Same	Same	Br	Pl
6374				

NEW YORK—Continued

Williamsville

NUMBER	OBVERSE	REVERSE	METAL	EDGE
6375	'Williamsville Express' around border—'Leaves/8 A M/Williamsville' in centre	'Williamsville Express' around border — 'Leaves/Buffalo/3 P M' in centre	C	R
6376				

Yonkers

6377	E E Hasse/Yonkers/N Y	85	C	Pl
6378	Same	180	C	Pl
6379	Same	291	C	Pl

OHIO

Adamsville

6400	Stoner & Shroyer/Dry Goods/Adamsville/Ohio	80	C	Pl
6401				
6402	Same	Same	N	Pl
6403	Same	Same	C-N	Pl
6404	Same	Same	W-M	Pl
6405	Same	Same	S	Pl
6406	Same	95	C	Pl
6407	Same	Same	Br	Pl
6408				
6409				
6410				
6411	Same	Same	S	Pl
6412				
6413	Same	104	C	Pl
6414	Same	Same	Br	Pl
6415				
6416				
6417	Same	Same	W-M	Pl
6418	Same	Same	S	Pl
6419				
6420	Same	113	C	Pl
6421	Same	Same	Br	Pl
6422				
6423				
6424	Same	Same	W-M	Pl
6425	Same	Same	S	Pl
6426				
6427				
6428				
6429	Same	211	N	Pl
6430				
6431	Same	Same	W-M	Pl
6432				

OHIO—Continued

Adamsville—Continued

NUMBER	OBVERSE	REVERSE	METAL	EDGE
6433	Same	263	C	Pl
6434	Same	Same	Br	Pl
6435				
6436	Same	Same	C-N	Pl
6437	Same	Same	W-M	Pl
6438	Same	Same	S	Pl
6439				
6440	Same	Bust of Franklin	C	Pl
6441				
6442				
6443				
6444	Same	Same	W-M	Pl
6445	Same	Same	S	Pl
6446	Same	Bust of Garfield	C	Pl
6447				
6448				
6449				
6450	Same	Same	W-M	Pl
6451				
6452	Same	Bust of Horace Greeley	C	Pl
6453	Same	Same	Br	Pl
6454				
6455				
6456	Same	Same	W-M	Pl
6457	Same	Same	S	Pl
6458				

Adelphi

6459	D H Strous/Flour/&/Woolen/Manuf'rs/Adelphi O	428	C	Pl
6460	Same	480	C	Pl
6461				

Barnesville

6462	N Patterson/Saddlery/Hardware/Barnesville/Ohio	Leather/and/shoe findings/wool/sheep pelts/shipping furs/&c &c	C	Pl
6463				
6464	W A Talbot & Son/Dry Goods/Barnesville/Ohio	428	C	Pl
6465	Same	445	C	Pl
—6466	Same	446	C	Pl
6467	Same	447	C	Pl
6468	Same	466	C	Pl
6469	Same	547	C	Pl
6470				

Bellaire

6471	Bellaire/Ferry/Ticket	478	C	Pl
6472				

OHIO—Continued

Bellaire—Continued

NUMBER	OBVERSE	REVERSE	METAL	EDGE
6473	J S Bonbright/hardware/and/stove/dealer/Bellaire/Ohio	423	C	Pl
6474	Same	443	C	Pl
6475				
6476				
6477	Richardson & Bro/Dry Goods/&/Groceries/Bellaire O	470	C	Pl
6478				
6479	E B Winans & Co/dry goods/notions / drugs and / medicines/Bellaire/Ohio	117	C	Pl
6480	Same	428	C	Pl
6481	Same	Same	Br	Pl
6482	Same	470	C	Pl
6483	Same	478	C	Pl
6484	Same	528	C	Pl
6485				
6486				

Bellevue

6487	Cheap Cash Store,'Applegate/& Co/Bellevue O	471	C	Pl
6488				
6489	P Brady/dealer/in/stoves tin/and house/furnishing/goods/Bellevue Ohio	442	C	Pl
6490	Same	521	C	Pl
6491				
6492	P Brady/dealer/in/stoves/tinware/&c/Bellevue O	519	C	Pl
6493	Same	Same	Br	Pl
6494	Same	Same	N	Pl
6495	Same	Same	C-N	Pl
6496	Same	Same	W-M	Pl
6497				
6498	C A Willard/dry goods/Bellevue O	446	C	Pl
6499				
6500				

Belmont

6501	O C Metcalf/Dry Goods/Belmont/Ohio	427	C	Pl

Berea

6502	'D E Stearns Berea O' above—grindstone in centre—'1863' below	Grindstones/mounted/with patent/adjustable rest/for/grinding/all sizes/harvest knives	C	Pl
6503	Same	Same	C	R

OHIO—Continued

Berea—Continued

NUMBER	OBVERSE	REVERSE	METAL	EDGE
6504	Same	Same	Br	Pl
6505	Same	Same	Br	R
6506	Same	Family/&/shop/reaper / & mower/mounted/grindstones	C	R
6507	Same	Same—'Shop' reads 'ship'	C	Pl
6508	Same	Same as die No 453 with '1863'	C-N	R
6509	Same	405	C	R
6510	Same	611	C	Pl
6511	Same	418	C	R
6512	Same	Same	Br	R
6513	Same—but reads 'D E Stearns Berea Ohio'	Same as reverse of No. 6502	C	Pl
6514	Same	Same as obverse of No 6502	C	Pl
6515				

Beverly

6516	P Burkholder/dealer/in/groceries/ provisions/confectionary/and/produce/Beverly/Ohio	421	C	Pl
6517				

Birmingham

6518	Craig & Foy/dry goods/Birmingham/Ohio	421	C	Pl
6519	Same	426	C	Pl
6520				

Bryan

6521	Jeff Miller/Dealer/in/hardware/Bryan/Ohio	542	C	Pl
6522				
6523	E G Selby & Co/dealers/in/hardware/Bryan/Ohio	Steroscopic/pictures/and/instruments/for/sale/P O Box 2566	C	Pl
6524	Same	549	C	Pl
6525				
6526	Good for one/cent/in goods/at/ E G Selby's/ store	442	C	Pl
6527	Same	465	C	Pl
6528				

Cadiz

6529	G B Barrett/dealer/in/watches/ clocks/jewelry/fancy goods/Cadiz Ohio	405	C	R
6530	Same	410	C	R
6531	Same	418	C	R
6532	Same	Same	Br	R

OHIO—Continued
Cadiz—Continued

NUMBER	OBVERSE	REVERSE	METAL	EDGE
6533	Same	419	C	R
6534	Same	469	C	Pl
6535	Same	470	C	Pl
6536	Same	471	C	Pl
6537	Same	656	C	R
— 6538	Same	656	C	Pl
6539	L M Robinson/dealer/in/hardware/ stoves/fire fronts &c/Cadiz O	404	C	R
6540	Same	410	C	R
6541				
6542	Same	418	C	R
6543	Same	Same	Br	F
6544				
6545	Same	Same as Die No 453—dated '1863'	C-N	R
6546				

Cambridge

6547	'A C Cochran' above—'Hardware/ dealer' on lock in centre—'Cambridge O' below	117	C	Pl
— 6548	Same	469	C	Pl
6549	Same	470	C	Pl
6550	Same	524	C	Pl
6551				
6552	J J Squier/Dry Goods/Cambridge O	117	C	Pl
6553	Same	423	C	Pl
6554	Same	424	C	Pl
— 6555	Same	425	C	Pl
6556	Same	442	C	Pl
— 6557	Same	445	C	Pl
6558	Same	465	C	Pl
6559	Same	469	C	Pl
6560	Same	478	C	Pl
6561				

Camden

6562	C Chadwick/dealer/in/dry goods/ Camden O	466	C	Pl
6563	Same	480	C	Pl
6564				
— 6565	J P Fornshell/grocer/&/oyster/ dealer/Camden O	417	C	Pl
6566	Same	418	C	R
6567	Same	Same	Br	R
6568				
6569	Same	419	C	R
6570				

OHIO—Continued

Canaan

NUMBER	OBVERSE	REVERSE	METAL	EDGE
6571	Grimes & Griner/dealers/in/dry goods/notions &c/Canaan/Ohio	443	C	Pl
6572				

Canton

6573	J A Meyer/watches/clocks/&/jewelry/Canton O	68	C	Pl
6574	Same	412	C	Pl
6575	Same	418	C	R
6576	Same	Same	Br	R
6577	Same	419	C	R
6578	Same	453—dated '1863'	C-N	R
6579				
6580	C Oberly/dealer/in/groceries/provisions/confectionery/wooden & willow/ware/Canton Ohio	442	C	Pl
6581	Same	560	C	Pl
6582	Same	Same	Br	Pl
6583				

Centreville

6584	James Matthews/dealer/in/dry goods/groceries/&c/Centreville O	423	C	Pl
6585	Same	Same	Br	Pl
6586	Same	464	C	Pl
6587				

Chesterville

6588	Bartlett Goble & Co/staple & fancy/dry/goods/groceries/&c/Chesterville O	419	C	R
6589	Same	Same	Br	R
6590				
6591				
6592	Same	420	C	R
6593				
6594	Miles & Sperry/dealers/in/dry/goods/groceries/&c/Chesterville O	419	C	R
6595	Same	Same	Br	R
6596				

Chillicothe

6597	John Bohm/Chillicothe/O	Similar to Die No 608—'5' instead of '25'	Br	Pl
6598				
6599	Jno F Bier & Bro/dealers/in/groceries/boots & shoes/101 Paint/street/Chillicothe O	117	C	Pl
6600	Same	423	C	Pl

OHIO—Continued

Chillicothe—Continued

NUMBER	OBVERSE	REVERSE	METAL	EDGE
6601	Same	443	C	Pl
6602	Same	469	C	Pl
6603				
—6604	H Keim/grocer/cor/Fourth & Hickory/Sts/Chillicothe O	480	C	Pl
6605				
6606	A S Kramer/dealer/in/confectionery/toys/notions &c/Allen/Block/Paint St/Chillicothe O	117	C	Pl
6607	Same	445	C	Pl
6608	Same	464	C	Pl
6609				
6610	Rufus Motter / book / periodical/ news cigar/tobacco/and/notion/ dealer/Chillicothe O	444	C	Pl
6611	Same	467	C	Pl
6612	Same	468	C	Pl
6613	Same	470	C	Pl
6614	Same	538	C	Pl
6615	Same	Same	Br	Pl
6616				
6617	Same	539	C	Pl
6618				
6619	Same	540	C	Pl
6620				
6621	Same	Same	C-N	Pl
6622				
6623	T Rupel & Co/grocers/No 52/4th St/Chillicothe O	444	C	Pl
6624	Same	469	C	Pl
6625	Same	470	C	Pl
6626	Same	471	C	Pl
6627	Same	552	C	Pl
6628				
6629				
6630	Wm M Sosman/baker/&/grocer/ Chillicothe/Ohio	444	C	Pl
6631	Same	445	C	Pl
6632				
6633	Same	Same	C-N	Pl
6634				
6635	A Wallace/news/depot/tobacco/ cigars/&/notions/Chillicothe O	466	C	Pl
6636	Same	478	C	Pl
6637	Same	539	C	Pl
6638	Same	540	C	Pl
6639				
6640				

OHIO—Continued

Cincinnati

NUMBER	OBVERSE	REVERSE	METAL	EDGE
6641	M Adleta/570/Cen/Avenue/Cincinnati	418	C	R
6642	Same	Same	Br	R
6643	Same	Same	Z	R
6644	Same	420	C	R
6645	Same	615	C	Pl
6646	Same	635	C	Pl
6647				
6648				
6649	W Alenburg/No 622/Central/Avenue/meat store	183	C	Pl
6650				
6651	B B Armstrong/Black/Bear/Hotel/9' & Sycamore/Sts/Cincinnati	418	C	R
6652	Same	Same	Br	R
6653				
6654	Same	420	C-N	R
6655				
6656	Same	622	C	Pl
6657				
6658	Gruhlers/garden/concert/saloon/ 470 Vine Sts/F Arnold	210	C	Pl
6659				
6660	Same	407	C	Pl
6661				
6662	Same	417	C	Pl
6663	Same	418	C	R
6664	Same	Same	Br	R
6665	Same	Same	Z	R
6666				
6667	Same	420	C	R
6668	Same	Same	C-N	R
6669				
6670	J S Austin/dealer/in/staple&fancy/ groceries/5th & Elm/Sts/Cincinnati	402	C	Pl
6671				
6672	Same	418	C	R
6673	Same	Same	Br	R
6674	Same	Same	Z	R
6675				
6676	Same	420	C-N	R
6677				
6678	H Avermaat/dealer/in/butter/&/ eggs/ 315 Findlay St/Cincinnati	401	C	Pl
6679				
6680	Same	405	C	Pl
6681	Same	406	C	Pl
6682				
6683	Same	418	C	R
6684	Same	Same	Br	R

OHIO—Continued

Cincinnati—Continued

NUMBER	OBVERSE	REVERSE	METAL	EDGE
6685				
6686	Same	420	C-N	R
6687				
6688	S Bacciocco/confectionery/and/ice/cream/saloon/176 Fifth St	Similar to Die 117—eagle flying to right	C	Pl
6689	Same	340	C	Pl
6690	Same	582	C	Pl
6692	'E Bacher' in script on plain planchet	Good/for/five cents/in/refreshment/Union saloon	C	Pl
6693	Same	Same	Br	Pl
6694	Same	561	C	Pl
6695	Same	Same	Br	Pl
6696	R Bathgate/dealer/in/boots shoes/&/groceries/198 W 6' St/Cincinati	401	C	Pl
6697				
6698	Same	418	C	R
6699	Same	Same	Br	R
6700				
6701	Same	420	C-N	R
6702				
6703	John Bauer / 29/Front/St/Cincinati	416	C	Pl
6704	Same	622	C	Pl
6705	Same	634	C	Pl
6706				
6707	Same	418	C	R
6708	Same	Same	Br	R
6709				
6710	Same	420	C-N	R
6711				
6712	C H Beer's/saloon/55/broadway/Cint'i O. Three stars on sides	Also/cutlery/notions/ &c	C	Pl
6713	Same	30	C	Pl
6714	Same	Same	C-N	Pl
6715	Same	467	C	Pl
6716				
6717	Same	468	C	Pl
6718	Same	Same	C-N	Pl
6719	Same	518	C	Pl
6720	Same	546	C	Pl
6721	Same	657	C	Pl
6722				
6723	Teeth/extracted/without/pain/by/ B P Belknap	560	C	Pl
6724				
6725	Dr Bennett's/Medicines/cure/sickness/& pain	30	C	Pl
6726	Same	Same	C-N	Pl
6727	Same	467	C	Pl
6728	Same	518	C	Pl

OHIO—Continued

Cincinnati—Continued

NUMBER	OBVERSE	REVERSE	METAL	EDGE
6729	Same	546	C	Pl
6730	Same	Same—incused	C	Pl
6731				
6732	Same	200000/families/now/use/Dr Bennetts/medicines	C	Pl
6733	Same	Same	C-N	Pl
6734	Same	509	C	Pl
6735	Same	565	C	Pl
6736	500000 / persons / annually/cured/by/Dr Bennett's/medicines	68	C	Pl
6737				
6738	Same	412	C	Pl
6739	Same	415	C	Pl
6740	Same	634	C	Pl
6741	Same	662	C	Pl
6742		622		
6743	Same	418	C	R
6744	Same	Same	Br	R
6745	Same	Same	Z	R
6746				
6747	Same	If you get sick/use/Dr/Bennett's/medicines	C	Pl
6748	Same	Same	C	R
6749				
6750	If you get sick/use/Dr/Bennett's/medicines	68	C	Pl
6751	Same	634	C	Pl
6752	Same	635	C	Pl
6753	Same	659	C	Pl
6754				
6755	Same	418	C	R
6756	Same	Same	Br	R
6757				
6758	Same	420	C	R
6759	Same	Same	C-N	R
6760				
6761	'C H Bennett' above — sheaf of wheat in centre—'steam' to left—'bakery' to right—'89 Court St' below	413	C	Pl
6762	Same	414	C	Pl
6763	Same	416	C	Pl
6764	Same	615	C	Pl
6765				
6766	Same	418	C	R
6767	Same	Same	Br	R
6768	Same	Same	Z	R
6769				
6770	'Frank Beresford' above—square and compass in centre—'Cincinnati' below	Buy your/meat/of/Frank Beresford/in/market	C	Pl
6771	Same	Same	C	R

OHIO—Continued

Cincinnati—Continued

NUMBER	OBVERSE	REVERSE	METAL	EDGE
6772	Same	418	C	R
6773	Same	Same	Br	R
6774	Same	Same	Z	R
6775				
6776	Buy your/meat/of/Frank/Beresford/in/market	418	C	R
6777	Same	Same	Br	R
6778	Same	Same	Z	R
6779				
6780	Same	420	C-N	R
6781				
6782				
6783	Lew Boman/sets a/Lunch/at the/Brighton/Hotel/at 10 o'clock/Sunday	68	C	Pl
6784	Same	402	C	Pl
6785	Same	507	C	Pl
6786	Same	615	C	Pl
6787				
6788	Same	418	C	R
6789	Same	Same	Br	R
6790	Same	Same	Z	R
6791	Same	429	C-N	R
6792				
6793	I promise/to pay/5/cents/Lew Boman	Steer to right in centre—'Brighton' above — 'House' below	C	Pl
6794	Same	Same	C	R
6795	Same	210	C	R
6796	Same	Same	Br	R
6797	Same	Same	Z	R
6798	Same	Same	C	Pl
6799				
6800	Same	Same	Z	Pl
6801				
6802	I promise/to pay/10/cents/Lew Boman	597	C	R
6803	Same	Same	Br	R
6804	Same	Same	Z	R
6805	Same	Same	C	Pl
6806				
6807	Same	Same as reverse of No 6793	C	Pl
6808	Same	Same	C	R
6809				
6810	Same	420	C-N	R
6811				
6812				
6813	Same as reverse of No 6793	404	C	Pl
6814	Same	Same	C	R
6815				
6816	Same	418	C	R

OHIO—Continued
Cincinnati—Continued

NUMBER	OBVERSE	REVERSE	METAL	EDGE
6817	Same	Same	Br	R
6818	Same	Same	Z	R
6819	Same	420	C	R
6820	Same	Same	C-N	R
6821				
6822				
6823				
6824	A Bruggeman/grocer/cor/Liberty/ & Walnut	183	C	Pl
6825				
6826				
6827	J Campbell/grocer/&/provision/ dealer/481 John St	408	C	Pl
6828	Same	412	C	Pl
6829	Same	415	C	Pl
6830				
6831	Same	418	C	R
6832	Same	Same	Br	R
6833				
6834	Same	420	C-N	R
6835				
6836	Same	C G Bruce/authorized/war/claim/agent/1863/Cleveland O	C	Pl
6837				
6838	Buy your coal now at Central Coal Office 56 W Fourth St Cinti	Good for one cents worth of coal. Portrait	C	Pl
6839				
6840	'Chamberlain Bros' around border —'1/glass/soda/water' in centre	529	C	R
6841	Same	Same	Br	R
6842	Same	623	C	Pl
6843	Same	420	C-N	R
6844				
6845	Cin & Cov/Ferry/Company	418	C	R
6846	Same	Same	Br	R
6847				
6848	Same	420	C-N	R
6849				
6850	Same	615	C	Pl
6851				
6852	Same	617	C	Pl
6853				
6854	City Hosiery Store/ladies/&/gents furnishing/&/fancy goods/ No 12 W 5' St	407	C	Pl
6855				
6856	Same	418	C	R
6857	Same	Same	Br	R
6858				
6859	Same	419	C	R

OHIO—Continued

Cincinnati—Continued

NUMBER	OBVERSE	REVERSE	METAL	EDGE
6860	Same	420	C-N	R
6861				
6862	Good for/one/shave/at/C E Clark's/ lightning/hair dyeing rooms/ No 4/ Burnet House	405	Br	Pl
6863				
6864	Same	418	C	R
6865	Same	Same	Br	R
6866				
6867	Same	419	C	R
6868	Same	420	C-N	R
6869				
6870	Same	453	C	R
6871	Same	Same	Br	R
6872	Same	Same	C	Pl
6873	Same	Same	Br	Pl
6874				
6875	Same	597	C-N	Pl
6876				
6877	Good for/one/cent/at/Cole's Bakery	402	C	Pl
6878				
6879	Same	417	C	Pl
6880	Same	418	C	R
6881	Same	Same	Br	R
6882				
6883	Same	419	C	R
6884	Same	420	C-N	R
6885				
6886	Same	617	C	Pl
6887	Same	Redeemed/in/par funds/in sums of/one/dollar	C	Pl
6888	Same as reverse of No 6887	401	C	Pl
6889				
6890	Same	419	C	R
6891				
6892	Conn Mutual Life Ins Co/capital/ 6000000/dollars/1864	420	C	R
6893				
6894	Commission/boots/&/shoes/154/ Main St/Cincinnati	401	C	Pl
6895				
6896	Same	418	C	R
6897	Same	Same	Br	R
6898	Same	Same	Z	R
6899	Same	420	C-N	R
6900				
6901	Charles Conroy/grocer/&/liquor/ dealer/3 & Cen Avenue	418	C	R
6902	Same	Same	Br	R
6903	Same	Same	Z	R

164

OHIO—Continued

Cincinnati—Continued

NUMBER	OBVERSE	REVERSE	METAL	EDGE
6904	Same	419	C-N	R
6905	Same	420	C	R
6906	Same	634	C	Pl
6907				
6908	Costello's/trimmings/&/fancy goods/ 138/Fifth St/Cincinnati	400	C	Pl
6909	Same	Same	C	R
6910	Same	Same	Br	R
6911	Same	401	C	Pl
6912	Same	405	C	Pl
6913	Same	406	C	Pl
6914	Same	407	C	Pl
6915	Same	408	C	Pl
6916	Same	413	C	Pl
6917	Same	414	C	Pl
6918	Same	418	C	Pl
6919	Same	Same	C	R
6920	Same	Same	Br	R
6921	Same	Same	N	R
6922	Same	Same	Z	R
6923	Same	420	C-N	R
6924	Same	617	C	Pl
6925				
6926	Crittenden/shades Star above and below	420	C-N	Pl
6927	Same	616	C	Pl
6928				
6929	Bates/House,/one/meal/ J M Daggert & Co	419	C	R
6930	Same	Same	C-N	R
6931				
6932	Geo R Dixon & Co/spice/mills/ Sycamore/bet 7 & 8' St/Cincinnati	210	C	Pl
6933	Same	400	C	Pl
6934	Same	401	C	Pl
6935	Same	Same	Br	Pl
6936	Same	402	C	Pl
6937	Same	407	C	Pl
6938	Same	418	C	R
6939	Same	Same	Br	R
6940	Same	Same	Z	R
6941	Same	420	C-N	R
6942	Same	453	Br	Pl
6943				
6944	J N Doniphan/188/East/Pearl/St/ Cincinnati	418	C	R
6945	Same	Same	Br	R
6946				
6947	Same	420	C-N	R
6948				
6949	Same	660	C	Pl

OHIO—Continued

Cincinnati—Continued

6950				
— 6951	Garret T Dorland/importer/of/ watches/and/Jewelry/N W Cor Main & Pearl/Sts/Cincinnati	401	C	Pl
— 6952	Same	413	C	Pl
6953	Same	418	C	R
6954	Same	Same	Br	R
6955	Same	Same	Z	R
6956	Same	420	C-N	R
6957	Same	Same as die No 453—dated '1863'	C	Pl
6958				
6959	R Downing/publisher/of/sheet songs/& dealer in/ old/coins/Cincinnati	A bunch of fruit in a circle of stars	Tin	Pl
6060	Same	419	C-N	R
6961				
6962	Same	Same as die No 453—dated '1863'	Br	Pl
6963	Same	577	C	R
6964	Same	Same	Br	R
6965				
6966	D B S/grocer/Main St	413	C	Pl
6967	Same	418	C	R
6968	Same	Same	Br	R
6969	Same	420	C	R
6970	Same	617	C	Pl
6971				
6972	L Eckert/bookbinder/stationer/&/ fancy goods/N W cor/Walnut .& 13' Sts/ Cincinnati	400	C	Pl
6973	Same	405	C	Pl
6974	Same	Same	Br	Pl
6975	Same	414	C	Pl
6976	Same	417	C	Pl
6977	Same	617	C	Pl
6978				
6979	C W Ellis/Gen Agt/35 W 3d St/ Cin O/Dayton Agency/44 Jeff St	Conn Mut Life Ins Co/ capital/ over/6000000/dollars/1864	C	R
6980	Same	420	C	R
6981				
6982	Fenton & Beck/daily / market/N W Cor/ 8' & Plum	414	C	Pl
6983	Same	418	C	R
6984	Same	Same	Br	R
6985				
6986	J Ferguson/grocer/cor 9' & Vine Sts/Cincinnati/goods delivered/. free of charge	401	C	Pl
6987	Same	407	C	Pl
6988	Same	418	C	R

OHIO—Continued

Cincinnati—Continued

NUMBER	OBVERSE	REVERSE	METAL	EDGE
6989	Same	Same	Br	R
6990	Same	Same	Z	R
6991	Same	420	C-N	R
6992				
6993	Same	453	C	Pl
6994				
6995	E Fiedler's/beer/hall/206/Vine St	418	C	R
6996	Same	Same	Br	R
6997	Same	Same	Z	R
6998	Same	615	C	Pl
6999	Same	617	C	Pl
7000	Same	622	C	Pl
7001	Same	658	C	Pl
7002	Same	661	C	Pl
7003				
7004	Emil Fiedler	'C3' in circle of stars	Lead	Pl
7005	F Fischer/214/Vine/St/Cincinnati	418	C	R
7006	Same	Same	Br	R
7007	Same	Same	Z	R
7008	Same	420	C-N	R
7009	Same	615	C	Pl
7010				
7011	'Fisler & Chance' above—'polar' below—'1/glass/soda/water' in centre	420	C	R
7012	Same	Same	C-N	R
7013	Same	529	Br	R
7014				
7015	J W Fitzgerald/grocer/cor/fifth/and/Broadway/Cincinnati	446	C	Pl
7016	Same	580	C	Pl
7017	Same	Blank Reverse	C	Pl
7018				
7019	Chas Flach/dealer/in/provisions/cor/Madison & Canal/Cincinnati	418	C	R
7020	Same	Same	Br	R
7021	Same	Same	Z	R
7022	Same	420	C-N	R
7023	Same	615	C	Pl
7024	Same	617	C	Pl
7025	Same	661	C	Pl
7026				
7027	'James Foster Jr & Co Cincinnati' around border—'Cor Fifth & Race Sts' in circle in centre—2 stars	420	C	R
7028				
7029				
7030	'John Frank' above—eight small circles around ornament in centre—5 stars below	one/half/pint/of/milk	C	R

OHIO—Continued

Cincinnati—Continued

NUMBER	OBVERSE	REVERSE	METAL	EDGE
7031	Same	Same	Br	R
7032	Same	Same	N	R
7033	Same	Same	Z	R
7034				
7035	Same	1/pint/of/milk	C	R
7036	Same	Same	Br	R
7037	Same	Same	Z	R
7038				
7039	Same	One/quart/of/milk	C	R
7040	Same	Same	Br	R
7041	Same	Same	Z	R
7042				
7043	Same	One/Gall/of/milk	C	R
7044				
7045				
7046				
7047	Same	420	C-N	R
7048				
7049	Use/Frost's/medicine/sold/by/druggists	416	C	R
7050	Same	Same	Br	R
7051	Same	Same	Z	R
7052	Same	418	C	R
7053	Same	419	C-N	R
7054				
7055	John Galvagni/fancy/goods/&/toys/513/Vine bet 14' & 15'/Sts/Cincinnati	400	C	Pl
7056				
7057	Same	418	C	R
7058	Same	Same	Br	R
7059	Same	Same	Z	R
7060	Same	420	C-N	R
7061				
7062	L Geilfus/grocer/701/Vine St	183	C	Pl
7063	Same	259	C	Pl
7064				
7065	J Geiser—ornament above and below	183	C	Pl
7066	Same	592	C	Pl
7067				
7068	W Gentsch/wine/&/beer/saloon/393 Vine St	418	C	R
7069	Same	Same	Br	R
7070	Same	Same	Z	R
7071	Same	420	C-N	R
7072	Same	Same	C	R
7073	Same	617	C	Pl
7074	Gilbert & Hotchkiss			
7075				
7076				

OHIO—Continued
Cincinnati—Continued

NUMBER	OBVERSE	REVERSE	METAL	EDGE
7077	Segars/O G/Tobacco—(O Goffery)	418	C	R
7078	Same	Same	Br	R
7079	Same	Same	Z	R
7080	Same	420	C	R
7081	Same	Same	Br	R
7082	Same	635	C	R
7083				
7084	J Grossius/Tinner/33/Court St/ CIN O	616	C	Pl
7085				
7086	Jacob Guth/S W Cor/Vine/&/Columbia/Sts/Cincinnati	418	C	R
7087	Same	Same	Br	R
7088	Same	Same	Z	R
7089				
7090	Same	634	C	Pl
7091				
7092				
7093	'Carl Haas' above—'Cincinnati O.' below—'493/Vine/St'within a beaded circle in centre	405	C	Pl
7094	Same	406	C	Pl
7095	Same	407	C	Pl
7096	Same	417	C	Pl
7097	Same	418	C	R
7098	Same	Same	Br	R
7099	Same	Same	Z	R
7100	Same	420	C-N	R
7101				
7102	Same	'Carl Haas' above—'493 Vine St' below—rabbit in centre	C	Pl
7103				
7104	'Carl Haas' above—'493 Vine St' below—rabbit in centre	68	C	Pl
7105	Same	406	C	Pl
7106	Same	408	C	Pl
7107	Same	413	C	Pl
7108	Same	418	C	R
7109	Same	Same	Br	R
7110	Same	Same	Z	R
7111	Same	420	C-N	R
7112	Same	617	C	Pl
7113	Same	659	C	Pl
7114	Same	660	C	Pl
7115	Same	662	C	Pl
7116	Same	663	C	Pl
7117	Same	Same	Br	Pl
7118				
7119	W W Hanley/wholesale/grocer/ 25/Main St/Cincinnati	401	C	Pl

OHIO—Continued

Cincinnati—Continued

NUMBER	OBVERSE	REVERSE	METAL	EDGE
7120	Same	402	C	Pl
7121	Same	417	C	Pl
7122	Same	418	C	R
7123	Same	Same	Br	R
7124	Same	Same	Z	R
7125	Same	420	C-N	R
7126				
7127	Harpel/superior/card/&/mercantile/printer/S E Cor 3rd & Vine St/Cincinnati	402	C	Pl
7128	Same	Same	C-N	Pl
7129	Same	Peebles/dealer / in / staple & fancy/groceries/5th&Race/Sts/Cincinnati	C	Pl
7130	Same	Harpel/mercantile/printer/ S E Cor/3rd & Vine Sts Cin O	C	Pl
7131	Same	Same	C	R
7132	Harpel/mercantile/printer/S E Cor/3rd & Vine Sts CIN O	402	C	Pl
7133	Same	Same	C	R
7134				
7135	C G Hartmann/grocer/140/Everett St/CIN O	259	C	Pl
7136				
7137	M Hartzel/grocer/&/commission/Merc't/N W Cor 3' & Elm/Sts/Cincinnati	259	C	Pl
7138	Same	402	C	Pl
7139	Same	Same	Br	Pl
7140	Same	405	C	Pl
7141	Same	418	C	R
7142	Same	Same	Br	R
7143				
7144	Same	420	C-N	R
7145				
7146	'J Hayes & Bro' above—'Cents' below—'5' in centre	479	C	Pl
7147	Same as preceeding—'1' instead of '5' 'Drink' below	479	C	Pl
7148	Same	Same	Br	Pl
7149	Same	518	C	Pl
7150	Same	471	C	Pl
7151	Buy/clothing/at/Heinman's/under the/Russell/House/&/save25 per ct	410	C	R
7152	Same	418	C	R
7153	Same	Same	Br	R
7154	Same	420	C-N	R
7155				
7156	E Heinzmann/No 12/Court St	183	C	Pl
7157	Same	419	C-N	R

OHIO—Continued
Cincinnati—Continued

NUMBER	OBVERSE	REVERSE	METAL	EDGE
7158	Same	592	C	Pl
7159				
7160	J Helmig/grocer/708/Freeman/St/Cincinnati	413	C	Pl
7161	Same	418	C	R
7162	Same	Same	Br	R
7163	Same	420	C-N	R
7164				
7165	B Hempleman/dealer/in/groceries/&/feed/N W Cor/Linn & Findlay/Sts/Cincinnati	405	C	Pl
7166	Same	407	C	Pl
7167	Same	410	C	Pl
7168	Same	417	C	Pl
7169	Same	418	C	R
7170	Same	Same	Br	R
7171	Same	420	C-N	R
7172	Same	615	C	Pl
7173	Same	661	C	Pl
7174				
7175	Same	Stanton steel stamps brand & stencils 139 Fifth St	C	Pl
7176				
7177	Farmers Hotel/cor/Court/&/Race/Sts/Cincinnati/V Heyl	414	C	Pl
7178	Same	417	C	Pl
7179	Same	418	C	R
7180	Same	Same	Br	R
7181				
7182	Same	419	C-N	R
7183	Same	617	C	Pl
7184	Same	661	C	Pl
7185				
7186	Farmers Hotel/good for/5/cents/V Heyl/Cincinnati	210	C	R
7187	Same	Same	Br	R
7188	Same	Same	Z	R
7189	Same	401	C	Pl
7190	Same	661	C	Pl
7191				
7192				
7193	Dr H H Hill & Co/dealers/in/drugs/&/medicines/S E Cor 5' & Race/Sts/Cincinnati O	401	C	Pl
7194	Same	414	C	Pl
7195	Same	417	C	Pl
7196	Same	418	C	R
7197	Same	Same	Br	R
7198	Same	Same	Z	R
7199	Same	420	C-N	R
7200				

OHIO—Continued

Cincinnati—Continued

NUMBER	OBVERSE	REVERSE	METAL	EDGE
7201	B Hintrick & C Glaser/636 & 638/Elm/St	406	C	Pl
7202	Same	418	C	R
7203	Same	Same	Br	R
7204	Same	Same	Z	R
7205	Same	420	C-N	R
7206	Same	Same as Die No 453—dated '1863'	C	Pl
7207	Same	615	C	Pl
7208				
7209	'J A Hughes' above—'Cincinnati' below—'metalic/cards'ina wreath	Try/Allen's/Blacklead/compound/Babbitt/metal/1863	C	Pl
7210	Same	Same	S	Pl
7211				
7212	Same	340	C	Pl
7213				
7214	Good for one/5/cent/loaf of bread/P Hughes	210	C	R
7215	Good for one/10/cent/loaf of bread/P Hughes	597	C	R
7216				
7217	C C Hyatt/staple/& Fancy/grocer/cor/Freeman & Poplar/Sts/Cincinnati	400	C	Pl
7218	Same	418	C	R
7219	Same	Same	Br	R
7220	Same	Same	Z	R
7221	Same	420	C	R
7222				
7223	B Jahr/549/Vine Str/Cin'ti O	419	C-N	R
7224	Same	420	C	R
7225				
7226	B Jahr & Co/549/Vine St/Cin'ti O	607	C	Pl
7227	Same	Same—but '15' instead of '10'	C	Pl
7228	H Johnston/die/sinker/154/Everett St/Cin O 'sinker' curved	592	C	Pl
7229	Same	Same—badly broken die	C	Pl
7230				
7231	W Johnston/die/sinker/154/Everett St/CIN O "sinker' straight	259	C	Pl
7232	Same	616	C	Pl
7233				
7234	W Johnston/die/sinker/Cin O	183	C	Pl
7235	Same	259	C	Pl
7236	Same—'Sinker' curved	592	C	Pl
7237	C Kahn & Co/No 73/Everett St/meat/store	183	C	Pl
7238	Same	616	C	Pl
7239				
7240	A Karman/No/627/Central/Avenue/Cin O	183	C	Pl

OHIO—Continued

Cincinnati—Continued

NUMBER	OBVERSE	REVERSE	METAL	EDGE
7241	Same	259	C	Pl
7242				
7243	J Katzenstein/No—row of ten dots below	210	Br	R
7244	Same	420	C-N	R
7245	Same	535	C	R
7246				
7247	Warren Kennedy/news/depot/160/Vine St	418	C	R
7248	Same	Same	Br	R
7249	Same	420	C	R
7250	Same	617	C	Pl
7251	Same	622	C	Pl
7252				
7253	Same—'news' curved	467	C	Pl
7254	Same	509	C	Pl
7255	Same	518	C	Pl
7256	Same	Same	C-N	Pl
7257	Same	546	C	Pl
7258	Same	30	C-N	Pl
7259				
7260	Frank Kern/grocer/692/Cen Avenue	413	C	Pl
7261	Same	418	C	R
7262	Same	Same	Br	R
7263				
7264	Same	420	C-N	R
7265				
7266	See best stock in city at King's Franklin St	Same as Die No 453—dated '1863'	C-N	R
7267	Same	420	C	R
7268				
7269	Good for/5/cents/at the/bar/ J Kirchenschlager	518	C	Pl
7270	Same	Same	Br	Pl
7271				
7272	J Kirker & Co/grocers/and/produce/dealers/Cincinnati O	462	C	Pl
7273	Same	464	C	Pl
7274	Same	565	C	Pl
—7275	'B Kittredge & Co 134 Main St Cin O' above—'1863' below—liberty head to left in centre—period after 'Co'	'Guns Pistols/and/Sporting' in wreath in centre—'dealers in military goods apparatus' around border	C	Pl
7276	Same—period and comma after 'Co'	Same	C	Pl
7277				
7278	J Klein/grocer/63/Hamilton Road	413	C	Pl
7279	Same	418	C	R
7280	Same	Same	Br	R

OHIO—Continued

Cincinnati—Continued

NUMBER	OBVERSE	REVERSE	METAL	EDGE
7281				
7282	Same	419	C-N	R
7283				
7284	Jacob Knauber/butcher/Cin O	210	C	Pl
7285	Same	400	C	Pl
7286	Same	417	C	Pl
7287	Same	418	C	R
7288	Same	Same	Br	R
7289				
7290	Same	420	C-N	R
7291				
7292	Wm Knecht/grocer/502/John St/ Cincinnati	418	C	R
7293	Same	Same	Br	R
7294	Same	Same	Z	R
7295	Same	420	C-N	R
7296	Same	617	C	Pl
7297	Same	659	C	Pl
7298	Same	661	C	Pl
7299				
7300	John Koch/No 10/Harrison Road	418	C	R
7301	Same	Same	Br	R
7302	Same	419	C-N	R
7303	Same	617	C	Pl
7304	'Koos/Restaurant' below—'Beer Check' above—'5' in centre	210	C	R
7305	Same	664	C	R
7306				
7307	B Kreager/grocer/cor/Home & Smith/Sts/Cincinnati	418	C	R
7308	Same	Same	Br	R
7309	Same	420	C-N	R
7310	Same	634	C	Pl
7311	Same	661	C	Pl
7312				
7313	H Kreber/grocer/Columbia/bet/ Rowe & Mill	182	C	Pl
7314	Same	467	C	Pl
7315	Same	468	C	Pl
7316	Same	546	C	Pl
7317				
7318	A Krengle's/Union/Exchange/ 218/Vine St	68	C	Pl
7319	Same	407	C	Pl
7320	Same	415	C	Pl
7321	Same	417	C	Pl
—7322	Same	418	C	R
7323	Same	Same	Br	R
7324				
7325	Same	617	C	Pl
7326	Same	656	C	Pl

OHIO—Continued
Cincinnati—Continued

NUMBER	OBVERSE	REVERSE	METAL	EDGE
7327	Same	661	C	Pl
7328				
7329	Jacob Krick	420	C	R
7330	Same	Same	C-N	R
7331				
7332	'W K Lanphear' above—Cincinnati O below—'Manu'fr/of/metallic /cards' in corn wreath in centre	423	C	Pl
7333	Same	Same	Br	Pl
7334	Same	425	C	Pl
7335	Same	Same	Br	Pl
7336	Same	442	C	Pl
7337	Same	Same	Br	Pl
7338	Same	444	C	Pl.
7339	Same	Same	Br	Pl
7340	Same	459	C	Pl
7341	Same	Same	Br	Pl
7342	Same	462	C	Pl
7343				
7344	Same	463	C	Pl
7345	Same	Same	Br	Pl
7346	Same	464	C	Pl
7347	Same	Same	Br	Pl
7348	Same	460	C	Pl
7349	Same	Same	Br	Pl
7350	Same	470	C	Pl
7351	Same	Same	Br	Pl
7352	Same	471	C	Pl
7353	Same	Same	Br	Pl
7354				
7355	Same	478	Br	Pl
7356	Same	479	C	Pl
7357	Same	Same	Br	Pl
7358	Same	499	C	Pl
7359	Same	Same	Br	Pl
7360	Same	618	C	Pl
7361	Same	Same	Br	Pl
7362	Same	520	C	Pl
7363	Same	Same	Br	Pl
7364	Same	521	C	Pl
7365	Same	Same	Br	Pl
7366				
7367	Same	523	C	Pl
7368	Same	Same	Br	Pl
7369	Same	524	C	Pl
7370	Same	Same	Br	Pl
7371	Same	528	C	Pl
7372	Same	Same	Br	Pl
7373	Same	532	C	Pl
7374	Same	Same	Br	Pl
7375	Same	536	C	Pl

OHIO—Continued

Cincinnati—Continued

NUMBER	OBVERSE	REVERSE	METAL	EDGE
7376	Same	Same	Br	Pl
7377	Same	537	C	Pl
7378	Same	Same	Br	Pl
7379	Same	539	C	Pl
7380	Same	Same	Br	Pl
7381	Same	542	C	Pl
7382	Same	Same	Br	Pl
7383	Same	551	C	Pl
7384	Same	Same	Br	Pl
7385	Same	552	C	Pl
7386	Same	Same	Br	Pl
7387	Same	554	C	Pl
7388	Same	Same	Br	Pl
7389	Same	556	C	Pl
7390	Same	Same	Br	Pl
7391	Same	558	C	Pl
7392	Same	Same	Br	Pl
7393	Same	560	C	Pl
7394	Same	Same	Br	Pl
7395	Same	561	C	Pl
7396	Same	Same	Br	Pl
7397	Same	564	C	Pl
7398	Same	Same	Br	Pl
7399	Same	623	C	Pl
7400	Same	Same	Br	Pl
7401	Same	'Also cutlery & notions &c' in a circle of dots—ornaments above and below	C	Pl
7402	Same	Same	Br	Pl
7403	Same	'Dealers/in/hoop/skirts/hats caps/and/notions'	C	Pl
7404	Same	Same	Br	Pl
7405	Same	'Stereocopic/pictures/and/instruments/for/sale/P O Box 2566	C	Pl
7406	Same	Same	Br	Pl
7407	Same	'Wm Senour'	C	Pl
7408				
7408A	"	Boots shoes + Yankee notions	C	Pl
7409	Same as reverse of No 7505	Boots shoes and Yankee notions		
7410			C	Pl
7411	Same	560	C	Pl
7412				
7413				
7414				
7415				
7416				
7417	W K Lanphear/manuf'r/of/metalic/cards/Cin'ti/Ohio	Same as obverse of preceeding	C	Pl
7418	Same	Same	Br	Pl

OHIO—Continued

Cincinnati—Continued

NUMBER	OBVERSE	REVERSE	METAL	EDGE
7419				
7420	Same	259	C	Pl
7421	Same	Same	Br	Pl
7422	Same	425	C	Pl
7423	Same	Same	Br	Pl
7424	Same	426	C	⌐Pl
7425	Same	Same	Br	Pl
7426	Same	442	C	Pl
7427	Same	Same	Br	Pl
7428	Same	444	C	Pl
7429	Same	Same	Br	Pl
7430	Same	446	C	Pl
7431	Same	Same	Br	Pl
7432	Same	459	C	Pl
7433				
7434	Same	460	C	Pl
7435	Same	Same	Br	Pl
7436	Same	463	C	Pl
7437	Same	Same	Br	Pl
7438	Same	464	C	Pl
7439	Same	Same	Br	Pl
7440	Same	469	C	Pl
7441	Same	Same	Br	Pl
7442	Same	471	C	Pl
7443	Same	Same	Br	Pl
7444	Same	478	C	Pl
7445				
7446	Same	479	C	Pl
7447	Same	Same	Br	Pl
7448	Same	499	C	Pl
7449	Same	Same	Br	Pl
7450	Same	518	C	Pl
7451	Same	Same	Br	Pl
7452	Same	520	C	Pl
7453	Same	Same	Br	Pl
7454	Same	521	C	Pl
7455	Same	Same	Br	Pl
7456	Same	523	C	Pl
7457	Same	Same	Br	Pl
7458	Same	524	C	Pl
7459				
7460	Same	532	C	Pl
7461	Same	Same	Br	Pl
7462	Same	536	C	Pl
7463	Same	Same	Br	Pl
7464	Same	537	C	Pl
7465	Same	Same	Br	Pl
7466	Same	539	C	Pl
7467	Same	Same	Br	Pl
7468	Same	540	C	Pl
7469	Same	Same	Br	Pl

OHIO—Continued

Cincinnati—Continued

NUMBER	OBVERSE	REVERSE	METAL	EDGE
7470	Same	542	C	Pl
7471	Same	Same	Br	Pl
7472	Same	551	C	Pl
7473	Same	Same	Br	Pl
7474	Same	552	C	Pl
7475	Same	Same	Br	Pl
7476	Same	554	C	Pl
7477	Same	Same	Br	Pl
7478	Same	555	C	Pl
7479	Same	Same	Br	Pl
7480	Same	556	C	Pl
7481	Same	Same	Br	Pl
7482	Same	558	C	Pl
7483	Same	Same	Br	Pl
7484	Same	560	C	Pl
7485	Same	Same	Br	Pl
— 7486	Same	561	C	Pl
7487	Same	Same	Br	Pl
7488	Same	564	C	Pl
7489	Same	Same	Br	Pl
7490	Same	591	C	Pl
7491	Same	Same	Br	Pl
7492	Same	623	C	Pl
7493	Same	Same	Br	Pl
7494	Same	'Also cutlery & notions' in a circle of dots—ornaments above and below	C	Pl
7495				
7496	Same	'Dealers/in/hoop/skirts/hats caps/and/notions	C	Pl
7497				
7498	Same	'Boots shoes and Yankee notions'	C	Pl
7499	Same	Same	Br	Pl
7500	Same	'Hardware/dealer' inscribed on lock in centre—'C W Potwin & Co' above—'Zanesville O' below	C	Pl
7501				
7502				
7503				
— 7504	'W K Lanphear'above—'Manuf'r/of/metalic/cards'in corn wreath in centre—'134 West 4th St Cin O'	'Seal presses/cancelling/and/hand/stamps' 3 starts on side	C	Pl
7505	Same	Same	Br	Pl
7506	Same	'W K Lanphear/seal/presses/Cin O	C	Pl
7507	Same	Same	Br	Pl
7508	Same as reverse of No7607	428	C	Pl
7509				
— 7510	Same	465	C	Pl

OHIO—Continued

Cincinnati—Continued

NUMBER	OBVERSE	REVERSE	METAL	EDGE
7511				Pl
7512	Same	532	C	Pl
7513				
7514	Same	Same as obverse of No 7432	C	Pl
7515				
7516	W K Lanphear/manufacturer/of/store cards/102/West Fourth St/Cincinnati O	499	C	Pl
7517				
7518	Same	509	C	Pl
7519	Same	Same	C-N	Pl
7520				
7521	Same	W K Lanphear/general/engraver/102/W 4' St/Cincinnati	C	Pl
7522	Same	Same	Br	Pl
7523				
7524	W K Lanphear/stencil/cutter/102 West 4' St Large star and five small stars between the radiations	467	C	Pl
7525				
7526	Same	546	C	Pl
7527				
7528	Same as obverse of No. 7417—'Manufr' spelled 'Manner'	442	C	Pl
7529				
7530				
7531	Good for/5/cents/in cigars/or tobacco/at/Lanphears/133 Vine St	Blank	Br	Pl
7532	Good for/25/cents/at/Lanphear's/133 Vine St/in/cigars or tobacco	Blank	Br	Pl
7533				
7534	JF Larwell Watchmaker	419	C	R
7535	Same	420	C-N	R
7536	S Lasurs/dealer in/rags & Metals 26/15 st Cin O	259	C	Pl
7537	Same	665	C	Pl
7538				
7539	H Lazaress/dealer/in/rags & metals/26/15 St	259	C	Pl
7540	H Lazaruss/dealer/in/rags &/metals/26 15th Cin O	666	C	Pl
7541				
7542	Leavitt & Bevis/gents/furnishing/goods/5th&Vine/sts/Cincinnati	402	C	Pl
7543	Same	418	C	Pl
7544	Same	Same	C	R
7545	Same	Same	Br	R
7546	Same	Same as Die No 453—dated '1863'	C	R
7547				

OHIO—Continued

Cincinnati—Continued

NUMBER	OBVERSE	REVERSE	METAL	EDGE
7548	Leavitt & Bevis/hosiery/&/gloves/ 5th & Vine/sts/Cincinnati	402	C	Pl
7549	Same	418	C	R
7550	Same	Same	Br	R
7551	Same	420	C	R
7552	Same	Same as Die No 453—dated '1863	C-N	R
7553				
7554	W Lindermann/cor/Elm/& Henry/check maker	259	C	Pl
7555	Same	665	C	Pl
7556	Same	667	C	Pl
7557				
7558	H Lowenstein/butcher/N W Cor 9th & John	416	C	Pl
7559	Same	418	C	R
7560	Same	Same	Br	R
7561	Same	420	C	R
7562	Same	Same as Die No 453—dated '1863'	C	R
7563				
7564	Same	615	C	Pl
7565	Same	660	C	Pl
7566	F W Luk/artist	520	C	Pl
7567	Marsh & Miner/Vest/manufacturers/207/Wade St/Cincinnati	401	C	Pl
7568	Same	402	C	Pl
7569	Same	Same	Br	Pl
7570	Same	405	C	Pl
7571	Same	418	C	R
7572	Same	Same	Br	R
7573	Same	Same as Die No 453—dated '1863'	C	R
7574	Same	617	C	Pl
7575				
7576				
7577	Same—'Manufacturer' instead of 'Manufacturers'	401	C	Pl
7578	Same	402	C	Pl
7579	Same	405	C	Pl
7580	Same	417	C	Pl
7581	Same	418	C	R
7582	Same	Same	Br	R
7583	Same	Same	Z	R
7584	Same	420	C-N	R
7585	Same	661	C	Pl
7586				
7587	Martin's/grocery/23/Water St/Cincinnati	418	C	R
7588	Same	Same	Br	R
7589	Same	Same	Z	R

OHIO—Continued

Cincinnati—Continued

NUMBER	OBVERSE	REVERSE	METAL	EDGE
7590	Same	Same as Die No 453—dated '1863'	C	R
7591	Same	617	C	Pl
7592	Same	622	C	Pl
7593				
7594	W C McClenahan & Co/grocer/ N E Cor/4 &/Sycamore	30	C	Pl
7595	Same	426	C	Pl
7596	Same	509	C	Pl
7597	Same	Same	C-N	Pl
7598				
7599	T W McDonald/boots/&/shoes/ 299/Cen Avenue/Cincinnati	400	C	Pl
—7600	Same	401	C	Pl
7601	Same	405	C	Pl
7602	Same	418	C	Pl
7603	Same	Same	C	R
7604	Same	Same	Br	R
7605	Same	Same as Die No 453—dated '1863'	C-N	R
7606				
7607	L Phil Meredith/& J N M'Clung/ dentists/at/M'Clung's/dental rooms/152/Sixth St/Cincinnati O	'W K Lanphear'above—'Cincinnati' below — 'Manu'fr/ metalic/cards' in a wreath in centre	C	Pl
7608	Same	558	C	Pl
7609				
7610	Adam Metz/Butcher/957/Cen Avenue	400	C	Pl
7611	Same	401	C.	Pl
7612	Same	405	C	Pl
7613	Same	417	C	Pl
7614	Same	418	C	R
7615	Same	Same	Br	R
7616	Same	420	C	Pl
7617	Same	453	C	Pl
7618	J & D Metz/pork/packers/Cincinnati	68	C	Pl
7619	Same	418	C	R
7620	Same	Same	Br	R
7621	Same	Same as Die No. 453—dated '1863'	C-N	R
7622	Same	615	C	Pl
7623	Same	622	C	Pl
7624				
7625	Geo Metzger/12/mile/house	413	C	Pl
7926	Same	418	C	R
7627	Same	Same	Br	R
7628	Same	420	C	R
7629	Same	Same as Die No. 453—dated '1863'	C-N	R

OHIO—Continued

Cincinnati—Continued

NUMBER	OBVERSE	REVERSE	METAL	EDGE
7630				
7631	L Meyer/West/End/Saloon/Cincinnati	418	C	R
7632	Same	Same	Br	R
7533	Same	Same	Z	R
7634	Same	Same as Die No. 453—dated '1863'	C-N	R
7635	Same	617	C	Pl
7636				
7637	Buy your/groceries / from/Miedeking/N E Cor/9' & John Sts	418	C	R
7638	Same	Same	Br	R
7639				
7640	Same	Same as Die No. 453—dated '1863'	C-N	R
7641	Same	622	C	Pl
7642	'S B Monarch' below—'Bar' above —'10' in centre	420	C-N	R
7643	Same	597	C	R
7644	Same	Murdock&Spencer/139/W' Fifth/Street/Cincinnati	Br	R
7645				
7646	J T Moore/fruit/dealer/164/ sixth St/Cincinnati	400	C	Pl
7647	Same	405	C	Pl
7648	Same	407	C	Pl
7649	Same	418	C	R
7650	Same	Same	Br	R
7651	Same	Same	Z	R
7652	Same	same as Die No 453—dated '1863'	C-N	R
7653	Same	Fruits and flowers	C	Pl
7654				
7655	Morgan & Ferry/5/No 20 E 5' St/Cincinnati	210	C	R
7656	Same	Same	Br.	R
7657	Same	400	C	Pl
7658	Same	401	C	Pl
7659	Same	same as Die No 453—dated '1863'	C-N	R
7660	Same	Fruits and Flowers	C	Pl
7661	Same	420	C	R
7662	Same	Same	Br	R
7663				

OHIO. Continued

7664	Morgan & Ferry/10/No 20 E 5' St/Cincinnati	400	C	Pl
7665	Same	401	C	Pl
7666	Same	418	C	R
7667	Same	same as Die No 453—dated '1863'	C-N	R

OHIO—Continued

Cincinnati—Continued

NUMBER	OBVERSE	REVERSE	METAL	EDGE
7668	Same	597	C	R
7669	Same	Same	Br	R
7670				
7671	'H J Moser Watchmaker' around border circle of 14 stars in centre	420	C	R
7672	Same	Same	C-N	R
7673				
7674	Jas Murdock Jr M'F'R' of lead seals wires & presses 165 Race St Cinti O	Around edge 'M'F'T'R of baggage checks wax seals & ticket stamps 'inside in three lines' 100 10 in wires'	B	Pl
7675	Same	Same	Br	R
7676				
7677	Jas Murdock Jr/die/sinker/139/Fifth St/Cincinnati O	210	C	R
7678	Same	345	C	R
7679	Same	same as Die No 453—dated '1863'	C-N	R
7680	Same	502	C	Pl
7681				
7682	Murdock & Spencer 139 W' Fifth Street Cincinnati	597	C	R
7683				
7684	E Myers & Co/dealers/in/foreign/fruit/&/confectionery/52 Main St Cin O	405	C	Pl
7685	Same	418	C	R
7686	Same	Same	Br	R
7687	Same	Same	Z	R
7688	Same	same as Die No 453—dated '1863'	C-N	R
7689	Same	615	C	Pl
7690				
7691	H Niebuhr/wine/&/beer/saloon 223/Central Ave	467	C	Pl
7692	Same	509	C	Pl
7693	Same	518	C	Pl
7694	Same	Same	C-N	Pl
7695	Same	589	C	Pl
7696	Same	667	C	Pl
7697	Same	Obverse die incused	C	Pl
7698	F J Niemer's/hotel/262/Front St/CIN O	30	C	Pl
7699	Same	Same	C-N	Pl
7700	Same	467	C	Pl
7701	Same	518	C	Pl
7702	Same	Same	C-N	Pl
7703	Same	546	C	Pl
7704	J H Nolwer/cor/Elm &/Findley/Grocer	592	C	Pl
7705				

OHIO—Continued

Cincinnati—Continued

NUMBER	OBVERSE	REVERSE	METAL	EDGE
7706	R D Norris/dry/goods/174/Fifth St	405	C	Pl
7707	Same	406	C	Pl
7708	Same	418	C	R
7709	Same	Same	Br	R
7710				
7711	Same	same as Die No 453—dated '1863'	C-N	Pl
7712	Same	615	C	Pl
7713				
7714	O'Donoghue & Naish/boots/&/shoes/164 West 5'St/Cincinnati	400	C	Pl
7715	Same	401	C	Pl
7716	Same	402	C	Pl
7717	Same	418	C	R
7718	Same	Same	Br	R
7719				
7720	Same	same as Die No 453—dated '1863'	C-N	R
7721	Same	622	C	Pl
7722				
7723	O'Reilly Bros/dry/goods/112/Fifth St/Cincinnati	418	C	R
7724	Same	Same	Br	R
7725	Same	same as Die No 453—dated '1863'	C-N	R
7726	Same	629	C	Pl
7727	Same	H H Robinson/dry/goods/groceries/&/produce/New London B Co	C	Pl
7728				
7729	'B Panzer' above—'cents' below—'10' in beaded circle in centre	Jos J Sayre/die/sinker/4th &/ Walnut Cin O	Br	Pl
7730				
7731	Peebles/dealer/in/staple & fancy/groceries/5th & Race/sts/Cincinnati	59	C	Pl
7732	Same	400	C	Pl
7733	Same	401	C	Pl
7734	Same	402	C	Pl
7735	Same	405	C	Pl
7736	Same	417	C	Pl
7737	Same	418	C	Pl
7738	Same	Same	C	R
7739	Same	Same	Br	R
7740	Same	same as Die No 453—dated '1863'	C-N	R
7741	Same	634	C	Pl
7742	Same	Fruits vegetables &c	C	Pl
7743				
7744	Philip/16/Walnut/St/Cincinnati	418	C	R

OHIO—Continued

Cincinnati—Continued

NUMBER	OBVERSE	REVERSE	METAL	EDGE
7745	Same	Same	Br	R
7746	Same	same as Die No 453—dated '1863'	C-N	Pl
7747	Same	615	C	Pl
7748				
7749	J G Pleisteiner/fancy/goods/&/notions/555 Vine St/bet 15' & Liberty/Cincinnati	400	C	Pl
7750	Same	418	C	R
7751	Same	Same	Br	R
7752	Same	Same	Z	R
7753	Same	same as Die No 453—dated '1863'	C-N	R
7754				
7755	Chas Plumb/huckster/market/Cincinnati	413	C	Pl
7756	Same	415	C	Pl
7757	Same	418	C	R
7758	Same	Same	Br	R
7759	Same	Same	Z	R
7760	Same	same as Die No 453—dated '1863'	C-N	R
7761	Same	659	C	Pl
7762				
7763	Pogue & Jones/dry/goods/128/Fifth St/Cincinnati	414	C	Pl
7764	Same	418	C	R
7765	Same	Same	Br	R
7766	Same	Same	Z	R
7767	Same	same as Die No 453—dated '1863'	C-N	R
7768	Same	615	C	Pl
7769	Henry Porter/95/Fifth/St/Cincinnati	'15' on plain planchet	Br	R
7770	'H A Ratterman' above—'Cincinnati' below—12 stars in circle in centre	210	C	Pl
7771	Same	400	C	Pl
7772	Same	401	C	Pl
7773	Same	418	C	R
7774	Same	Same	Br	R
7775	Same	Same	Z	R
7776	Same	same as Die No 453—dated '1863'	C-N	R
7777	Same	blank planchet	C	Pl
7778				
7779	John Ravy/confectioner/185/Race/street/Cincinnati	400	C	Pl
7780	Same	401	C	Pl
7781	Same	407	C	Pl
7782	Same	417	C	Pl

OHIO—Continued

Cincinnati—Continued

NUMBER	OBVERSE	REVERSE	METAL	EDGE
7783	Same	418	C	R
7784	Same	Same	Br	R
7785				
7786	Same	453	C	Pl
7787	Same	same as Die No 453—dated '1863'	C-N	R
7788	Same	622	C	Pl
7789	Same	blank planchet	C	Pl
7790				
7791	I Rees/401/Central/Ave/Cincinnati O	467	C	Pl
7792	Same	657	C	Pl
7793	Same	Same	C-N	Pl
7794	J Reis & Co/cor 7th &/Walnut/meat store	183	C	Pl
7795				
7796	J F Resta/3' & Smith/Sts/Cincinnati/sausage maker	418	C	R
7797	Same	Same	Br	R
7798				
7799	Same	617	C	Pl
7800	Same	622	C	Pl
7801	Same	661	C	Pl
7802	Same	same as Die No453—dated '1863'	C-N	R
7803	Same	same as obverse No7104	C	Pl
7804				
7805	'A Ricke' above—'Cincinnati' below—square ornament in circle of eleven stars in centre	418	C	R
7806	Same	Same	Br	R
7807	Same	same as Die No453—dated '1863'	C-N	R
7808	Same	615	C	Pl
7809	Same	622	C	Pl
7810	Same	659	C.	Pl
7811				
7812	'A Ricke' above—'Cincinnati'below—square ornament in circle of nine stars—all surrounded by a beaded circle	400	C	Pl
7813	Same	401	C	Pl
7814	Same	210	C	Pl
7815	Same	405	C	Pl
7816	Same	417	C	Pl
7817	Same	418	C	R
7818	Same	Same	Br	R
7819	Same	Same	Z	R
7820	Same	same as Die No453—dated '1863'	C-N	R
7821	Same—smaller letters	615	C	Pl

OHIO—Continued

Cincinnati—Continued

NUMBER	OBVERSE	REVERSE	METAL	EDGE
7822				
7823	B J Ricking/grocer/49/Plum St/ Cinti O	30	C	Pl
7824	Same	259	C	Pl
7825	Same	425	C	Pl
7826	Same	427	C	Pl
7827	Same	428	C	Pl
7828	Same	460	C	Pl
7829	Same	463	C	Pl
7830	Same	467	C	Pl
7831	Same	Same	C-N	Pl
7832	Same	519	C	Pl
7833	Same	546	C	Pl
7834	Same	657	C	Pl
7835				
7836	Geo W Ritter's/meat/store/241/ Fourth St	509	C	Pl
7837	Same	Same	C-N	Pl
7838				
7839	'F H Rollins' above—'18 Public Landing Cin'ti O' below—Indian head to left in centre	Stationery / printing / &/ blank/books	Br	R
7840				
7841	'Yankee Robinson' above — 'The great Comedian' below—portrait of man in centre with gun resting on right shoulder	'Yankee Robinson' above— 'Big Show' below—infield a triangle inclosing hand pointing downward to 'Triad'—at sides of triangle the words 'Past' 'Present' 'Future'	C	Pl
7842	Same	Blank Planchet	Tin	Pl
7843	Same	415	C	Pl
7844	Same as reverse of 7841	656	C	Pl
7845	Bust of Same Yankee Robinson	Similar to reverse of No 7841—but hand is shorter and divides the date '1863'	C	R
7846	Same	Same	Br	R
7847				
7848				
7849	Same as reverse of No. 7845	419	C	R
7850	Same	420	C	R
7851				
7852	Albert Ross Druggist / corner/of Central/Avenue/&/8th Street/ Cincinnati	527	C	Pl
7853	Same	Same	Br	Pl
7854	Same	Same	C-N	Pl
7855	Same	Same	S	Pl
7856				

OHIO—Continued

Cincinnati—Continued

NUMBER	OBVERSE	REVERSE	METAL	EDGE
7857	John Sacksteder / Man'fr/of/sewing/machines/419/Cen Ave/Cin O	Sewing/machines / neatly/ repaired/1863 star on sides of date	C	Pl
7858	Same	657	C	Pl
7859				
7860	Chr Schloendorn/paper/hangings,/ &/fancy goods/492/Main St/Cincinnati	400	C	Pl
7861				
7862	Same	418	C	R
7863	Same	Same	Br	R
7864	Same	Same	Z	R
7865	Same	same as No 453—dated '1863'	C-N	R
7866				
7867	H Schmidt's/auction/&/commission/goods/27 Elder St/Cincinnati	418	C	R
7868	Same	Same	Br	R
7869	Same	Same	Z	R
7870	Same	same as No 453—dated '1863'	C-N	R
7871	Same	634	C	Pl
7872				
7873	L Schneider/557/Walnut/St/Cincinnati	406	C	Pl
7874	Same	413	C	Pl
7875	Same	418	C	R
7876	Same	Same	Br	R
7877				
7878	Same	Same as Die No 453—dated '1863'	C-N	R
7879	Same	615	C	Pl
7880	Same	663	C	Pl
7881				
7882	H Schott/248/Liberty/St Cin'ti O	Blank planchet	Br	R
7883				
7884	Schultz & Negley Druggists N E Cor 5' & Main St Cin'ti O	210	W-M	R
7885				
7886	M Mendal Shafer/Attorney/&/ counselor/at/law/57 Third St/ Cincinnati	The/ federal / government/ a/national/ currency / free trade/and/human rights	C	Pl
7887	Same	402	C	Pl
7888	Same	407	C	Pl
7889	Same	418	C	R
7890	Same	Same	Br	R
7891	Same	Same	Z	R
7892	Same	615	C	Pl
7893	Same	663	C	Pl
7894				

OHIO—Continued

Cincinnati—Continued

NUMBER	OBVERSE	REVERSE	METAL	EDGE
7895	'Wm Senour' in script	Same as obverse of No 7417	C	Pl
7896				
7897	Same	Continental / hotel/money/ check	Br	Pl
7898	Same	185	C	Pl
7899	Same	426	C	Pl
7900	Same	471	C	Pl
7901	Same	520	C	Pl
7902	Same	560	C	Pl
7903	Same	621	C	Pl
7904	Same	S E Hustler Browne's old corner Troy O	C	Pl
7905				
7906	H E Shaw/new/and/second hand/ furniture/18/East 4 St/Cin O	30	C	Pl
7907	Same	Same	C-N	Pl
7908	Same	467	C	Pl
7909	Same	518	C	Pl
7910	Same	546	C	Pl
7911				
7912				
7913	F Sheen/groceries/&/bread/ Stuffs/70/E Pearl St	406	C	Pl
7914	Same	418	C	R
7915	Same	Same	Br	R
7916	Same	Same	Z	R
7917	Same	615	C	Pl
7918	Same	659	C	Pl
7919	Same	661	C	Pl
7920				
7921	Frank Smith/grocery/&/liquor/ store/119 Sycamore St/Cincinnati	60	C	Pl
7922	Same	411	C	Pl
7923	Same	418	C	R
7924	Same	Same	Br	R
7925	Same	Same	Z	R
7926	Same	420	C	R
7927	Same	Same as Die No 453—dated '1863'	C-N	R
7928	Same	629	C	Pl
7929				
7930	J Smith's meat/store/143 Lock St	418	C	R
7931	Same	Same	Br	R
7932				
7933	Same	Same as Die No 453—dated '1863'	C-N	R
7934	Same	615	C	Pl
7935	Same	617	C	Pl
7936	Same	659	C	Pl
7937	Same	663	C	Pl
7938				

OHIO—Continued

Cincinnati—Continued

NUMBER	OBVERSE	REVERSE	METAL	EDGE
7939	S & L Smith/grocers/Cincinnati	A B Wilson/staple/&/fancy/grocer/224/W 6'th St/ Cincinnati	C	Pl
7940	Same	417	C	Pl
7941	Same	418	C	Pl
7942	Same	Same	C	R
7943				
7944	Same	Same as Die No 453—dated '1863'	C-N	R
7945	Same	615	C	Pl
7946	Same	634	C	Pl
7947				
7948	F Snyder Grocer 53 Court St Cin O	259	C	Pl
7949				
7950	Chas Spreen/grocer/&/produce/dealer/Cor Court & Linn Sts	406	C	Pl
7951	Same	407	C	Pl
7952	Same	418	C	R
7953	Same	Same	Br	R
7954	Same	Same	Z	R
7955	Same	Same as Die No 453—dated '1863'	C-N	R
7956	Same	661	C	Pl
7957				
7958				
7959	H Stalkamp/grocer/10/Green St/Cincinnati	414	C	Pl
7960	Same	418	C	R
7961	Same	Same	Br	R
7962				
7963	Same	Same as die No 453—dated '1863'	C-N	R
7964	Same	615	C	Pl
7965				
7966	John Stanton/manufacturer/of/store/cards/stencils/stamps & brands/Cincinnati Ohio	68	C	Pl
7967	Same	345	C	R
7968	Same	Same	Br	R
7969	Same	Same	Z	R
7970	Same	402	C	Pl
7971	Same	Same	Z	Pl
7972	Same	418	C	R
7973	Same	Same	Br	R
7974	Same	Same	Z	R
7975	Same	420	C	R
7976	Same	Same as die No 453—dated '1863'	C-N	R
7977	Same	453	C	Pl
7978	Same	495	C	R

OHIO—Continued
Cincinnati—Continued

NUMBER	OBVERSE	REVERSE	METAL	EDGE
7979	Same	Same	Br	R
7980	Same	500	C	R
7981	Same	Same	Br	R
7982	Same	Same	Z	R
7983	Same	501	C	R
7984	Same	Same	Br	R
7985	Same	502	C	R
7986	Same	Same	Br	R
7987				
7988				
7989				
7990				
7991	John Stanton/steel/stamp/brand & stencil/cutter/139 Fifth St/ Cincinnati Ohio	418	C	R
7992	Same	Same	Br	R
7993				
7994	Same	419	C	R
7995	Same	Same	C-N	R
7996				
7997				
7998	C Sutton's/new/grocery/store/ 202 Fifth St	418	C	R
7999	Same	Same	Br	R
8000	Same	Same	Z	R
8001	Same	Same as die No 453—dated '1863'	C-N	R
8002	Same	617	C	Pl
8003				
8004	Wm Tell/House/225/Sixth ST/ Cincinnati	418	C	R
8005				
8006	Same	Same	Z	R
8007	Same	same as die No 453—dated '1863'	C-N	R
8008	Same	659	C	Pl
8009	Same	660	C	Pl
8010				
8011	E Townley/hives/&bees/Mount Auburn/Cincinnati	68	C	Pl
8012	Same	406	C	Pl
8013	Same	415	C	Pl
8014	Same	418	C	R
8015	Same	Same	Br	R
8016				
8017	Same	same as die No 453—dated '1863'	C-N	R
8018	Same	622	C	Pl
8019	Same	659	C	Pl
8020	Same	661	C	Pl
8021				

OHIO—Continued

Cincinnati—Continued

NUMBER	OBVERSE	REVERSE	METAL	EDGE
8022	Buy meat/at/Van Wunder/in/market	68	C	Pl
8023	Same	401	C	Pl
8024	Same	402	C	Pl
8025	Same	418	C	R
8026	Same	Same	Br	R
8027	Same	Same	Z	R
8028	Same	same as die No 453—dated '1863'	C-N	R
8029	Same	507	C	Pl
8030				
8031				
8032				
8033	Jacob Vogel/butcher/985/Cen Avenue	418	C	R
8034	Same	Same	Br	R
8035				
8036	Same	420	C	R
8037	Same	same as die No 453—dated '1863'	C-N	R
8038	Same	656	C	Pl
8039	Same	663	C	Pl
8040				
8041	Waldo & Brandon's/Emporium/1863	Dry goods/and/groceries	C	Pl
8042	Same	478	C	Pl
8043	Same as reverse of No 8041	478	C	Pl
8044				
8045	Weatherby's/cheap/dry/goods/emporium/Cincinnati	68	C	Pl
8046	Same	405	C	Pl
8047	Same	414	C	Pl
8048	Same	418	C	R
8049	Same	Same	Br	R
8050	Same	same as die No 453—dated '1863'	C-N	R
8051	Same	661	C	Pl
8052				
8053	H C Wehrman/baker/217 Everett St sheaf of wheat in centre	418	C	R
8054	Same	Same	Br	R
8055	Same	Same	Z	R
8056	Same	same as die No 453—dated '1863'	C-N	R
8057	Same	615	C	Pl
8058	Same	617	C	Pl
8059	Same	660	C	Pl
8060	Same	661	C	Pl
8061				
8062	W W Wert/auction/&/commission/boots & shoes/whoesale/&/retail/154 Main St	418	C	R

OHIO—Continued

Cincinnati—Continued

NUMBER	OBVERSE	REVERSE	METAL	EDGE
8063	Same	Same	Br	R
8064	Same	Same	Z	R
8065	Same	same as die No 453—dated '1863'	C-N	R
8066	Same	615	C	Pl
8067	Same	622	C	Pl
8068	Same	634	C	Pl
8069	Same	668	C	Pl
8070				
8071	A B Wilson/staple/&/fancy/grocer/224/W 6'th St/Cincinnati	59	C	Pl
8072	Same	401	C	Pl
8073	Same	406	C	Pl
8074	Same	418	C	R
8075	Same	Same	Br	R
8076				
8077	Same	453	C	Pl
8078	Same	617	C	Pl
8079				
8080	Good for/5/cents/H Wind	210	C	Pl
8081	Same	Same	C	R
8082	Same	Same	Br	R
8083				
8084	Same	405	Br	Pl
8085	Same	same as die No 453—dated '1863'	C-N	R
8086				
8087	Good for 25 cents at Wilkinson 110 West 4th St	Redeemed in par sums of one dollar	Br	Pl
8088				
8089	Winesteiner/35/East/Third/St/Cincinnati	210	C	Pl
8090	Same	405	C	Pl
8091	Same	Same	Br	Pl
8092	Same	418	C	R
8093	Same	Same	Br	R
8094	Same	Same	Z	R
8095	Same	same as die No 453—dated '1863	C-N	R
8096				
8097	John Woessner's / Jefferson/saloon/cor/12 & Main Sts/Cincinnati	400	C	Pl
8098	Same	405	C	Pl
8099	Same	406	C	Pl
8100	Same	407	C	Pl
8101	Same	417	C	Pl
8102	Same	418	C	R
8103	Same	Same	Br	R
8104	Same	Same	Z	R

OHIO—Continued

Cincinnati—Continued

NUMBER	OBVERSE	REVERSE	METAL	EDGE
8105	Same	same as die No 453—dated '1863'	C-N	R
8106				
8107	Wright/Cincinnati/1863	657	C	Pl
8108				
8109	C Wolfer/tin/shop/62 Findlay St/Cincinnati	418	C	R
8110	Same	Same	Br	R
8111				
8112	Same	same as die No 453—dated '1863'	C-N	R
8113	Same	659	C	Pl
8114				
8115	Robert Wright/dry/goods/397/Cen Avenue	210	C	Pl
8116	Same	400	C	Pl
8117	Same	401	C	Pl
8118	Same	404	C	Pl
8119	Same	405	C	Pl
8120	Same	407	C	Pl
8121	Same	415	C	Pl
8122	Same	417	C	Pl
8123	Same	418	C	R
8124	Same	Same	Br	R
8125				
8126	Same	453	C	Pl
8127	Same	same as die No 453—dated '1863'	C-N	R
8128	Same	615	C	Pl
8129	Same	617	C	Pl
8130	Same—more space at each end of the word 'Goods'	453	C	Pl
8131				
8132	H B Xelar/wine/&/Beer/saloon	442	C	Pl
8133	Same	582	C	Pl
8134				
8135	'S Y'—Stephen Yeatman	416	C	R
8136	Same	418	C	R
8137	Same	Same	Br	R
8138	Same	Same	Z	R
8139	Same	420	C	R
8140				
8141	L Young—scrolls above and below	557	C	Pl
8142				
8143	Jos Zandt Ice Cream Saloon 285 Central Avenue	582	C	Pl
8144				
8145	Jos Zanone Ice Cream Saloon 285 Central Avenue	582	C	Pl
8146	Same	657	C	Pl

OHIO—Continued
Cincinnati—Continued

NUMBER	OBVERSE	REVERSE	METAL	EDGE
8147	Same	'J A Hughes' above— 'Cincinnati' below — 'metalic/ cards' in wreath	W-M	Pl
8148	Same	S Bacciocci/confectionery/ and/ice/cream/ saloon/176 Fifth St	C	Pl
8149				
8150	John Zeltner/Vine/St/Hill	416	C	Pl
8151	Same	418	C	R
8152	Same	Same	Br	R
8153	Same	Same	Z	R
8154	Same	420	iC	R
8155	John Zeltner/National/Hall/400/ Vine St/Cincinnati O	405	C	Pl
8156	Same	416	C	Pl
8157	Same	417	C	Pl
8158	Same	418	C	R
8159	Same	Same	Br	R
8160	Same	Same	Z	R
8161	Same	615	C	Pl
8162	Same	617	C	Pl
8163	Same	634	C	Pl
8164	Same	Same as obverse	Br	R
8165				
8166	John E Zeltner/National/Hall/ 400/Vine St/Cincinnati O	59	C	Pl
8167	Same	400	C	Pl
—8168	Same	401	C	Pl
—8169	Same	405	C	Pl
8170	Same	407	C	Pl
8171	Same	417	C	Pl
— 8172	Same	615	C	Pl
8173				
8174				

Circleville

8175	C H Fickardt & Co/druggist/ Circleville/Ohio	30	C	Pl
8176	Same	469	C	Pl
8177	Same	621	C	Pl
—8178		ナンレ		
8179	J L King/grocer/and/provisions/ store/Circleville O	30	C	Pl
8180	Same	469	C	Pl
8181	Same	546	C	Pl
8182	Same	Blank planchet	C	Pl
8183	Same	Railroad/1863/Warehouse	C	Pl
8184	Mason & Son/grocers/and/ liquor/dealers/Circleville O	30	C	Pl
8185	Same	Same	C-N	Pl

OHIO—Continued

Cincinnati—Continued

NUMBER	OBVERSE	REVERSE	METAL	EDGE
8186	Same	469	C	Pl
8187	Same	546	C	Pl

Clarksburg

8188	Groceries & Notions/sold by/one/ French/Clarksburg O	669	C	Pl
8189	James & French/have/it/Clarksburg/Ohio	669	C	Pl
8190				
8191				

Cleveland

— 8192	C G Bruce/authorized/war/claim/ Agent/1863/Cleveland O 'A' of 'Agent' between 'C' and 'L'	$100 bounty/pensions/back pay/&c / collected/& cashed/ '$' above 'E' of pension	C	Pl
8193	Same	Blank	C	Pl
8194				
8195	same—dash on each side of 'war' —'A' of 'Agent' under 'L' of 'claim'	Same—'$' opposite to 'E' of 'pension'	C	Pl
8196	Same	Same	C	R
8197	Same	Same	C-N	R
8198				
— 8199	same—'A' almost directly between 'C' and 'L'	Same—'$' opposite 'P' of 'pension'	C	Pl
8200	Same	Same	C	R
8201	Same	Same	Br	R
8202	Same—incused	Same—incused	C	R
8203				
8204	Same	412	C	R
8205	Same	Same	C-N	R
8206				
8207	Same as reverse of No8192	60	C	Pl
8208	Same	blank	C	Pl
8209				
8210	Same as obverse of No 8195	Same as reverse of No8199	Z	R
8211				
— 8212	Same as obverse of No 8199	408	C	Pl
8213				
8214	C Chandler/fruit/&Seed/dealer/ Cleveland O	470	C	Pl
8215				
8216	Deckand & Englehart/fashionable/hatters/Cleveland/Ohio	209	C	Pl
8217	Same	433	C	Pl
8218				
8219	Dunn Goudy & Bro/groceries/&c/ 149/Ontario St/Cleveland O	444	C	Pl
8220				

OHIO—Continued

Cleveland—Continued

NUMBER	OBVERSE	REVERSE	METAL	EDGE
8221	D W Gage/authorized/war/claim/agent/1863/Cleveland O	$100 bounty/pensions/back pay/&c/collected/&/cashed	C	Pl
8222	Same	Same	C	R
8223	Same	Same	Br	R
8224	Same	Same	Z	R
8225	Same	Same	419	R
8226				
8227	J H & A S Gorham/grocers/manufacturers/of/crackers/and/confectionery/Cleveland O	469	C	Pl
8228	Same	470	C	Pl
8229				
8230	'John Hawkins' above—'The Ladies man' below—bust to right	Newburg House/226/Ontario St/Cleveland/Ohio	C	Pl
8231				
8232	J Langhorn/meat/store/Banks St/Cleveland O	470	C	Pl
8233				
8234				
8235	C L Marvin/stove &/grate/depot/50/Public Square/Cleveland O	470	C	Pl
8236				
8237				
8238	T J Quinlan/bill/poster/and/distributor/174/Ontario St/ Cleveland O	T J Quinlan/news/papers/stationery/songs/and/yankee/notions	C	Pl
8239	Same	Same as obverse die	C	Pl
8240	Same	478	C	Pl
8241	Same	560	C	Pl
8242				
8243	I P Sherwood/dry/goods/millinery/Cleveland O	409	C	R
8244	Same	416	C	R
8245	Same	418	C	R
8246	Same	Same	Br	R
8247	Same	Same	Z	R
8248	Same	420	C-N	R
8249				
8250	J P Sherwood/dry/goods/millinery/Cleveland O	60	C	R
8251	Same	418	C	R
8252	Same	Same	Br	R
8253				
8254	Same	Same as die NO 453—dated '1863'	C-N	R
8255				
8256	'Chas W Stearns' above—'Ohio' below—'foot/of/Vinyard/St/Cleveland' inscribed on grindstone in centre	Grindsone/flagging/&/building/stones	C	R
8257	Same	Same	Br	R

OHIO—Continued

Cleveland—Continued

NUMBER	OBVERSE	REVERSE	METAL	EDGE
8258	Same	Same as die No 453—dated '1863'	C-N	R
8259				
—8260	Same as reverse of No 8256	419	C	R
8261				
8262	Tages/London/Yoke shirt/Manufy/243/SuperiorSt/Cleveland Ohio	Send for a/circular/a perfect/fit/guaranteed	C	Pl
8263	Tages/London/Yoke shirts/Manufy/243/Superior St/Cleveland O	Same	Br	Pl
8264				
8265	'Wards/Lake/Superior/Line/Steamboat/Planet' in centre—'Cleveland Detroit & Lake Superior' around border	418	C	R
8266	Same	Same	Br	R
8267				
8268	Same	419	C-N	R
8269				
8270	'Geo Worthington & Co' above—'Cleveland O' below—in centre a circular saw inscribed 'Hardware dealer'	Try/Allen's/Blacklead/compound/Babitt/metal/1862	C	Pl
8271	Same	Same	Br	Pl
8272	Same as preceeding—dated '1863'	470	C	Pl
8273	Same	670	C	Pl
8274				
8275	'Geo Worthington & Co' above—'Cleveland O' below—a padlock in centre inscribed 'Hardware Dealer'	Try/Allen's/Blacklead/compound/Babitt/metal/1863	C	Pl
8276	Same	Same	C-N	Pl
8277	Same	528	C	Pl
8278	Same	Same	Br	Pl
8279	Same	582	C	Pl
8280	Same	same as reverse of No 7406	C	Pl
8281	Same	Same	Br	Pl
8282	Same	same as obverse of No 7209	C	Pl
8283				
8284				

Collinsville

8285	P Carle & Son/grocers/&/grain/dealers/Collinsville O	210	C	Pl
8286	Same	405	C	Pl
8287	Same	Same	Br	Pl
8288	Same	418	C	R
8289	Same	Same	Br	R
8290				
8291				
8292				
8293				

OHIO—Continued

Columbus

NUMBER	OBVERSE	REVERSE	METAL	EDGE
8294	John Grether/importer/of/china/&/queensware/Columbus O	416	C	R
8295	Same	Same	Br	R
8296	Same	Same	Z	R
8297	Same	418	C	R
8298	Same	Same	Br	R
8299				
8300	Same	420	C-N	R
8301				
8302	Heintz & Henkle/dealers/in/groceries/136 Cor 4th/and/Friend/Columbus O	422	C	Pl
8303	Same	444	C	Pl
8304	Same	468	C	Pl
8305				
8306	J M & V Koerner/grocers/S E Cor/Broad/&/Front/Columbus O	421	C	Pl
—8307	Same	423	C	Pl
8308	Same	444	C	Pl
8309	Same	469	C	Pl
8310	Same	478	C	Pl
8311				
8312	S T Martin/eating/house/160/South Fourth St/Columbus/Ohio	421	C	Pl
8313	Same	426	C	Pl
8314	Same	446	C	Pl
8315	Same	469	C	Pl
8316				
8317	S T Martin/eating/house/160/South/Fourth St/Columbus O small letters	443	C	Pl
8318	Same	444	C	Pl
8319	Same	470	C	Pl
8320	Same	621	C	Pl
8321	Same	671	C	Pl
8322	Same	same as obverse of No 7332	C	Pl
8323	Merchants Exchange/Columbus/Ohio	Similar to Die No 597—16 stars	Br	Pl
8324	Wm H Restieaux/Grocer/Columbus O	459	C	Pl
8325	Same	470	C	Pl
8326	Same	558	C	Pl
8327				
8328	H Schreiner/groceries/and/provisions/169/East/Friend ST/Columbus O	445	C	Pl
8329	Same	470	C	Pl
8330				
8331	Mrs M A Van Houten/milliner/68/E Town St/Columbus/Ohio	446	C	Pl
8332				

OHIO—Continued

Columbus—Continued

NUMBER	OBVERSE	REVERSE	METAL	EDGE
8333				
8334	Wagner's/Dining/Hall/Columbus O	30	C	Pl
8335	Same	421	C	Pl
8336	Same	469	C	Pl
8337	Same	470	C	Pl
8338				
8339				
8340	Wiatt & Bro/Bakers/&/Confectioners/Columbus O	30	C	Pl
8341	Same	467	C	Pl
8342	Same	Same	C-N	Pl
8343	Same	468	C	Pl
8344	Same	518	C	Pl
8345				

Columbiana

8346	Icenhour & Co/produce/&/commission/merchants/Columbiana O	530	C	R
8347	Same	Same	Br	R
8348	Same	Same	N	R
8349	Same	Same	Tin	R
8350				
8351	Same	419	C-N	R
8352				
8353	G Kipp/produce/dealer/Columbiana O	419	C	R
8354	Same	Same	Br	R
8355	Same	Same	C-N	R
8356				

Crestline

8357	Jacob Stump/merchant tailor/&/ready made/clothing/Crestline/Ohio	556	C	Pl
8358				

Dayton

8359	J C Cain/notions/305 Third St/Dayton/Ohio	422	C	Pl
8360				
8361	J Durst/grocer/Dayton O	404	C	R
8362	Same	408	C	R
8363	Same	418	C	R
8364	Same	Same	Br	R
8365	Same	Same	C-N	R
8366	Same	419	C	R
8367	Same	420	C	R
8368	Same	Same	Br	R

OHIO—Continued
Dayton—Continued

NUMBER	OBVERSE	REVERSE	METAL	EDGE
8369	Same	Same	C-N	R
8370				
8371	Henry Kline Clocks watches & Jewelry Dayton O	Blank	C	Pl
8372				
8373	S Wild/coffee/house/Dayton O	419	C	R
—8374	Same	420	C	R
8375	Same	Same	Br	R
8376				

Defiance

8377	Ruhl's/premium/steel/pens/Defiance O	68	C	Pl
8378	Same	401	C	Pl
8379	Same	418	C	R
8380	Same	Same	Br	R
8381	Same	Same	Z	R
8382	Same	same as Die No 453—dated '1863'	C-N	R
8383				
8384				

Delphos

8385	J W Hunt/druggist/&/express/Agt/Delphos O	416	C	R
8386	Same	419	C	R
8387	Same	Same	C	Pl
8388				

Edgerton

8389	D Farnham & Co/dealers/in/dry goods/Edgerton/Ohio	425	C	Pl
8390	Same	460	C	Pl
8391	Same	478	C	Pl
8392	Same	552	C	Pl
8393	Same	556	C	Pl
8394				

Elyria

—8395	'W B Eager Elyria O' above—'wholesale Agt' below—Indian head to left in centre	Try/Allen's/blacklead/compound/Babitt/metal/1862	Br	Pl
8396	Same—star before and after 'wholesale Agt'	Same	Br	Pl
8397	same as reverse of No 8395	478	C	Pl
8398	same as No 8397—dated '1863'	210	C	Pl
8399	Same	670	C	Pl
8400				

OHIO—Continued

Findlay

NUMBER	OBVERSE	REVERSE	METAL	EDGE
8401	I Boger/watch maker/&/jeweler/ Findlay O	536	C	Pl
8402				
8403	Osborne & BRO/grocers/&/produce/dealers/ Findlay O	418	C	R
8404	same	same	Br	R
8405	same	same	Z	R
8406	same	419	C-N	R
8407				

Frazeysburg

8408	E L Lemert/dry/goods/&/groceries/Frazeysburg O	416	C	R
8409	same	same	Br	R
8410	same	419	C	R
8411	same	420	C	R
8412	same	same	C-N	R
8413				

Fredericktown

8414	Bartlett & Rigby/dry/goods/groceries/&c/Fredericktown O	419	C	Pl
8415	same	same	C	R
8416	same	same	Br	R
8517	same	same	C-N	R
8418	same	420	C	R
8419				
8420	Mosure Bro & Lemon/clothiers/&/dry goods/Fredericktown O	560	C	Pl
8421				
8422	Rogers & Cassell/hardware/iron &/nails/Fredericktown/Ohio	524	C	Pl
8423				
8424	S S Tuttle/produce/commission/&/forwarding/merchant/Fredericktown O	419	C	R
8425	same	same	C-N	R
8426				
8427				
8428				

Fremont

8429	P Close/groceries/wines/liquors & cigars/wholesale/&/retail/Fremont O	423	C	Pl
8430	same	same	Br	Pl
8431				
8432	'Dr E Dillon & Son/Druggists' above—'Fremont/Ohio' below—small mortar and pestle in centre	528	C	Pl

OHIO—Continued

Fremont—Continued

NUMBER	OBVERSE	REVERSE	METAL	EDGE
8433	same	same	Br	Pl
8434				
8435	M Dryfoos/merchant/tailor/and dealer in/ready made/clothing/Fremont O	552	C	Pl
8436	same	same	Br	Pl
9437				
8438	Emrich & Co/dry goods/clothing/Fremont O	423	C	Pl
8439	same	same	Br	Pl
8440				
8441	Hoot & Meng/Manufr's/and/dealers in/boots & shoes/Fremont Ohio	533	C	Pl
8442	same	same	Br	Pl
8443				
8444	D W Krebs & Co/dealers/in/dry goods/clothing/&c/Fremont O	423	C	Pl
8445	same	same	Br	Pl
8446				
8447	Roberts & Sheldon/dealers in/stoves/tin/and/hardware/Fremont Ohio	526	C	Pl
8448	same	same	Br	Pl
8449				
8450	Thompson & Spicer/stoves/tin/& house/furnishing/goods/Fremont/Ohio	523	C	Pl
5451	same	same	Br	Pl
8452				

Galion

| 8453 | 'D & W Riblet' above'--Galion Ohio' below—U S shield in centre | 548 | C | Pl |
| 8454 | same | same | Br | Pl |

Gallipolis

8455	J D Bailey fancy dry goods/notions & groceries Gallipolis O	420	C-N	R
8456				
8457				
8458	J J Cadot & Bro/grocers/Gallipolis/Ohio	442	C	Pl
8459	same	same	Br	Pl
8460	same	471	C	Pl
8461				
8462				
8463	Good for 5 cts at S Goetz Cor Grape & 3 Sts Gallipolis O	5 cents—11stars	N	R
8464				

OHIO—Continued

Greenville

NUMBER	OBVERSE	REVERSE	METAL	EDGE
8465	F H Hafer & Co/staple/&/fancy/ groceries/Greenville O	400	C	Pl
8466	same	same	C	R
8467	same	same	Br	R
8468	same	417	C	Pl
8469	same	418	C	R
8470	same	same	Br	R
8471	same	419	C-N	R
8472	same	210	C	Pl
8473				
8474	T P Turpen/grocer/&/tobacco/ dealer/Greenville O	418	C	R
8475	same	same	Br	R
8476	same	same	Z	R
8477	same	Same as Die No 453—dated '1863'	C-N	R
8478	same	629	C	Pl
8479				

Hamilton

8480	John Deinzer/family/Grocery/No/ 19/High St/Hamilton O	407	C	Pl
8481	same	418	C	Pl
8482	same	same	C	R
8483	same	same	Br	R
8484				
8485	H & W Frechtling/dealers/in/dry/ goods/& groceries/Hamilton O	418	C	R
8486	same	same	Br	R
8487	same	same	Tin	R
8488				
8489	John Schubert/Hamilton/Saloon/ High/Street/Hamilton O	405	C	Pl
8490	same	407	C	Pl
8491	same	418	C	R
8492	same	same	Br	R
8493				
8494	same	Same as Die No. 453—dated '1863'	C-N	R
8495	same	615	C	Pl
8496	same	same	Br	Pl

Hillsboro

8497	Black & Kibler/dealers/in/hard- ware/iron/&/nails/Hillsboro O	542	C	Pl
8498	same	547	C	Pl
8499	same	549	C	Pl
8500	same	560	C	Pl
8501	Chaney & Harris dealers in dry goods Hillsboro Ohio	443	C	Pl

OHIO—Continued

Hillsboro—Continued

NUMBER	OBVERSE	REVERSE	METAL	EDGE
8502				
8503	O J Eckley/dairy/meat/market/Hillsboro/Ohio	506	C	Pl
8504				
8505	Herron & Amen/dry goods/&/notions/Hillsboro/Ohio	460	C	Pl
8506				
8507	Geo March/dealer/in/dry goods/Hillsboro/Ohio	460	C	Pl
8508	same	480	C	Pl
8509				
8510		.		

Jackson

8511	John Chestnut's/Exchange/Jackson O	Good for /10/cents/1862	Br	Pl
8512				

Kenton

8513	J M Brunson/dealer/ in/dry goods/&c/Kenton Ohio	Flag on staff in centre—'Fancy & staple' above—'dry goods &c' below	C	Pl
8514	same	blank	C	Pl
8515				

Lancaster

8516	J Armbruster/grocer/Lancaster/Ohio	469	C	Pl
8517	J Armbruster/grocer/Lancaster/Ohio	423	C	Pl
8518	J Block Agt/ready/made/clothing/Talmage/block/Lancaster O	552	C	Pl
8519				
8520				
8521	Chas Pairan/grocer/and/liquor/dealer/Lancaster O	445	C	Pl
8522	same	446	C	Pl
8523	same	464	C	Pl
8524	same	671	C	Pl
8525	same	same	C-N	Pl
8526				
8527	Andrew Reid/dry goods/and/shoes/Lancaster O	329	C	Pl
8528	same	same	C-N	Pl
8529				
8530				

Laurelville

—8531	Geo D Reigel/dry goods/and/groceries/Laurelville/Ohio	421	C	Pl
8532	same	same	Br	Pl

OHIO—Continued

Laurelville—Continued

NUMBER	OBVERSE	REVERSE	METAL	EDGE
8533	same	423	C	Pl
8534	same	465	C	Pl
8535	same	499	C	Pl
8536				

Lima

8537	R Boose/dry goods/Lima/Ohio	428	C	Pl
8538	same	same	Br	Pl
8539	same	460	C	Pl
8540	same	480	C	Pl
8541				

London

8542	Jas Mc Laughlin dealer in cigars & tobacco London O	598	W-M	R
8543				

Loudenville

— 8544	F Schuch/dealer/in/groceries/ Loudenville/Ohio	421	C	Pl
8545				

Mansfield

— 8546	H Endly/dealer/in/hats/and/caps/ Mansfield O	303	C	Pl
8547	same	same	N	Pl
8548	F B Orr/dealer in/hardware/iron & nails/Mansfield O	29	C	Pl
8549	same	same	Br	Pl
8550				
8551	same	99	C	Pl
8552	same	same	Br	Pl
8553	same	same	N	Pl
8554	same	same	C-N	Pl
8555	same	same	W-M	Pl
8556	same	same	S	Pl
8557				
8558	same	108	Br	Pl
8559				
8560				
8561	same	185	Br	Pl
8562	same	same	N	Pl
8563	same	302	Br	Pl
8564				
8565				
8566				
8567	same	303	C	Pl
8568				
8569				

OHIO—Continued

Mansfield—Continued

NUMBER	OBVERSE	REVERSE	METAL	EDGE
8570	same	645	Br	Pl
8571	same	same	N	Pl
8572				
8573				

Marion

8574	'A E Griffin/dentist' above—Marion/Ohio' below—plate of teeth in centre	422	C	Pl
8575	same	425	C	Pl
8576				

Martinsburg

8577	A & W H Barnes/dry goods/Martinsburg/Ohio	442	C	Pl
8578	same	same	Br	Pl
8579	'M N Dayton' above—"Martinsburg/Ohio 'below—mortar and pestle in centre	Dealer in/drugs/medicines/&/groceries	C	Pl
8580				

Massillon

— 8581	P G Albright/wholesale/and/retail/grocer/Massillon O—name and address in large letters	424	C	Pl
8582	same	same	Br	Pl
8583	same	444	C	Pl
8584	same	461	C	Pl
8585				
8586	Same—this variety uses '&' instead of 'and' in legend—no star at sides	423	C	Pl
8587	same	446	C	Pl
8588	same	461	C	Pl
8589	same	same	Br	Pl
— 8590	same	462	C	Pl
— 8591	Similar to No 8581—letters all small—four stars at sides	423	C	Pl
8592	same	426	C	Pl
8593	same	461	C	Pl
8594	J B Dangler/dealer/in/dry goods/Massillon/Ohio	446	C	Pl
8595	same	479	C	Pl
8596				
8597				
8598	Fred Loeffler/retail/grocer/Main St/Massillon/Ohio	426	C	Pl
8599	same	621	C	Pl
8600	H Knobloch/retail/grocer/Erie St/Massillon Ohio	421	C	Pl
8601	same	426	C	Pl
8602	same	461	C	Pl
8603				
8604				

OHIO—Continued

Maumee City

NUMBER	OBVERSE	REVERSE	METAL	EDGE
8605	H Burritt/drugs/medicines/oils/ dye stuffs &c/Maumee City/Ohio	528	C	Pl
8606	same	same	Br	Pl
8607				
8608	Maumee / and / Perrysburg / toll / Bridge Co	442	C	Pl
8609	same	same	Br	Pl
8610				

McConnelsville

8611	H M Cochran/tobacco/manufacturer/McConnelsville/Ohio/1863	546	C	Pl
8612	same	same	Br	Pl
8613				

Middletown

8614	P L Potter/dealer/in/groceries/&/ queensware/Middletown O	405	C	Pl
8615	same	418	C	R
8616	same	same	Br	R
8617				
8618	same	420	C-N	R
8619	same	478	C	Pl
8620	same	Same as obverse of No 8166	C	Pl
8621				

Monroeville

8622	R G Martin/Man'fr/tin/sheet iron/ and/copperware/Monroeville/Ohio	424	C	Pl
8623	same	same	Br	Pl
8624	same	447	C	Pl
8625	same	478	C	Pl
8626	same	523	C	Pl
8627	R G Martin/hardware/stoves and/ tinware/Monroeville/Ohio	447	C	Pl
8628	same	523	C	Pl
8629				
8630	R G Martin/hardware stores/&/ tinware/Monroeville O	424	C	Pl
8631				
8632				
8633	A W Prentiss/dry goods/groceries/ boots & shoes/Monroeville O	447	Br	Pl
8634	same	479	C	Pl
8635	same	same	Br	Pl
8636	same	533	C	Pl
8637	same	same	Br	Pl
8638				

OHIO—Continued

Morristown

8639	P Lochary/new/store/Morristown O	442	C	Pl
8640	same	447	C	Pl
8641	same	same	Br	Pl
8642				

Morrow

8643	J M Dynes/dry goods/and/groceries at/auction/Morrow Ohio	524	C	Pl
8644				
8645	E Levy/dry goods/clothing/boots/shoes &c/Morrow Ohio	444	C	Pl
8646	same	469	C	Pl
8647				

Mt Eaton

8648	D Giaugue/dealer/in/groceries/and/provisions/Mt Eaton/O	423	C	Pl
8649				

Mussey

8650	E C Morse/dry/goods/Groceries/&c/Mussey	416	C	R
8651	same	418	C	R
8652	same	same	Br	R
8653	same	420	C	R
8654	same	same	C-N	R
8655				

Navarre

8656	Hall & Frymire/dealers/in/stoves/and/tinware/Navaree/Ohio	521	C	Pl
8657	same	same	Br	Pl
8658	same	523	C	Pl
8659				

Newcomerstown

8660	A S Twiford/photograph/artist/and/druggist/Newcomerstown/Ohio	528	C	Pl
8661	same	same	Br	Pl
8662				

New London

8663	H H Robinson/dry/goods/groceries/&/produce/New London B Co	68	C	Pl
8664	same	same as preceeding—incused	C	Pl
8665	same	418	C	R
8666	same	same	Br	R

OHIO—Continued

New London—Continued

NUMBER	OBVERSE	REVERSE	METAL	EDGE
8667				
8668	same	629	C	Pl
8669	same	656	C	Pl
8670	same	Blank	C	Pl
8671				
8672	Cheap/cash/store/C M Shaw/New London/Butler Co/Ohio	467	C	Pl
8673	same	468	C	Pl
8674	same	518	C	Pl
8675	same	546	C	Pl
8676	same	30	C	Pl
8677				

North Hampton

8678	M Hartman dry goods hardware boots & Shoes North Hampton O	419	C	R
8679	same	same	C-N	R
8680	same	420	C	R
8681				
8682	G W McLean/produce/dealer/ North Hampton O	416	C	R
8683	same	419	C	R
8684	same	same	Br	R
8685	same	same	C-N	R
8686				

North Liberty

8687	Sam'l Bishop/dealer/in/dry goods/ groceries &c/North Liberty/Ohio	442	C	Pl
8688	same	462	C	Pl
8689				

Norwalk

8690	P Timmins/groceries &/provisions/ Norwalk O	423	C	Pl
8691	same	426	C	Pl
8692				

Oberlin

8693	R H Birge/drugs/groceries &c/ sign big mortar/Main St/Oberlin O	528	C	Pl
8694				
8695	Frank Hendry/man'fr/of/spectacles &/eye glasses/Oberlin O	426	C	Pl
8696	same	471	C	Pl
8697				

Orville

8698	J F Seas/dealer/in/hardware/books /paints oils/&c/Orville O	400	C	Pl

OHIO—Continued
Orville—Continued

NUMBER	OBVERSE	REVERSE	METAL	EDGE
8699	same	405	C	Pl
8700	same	418	C	R
8701	same	same	Br	R
8702				
8703	same	same as die No 453—dated '1863'	C-N	R
8704				

Oxford

8705	McGaw & Richey/dealers/in/drugs /books/and/wall paper/Oxford O	30	C	Pl
8706	same	470	C	Pl
8707				
8708	Newton & Kumlers/dealers/in/dry/ goods/Oxford O	670	C	Pl
8709				

Perrysburg

8710	G Beach/dry goods/clothing/boots shoes &c/Perrysburg/Ohio	468	C	Pl
8711	same	471	C	Pl
8712	same	same	Br	Pl
8713				
8714	D Krebs/dealer in agricultural implements & farm tools Perrysburg Ohio	Portable steam engine reapers mowers cane mills & evaporators	Br	Pl
8715				

Piqua

8716	Drs Brown & Dills/dentists/Piqua/ Ohio	468	C	Pl
8717	same	421	C	Pl
8718	same	444	C	Pl
8719	same	445	C	Pl
8720	same	446	C	Pl
8721				
8722	Same—eagle in glory	plate of teeth in centre— 'Branch Office' above—'Troy/ Ohio' below	C	Pl
8723	same	same	Br	Pl
8724				
8725	French & Swonger/daily meat/ market/Piqua O	506	C	Pl
8726				
8727	Martin Hoegner/daily/meat/market/Piqua O	506	C	Pl
8728				
8729	Smart & Co/grocers/136/Main St/ Piqua O	442	C	Pl
8730	same	479	C	Pl

OHIO—Continued

Piqua—Continued

NUMBER	OBVERSE	REVERSE	METAL	EDGE
8731	-			
8732	-			

Pomeroy

NUMBER	OBVERSE	REVERSE	METAL	EDGE
8733	J P Tou/grocer/104/Front/St/ Pomeroy O	68	C	Pl
8734	same	418	C	R
8735	same	same	Br	R
8736	same	Same as Die No 453—dated '1863'	C-N	R
8737	same	656	C	Pl
8738				
8739				
8740				

Portsmouth

NUMBER	OBVERSE	REVERSE	METAL	EDGE
8741	Burton's/exchange/Portsmouth O	Good for/10/cents/1862	Br	Pl
8742				
8743	S W Cunning/wholesale/liquors/ No 6/Front St/Portsmouth O	417	C	Pl
8744	same	418	C	R
8745	same	same	Br	R
8746	same	420	C-N	R
8747				

Putnam

NUMBER	OBVERSE	REVERSE	METAL	EDGE
8748	L Wiles/dry goods/&c/Putnam O	445	C	Pl
8749	same	469	C	Pl
8750	same	671	C	Pl
8751				

Ravenna

NUMBER	OBVERSE	REVERSE	METAL	EDGE
— 8752	Butler Witter & Co/dealers/in/ W R/butter/and cheese/Ravenna/ Ohio	Butler Witter & Co/dealers/ in/family/groceries/8 Phoenix /block/Ravenna/Ohio	C	Pl
8753	same	30	C	Pl
8754	same	same—incused	C	Pl
8755				
8756	Dr D R Jennings/surgeon/dentist/ Ravenna/Ohio	421	C	Pl
8757	same	443	C	Pl
8758	same	558	C	Pl
8759				
8760	C A Pease/dealer/in/groceries/ fruits &c/4Phoenix Block/Ravenna/Ohio	421	C	Pl
8761	same	471	C	Pl
8762	same	478	C	Pl
8763				

OHIO—Continued
Ravenna—Continued

NUMBER	OBVERSE	REVERSE	METAL	EDGE
8764	Mrs Reed/millinery/and/fancy/ goods/Ravenna/Ohio	329	C	Pl
8765				
8766	Buy/your/dry goods/of/Wm Ward/ Ravenna/Ohio/1863	Wm Ward/pays/the/highest/ market/price for/butter/and/ cheese	C	Pl
8767				
8768				
8769				

Richmond

8770	B L Crew/dry/goods/&/groceries/ Richmond O	68	C	Pl
8771	same	418	C	R
8772	same	same	Br	R
8773				
8774	same	419	C-N	R
8775	same	656	C	Pl
8776				

Sharonville

8777	W J McMillins/store/Sharonville O	418	C	R
8778	same	same	Br	R
8779	Same			Pl
8780	same	same as Die No 453—dated '1863'	C-N	R
8781				

Shelby

8782	Cummings & Anderson/dry/goods/ groceries/&/millinery/Shelby O	416	C	R
8783	same	672	C	R
8784	same	same	Br	R
8785				
8786				
8787	Thos Mickey/Shelby/Ohio/dry goods/groceries/hats caps/and/millinery goods/	Highest/cash/ price/paid/for/ country produce	C	Pl
8788				

Sidney

8789	Fry & Johnson/dry goods/boots/ & shoes/Sidney O	428	C	Pl
8790	same	442	C	Pl
8791	same	462	C	Pl
8792				
8793	Jason McVay/dry goods/boots/ shoes &c/Sidney O	552	C	Pl
8794				

OHIO—Continued

Sidney—Continued

NUMBER	OBVERSE	REVERSE	METAL	EDGE
8795	S N Todd & Co/druggists/&/ stationers/Sidney O	532	C	Pl
8796				

Sonora

8797	William Leas/call/at the /cash/ store/Sonora O	428	C	Pl
8798				
8799				

Springfield

8800	W G Brain/cash/druggist/Market St/Springfield O	404	C	R
8801	same	410	C	R
8802	same	411	C	R
8803	same	415	C	Pl
8804	same	418	C	R
8805	same	same	Br	R
8806	same	same	Z	R
8807	same	615	C	Pl
8808	same	661	C	Pl
8809				
8810	Kaufman & Co/cigars/&/ liquors/ Market/St/Springfield O	415	C	Pl
8811	same	418	C	R
8812	same	same	Br	R
8813	same	same	Z	R
8814	same	419	C-N	R
8815	same	656	C	Pl
8816				
— 8817	J W Low/books/&/wall paper/ Market/St/Springfield O	416	Br	R
8818	same	418	C	R
8819	same	same	Br	R
8820	same	same	Z	R
8821	same	419	C	R
8822	same	same	Br	R
8823	same	663	C	Pl
8824	same	672	Br	Pl
8825				
8826	Ludlow & Bushnell/druggists/85/ Main St/Springfield O	404	C	R
8827	same	406	C	Pl
8828	same	418	C	R
8829	same	same	Br	R
8830	same	same	Z	R
8831	same	420	C	R
8832	same	same as die No 453—dated '1863'	C	R
8833	same	615	C	Pl

214

OHIO—Continued

Springfield—Continued

NUMBER	OBVERSE	REVERSE	METAL	EDGE
8834				
8835	G W McLean/produce/dealer/Springfield O	418	C	R
8836	same	same	Br	R
8837				
8838	same	419	C-N	R
8839				
8840	Murphy & Bro/dry/goods/Market/St/Springfield O	416	C	Pl
8841	same	418	C	R
8842	same	same	Br	R
8843				
8844	same	same as die No 453—dated '1863'	C-N	R
8845	C Runyon/groceries/Market/St/Springfield O	416	C	R
8847	same	same	Br	R
8848	same	same	Z	R
8849	same	419	C-N	R
8850				

The obverse die of Runyon cards has 'Springfield' misspelled 'Spingfield'

Steubenville

8851	Wm Dunlap dry goods & groceries Fourth St Steubenville Ohio	671	C	Pl
8852	same	same	C-N	Pl
8853				
8854	J H Bristor/cor/Fourth/and/Market/Steubenville O	432	C	Pl
8855	Same	542	C	Pl
8856	Same	Same as obverse of No 7332	C	Pl
8857	J W Gray/groceries/and/dry goods/Cor Adams/&/Sixth/Steubenville O	446	C	Pl
8858	Same	471	C	Pl
8859	Same	Same	Br	Pl
8860	Same	478	C	Pl
8861	Same	621	C	Pl
8862				
8863	J H Hind's/news/depot/cor/4th & Market/Steubenville/Ohio	Same as obverse of No 7332	C	Pl
8864	Same	538	C	Pl
8865	Same	671	C	Pl
8866				
8867	C M May/merchant/tailor/and/clothier/Steubenville/Ohio	552	C	Pl
8868	Same	556	C	Pl
8869				
8870	J McCauley/grocer/Fourth St/Steubenville/Ohio	464	C	Pl

OHIO—Continued

Steubenville—Continued

NUMBER	OBVERSE	REVERSE	METAL	EDGE
8871				
8872	D McConville/dry goods/and/notions/ Steubenville/Ohio	469	C	Pl
8873	Same	671	C	Pl
8874				
8875				

Stryker

8876	'John S. Kingsland/& Bro' above—small mortar and pestle in centre—'Druggists/Stryker/Ohio' below	20	C	Pl
8877	Same	594	C	Pl
8878				
8879	G W Hamblin/general/goods/dealer/Stryker—Ohio	26	C	Pl
8880	Same	27	C	Pl

Syracuse

8881	H Bartels/dry/goods/groceries/boots/&/shoes/Syracuse O	419	C	R
8882	Same	Same	C-N	R
8883	Same	420	C	R

Tiffin

8884	M J Kirchner/groceries/Washington/St/Tiffin O	416	C	R
8885	Same	419	C-N	R
8886	Same	420	C	R
8887				
— 8888	'Souder/&/Carpenter's/card' within a wreath	Dry goods/dealers / Tiffin Ohio	Bronze	Pl
8889	Same	Wholesale/&/retail/dry goods/ Tiffin Ohio	Bronze	Pl
3390				

Tippecanoe

8891	E C Saylor/daily/meat/market/Tippecanoe O	465	C	Pl
8892	Same	506	C	Pl
8893	Same	Same	C-N	Pl
8894				

Toledo

— 8895	C P Curtis/auction/& commission/merchant/157 Summit St/Toledo/Ohio	423	C	Pl
— 8896	Same	446	C	Pl
8897	Same	471	C	Pl

OHIO—Continued

Toledo—Continued

NUMBER	OBVERSE	REVERSE	METAL	EDGE
8898	Same	479	C	Pl
8899				
8900	Hough & Hall/dry goods/carpets/ oil cloths &c/23 Summit St/Toledo/ Ohio	471	C	Pl
8901	Same	Same	Br	Pl
8902	Same	478	C	Pl
8903	Same	Same	Br	Pl
8904	Hough & Hall/dry goods/carpets/ oil cloths &c/113 Summit St/Toledo Ohio	422	C	Pl
8905				
8906	Ketcham & Barker/dealers/in/ hardware/stoves &/tinware/Toledo Ohio	525	C	Pl
8907	Same	Same	Br	Pl
8908				
8909	Plessner & Son/druggists/23/ Summit St/ Toledo Ohio Small mortar and pestle in field	528	C	Pl
8910	Same	Same	Br	Pl
8911				

Troy

8912	J Hall/Grain/dealer/Troy O	Railroad/1863/Warehouse	C	Pl
8913				
8914	S K Harter/dealer/in/iron nails/ hardware/guns pistols/&c/Troy O	547	C	Pl
8915				
8916				
8917	S E Hustler/Brown's/old/corner/ Troy O	428	C	Pl
8918	Same	460	C	Pl
8919	Same	480	C	Pl
8920	Same	534	C	Pl
8921	Same	Same	Br	Pl
8922	Same	'Wm Senour' in script	C	Pl
8923				
8924	Julian & Co/watchmakers/&/ jewelers/Troy O	427	C	Pl
8925	Same	536	C	Pl
8926				
8927	David Kelly/dealer/in/books/ stationery/&c/Troy O	30	C	Pl
8928	Same	470	C	Pl
8929				
8930				
8931	Pearson & Bro/wholesale/&/retail/grocers/Troy O	460	C	Pl
8932	Same	465	C	Pl

OHIO—Continued

Troy—Continued

NUMBER	OBVERSE	REVERSE	METAL	EDGE
8933	Same	480	C	Pl
8934	Same	560	C	Pl
8935	Same	671	C	Pl
8936				
8937	Rinehart & Gray/cash/druggists/ successors/to/R Wright/Troy O	445	C	Pl
8938	Same	470	C	Pl
8939				
8940				

Uniontown

8941	Fanley & Brechbill dry goods clothing & groceries Uniontown	549	C	Pl
8942		425	C	Pl

Urbana

8943	Washington McCarty Urbana O	Same as die No 453—dated '1863'	C-N	R
8944	Washington House, C. McCarty, Urbana O.	420	C	R

Van Wert

8945	A Jacobs/merchant tailor/&/ready made/clothing/Van Wert/Ohio	556	C	Pl
8946				
8947				

Wappakoneta

8948	Davis & Whitman/grocers/and/commission/merchants/Wappakoeta/Ohio	423	C	Pl
8949	Same	463	C	Pl
8950	Same	550	C	Pl
8951	Same	551	C	Pl
8952				
8953	A A C Miles/groceries/&/stationery/Wappakoneta O	541	C	Pl
8954				
8955	Momento of the Sanitary Fair of Wappakoneta O	Trophy of flags and arms with eagle perched on drum in centre	C	Pl
8956				
8957	J H Timmermeister/dry goods/&/groceries/Wappakoneta O	471	C	Pl
8958				

Warren

8959	'Robbins/Card' within a wreath	Photographic/albums/15/Market St/Warren Ohio	C	Pl

8944a   Walker's Ale Depot   404   C   R

OHIO—Continued
Warren—Continued

NUMBER	OBVERSE	REVERSE	METAL	EDGE
8960	Same	Same	Bronze	Pl
8961				

Wellsville

8962	Hoover & Camp/pianos/melodians/and/musical/Mds/Wellsville O	469	C	Pl
8963	Same	538	C	Pl
8964				
8965	Wm Lawrence/clothier/and/photographic/artist/Wellsville O	469	C	Pl
8966				

West Jefferson

8967	'John Tressler/grocery/store'in centre—'West Jefferson Wms Co Ohio' above—'1863' below	551	C	Pl
8968	Same	Same	Br	Pl
8969	Same	560	C	Pl
8970	Same	Same	Br	Pl
8971				
8972				

West Newton

8973	C M Coffin/dealer/in/dry/goods/&c/West Newton Ohio	419	C	R
8974				
8975				
8976				
8977				
8978				
8979				

West Unity

8980	Davies & Maxwell/dealers/in/hardware/and/agricultural/machinery West Unity/Ohio	445	C	Pl
8981				
8982	W H McGrew/druggist/West Unity/Ohio small mortar and pestle in centre	426	C	Pl
8983	Same	446	C	Pl
8984	Same	447	C	Pl
8985				
8986	S Pierce & Son/dealers/in/dry goods/groceries/&c/West Unity O	422	C	Pl
8987	Same	461	C	Pl
8988	Same	Same	Br	Pl
8989				

OHIO—Continued

West Unity—Continued

NUMBER	OBVERSE	REVERSE	METAL	EDGE
8990	S F Snow/dentist/West Unity/ Ohio plate of teeth in centre	446	C	Pl
8991	Same	621	C	Pl
8992				

Wilmington

8993	Mrs Owen & Taylor Millinery and fancy store South St near depot Wilmington O	182	C	Pl
8994	Same	339	C	Pl
8995	Same	446	C	Pl
8996	Same	469	C	Pl
8997				
8998	H Perrin/hardware/groceries/&c/ Wilmington O	469	C	Pl
8999	Same	Same	C-N	Pl
9000				
9001	Cheap/cash/store/Wm Preston/ Wilmington/Ohio	624	C	Pl
9002				
9003	T R Wraith/hardware/merchant/ Wilmington O	Sugar/mills/and/evaporators	C	Pl
9004	Same	Same	C-N	Pl
9005	Same	469	C	Pl
9006				
9007				

Woodsfield

9008	J W Walton/grocer/Woodsfield/ Ohio	J W Walton/pension/Agent	C	Pl
9009	Same	Same	Br	Pl
9010	Same	460	C	Pl
9011	Same	Same	Br	Pl
9012				

Wooster

9013	'P E Beach' above—silk hat in centre—'Wooster Ohio' below	Dealer in/hats/caps/&/ fancy goods	C	Pl
9014	Same	Same	Br	Pl
9015	Same	Same	N	Pl
9016	Same	Same	C-N	Pl
9017	Same	Same	W-M	Pl
9018	Same	Same	S	Pl
9019				
9020	J R Bowman/dealer/in/watches/ cloths/&/jewelry/West Liberty St/Wooster O	418	C	R
9021	Same	Same	Br	R
9022	Same	Same	Z	R

OHIO—Continued

Wooster—Continued

NUMBER	OBVERSE	REVERSE	METAL	EDGE
9023	Same	419	C-N	R
9024	Same	615	C	Pl
9225	Same	634	C	Pl
9026	G Brumter/dealer/in/groceries/ W Liberty St/Wooster/Ohio	423	C	Pl
9027	Same	426	C	Pl
9028	Same	469	C	Pl
9029	Same	471	C	Pl
9030	James B Childs/clothing/hats Caps/&/trunks/Wooster Ohio	601	C	Pl
9031	Same	602	C	Pl
9032				
9033	J S Duden/dealer/in/groceries/ and/provisions/Wooster/Ohio	445	C	Pl
9034				
9035	Samuel Geitgey/dealer/in/stoves and/tinware/of/all kinds/Wooster O	470	C	Pl
9036	Same	Same incused	C	Pl
9037	Same	524	C	Pl
9038				
9039	'John Leis' above—figure '5' in centre— 'Wooster O' below	557	C	Pl
9040	Same	Same	Br	Pl
9041	S C Martin/Wooster/Ohio	Good for/5 cents/in trade	Br	Pl
9042	Miller & Co/queensware/and/ glassware/near/post office/Wooster O	Dealer/in hoop/skirts/hats caps/and/notions	C	Pl
9043	Same	30	C	Pl
9044	Same	446	C	Pl
9045	Same	468	C	Pl
9046	Same	469	C	Pl
9047	Same	546	C	Pl
9048				
9049	Nold & Co/dealers/in/pork/and/ beef/Wooster/Ohio	423	C	Pl
9050	Same	469	C	Pl
9051				
9052	James Patrick/butter/packer/ Wooster Ohio	443	C	Pl
9053				
9054	C Roth/Manuf'r/and dealer/in boots/and shoes/Wooster/Ohio	533	C	Pl
9055				
9056	Rowe & Bro/watches/clocks and/ jewelry/S E Cor Pub/Square/ Wooster O	445	C	Pl
9057	Same	536	C	Pl
9058				

OHIO—Continued

Xenia

NUMBER	OBVERSE	REVERSE	METAL	EDGE
9059	F J Halls/wholesale/&/retail/ grocery &/confectionery/store/ Xenia O	423	C	Pl
9060				

Youngstown

9061	'W & A J Packard' above—U S shield in centre—'Youngstown Ohio' below	Warren Packard/hardware/ and/iron/Warren Ohio	C	Pl
9062	Same	Same	Br	Pl

Zanesville

9063	Barrell's/worm/confections/ H G O Cary/Zanesville/Ohio	Cary's/C C C/cough/cure— four stars at each side	C	Pl
9064	Same	Same	Br	Pl
9065	Address/H G O Cary/druggist/ and/chemist/Zanesville O	Same	C	Pl
9066	Same	Same	C-N	Pl
9067	Same	Same—four stars omitted	C	Pl
9068	Same	Same	C-N	Pl
9069				
9070				
9071	Joseph Crosby/grocer/and/tea dealer/83/Main St/Zanesville O	444	C	Pl
9072	Same	445	C	Pl
9073	Same	469	C	Pl
9074	Same	671	C	Pl
9075	Same	Same as obverse of No 7332	C	Pl
9076				
9077	Everich & Barton/grocer/and/ liquor/dealer/Zanesville/Ohio	329	C	Pl
9078				
9079	Alexr Grant & Co/dry goods/ Zanesville/Ohio	444	C	Pl
9080	Same	Same	C-N	Pl
9081	Same	Same as obverse of No 7332	C	Pl
9082				
9083	G W Griffee/news/dealer/sta- tioner/&c/Zanesville O	428	C	Pl
9084	Same	538	C	Pl
9085				
9086	Same	540	C	Pl
9087	Same	Same	C-N	Pl
9088	W B Harris & Bro/dry goods/ groceries/hardware/&c/Zanes- ville O	422	C	Pl
9089	Same	442	C	Pl
9090	Same	446	C	Pl
9091	Same	447	C	Pl
9092	Same	469	C	Pl

OHIO—Continued

Zanesville—Continued

NUMBER	OBVERSE	REVERSE	METAL	EDGE
9093	Same	Same as obverse of No 7332	C	Pl
9094	Same	470	C	Pl
9095				
9096				
9096	Herendeen & Witter/Singer/sewing/machines/Zanesville/Ohio	556	C	Pl
9098				
9099	John Irwin/wholesale/dealer in/wines & liquors/cor Main & Sixth/Zanesville/Ohio	421	C	Pl
9100	Same	426	C	Pl
9101	Same	621	C	Pl
9102				
9103	'C W Potwin & Co' above—padlock in centre—'Zanesville O' below	Agricultural implement/ sadlery/and/carriage/trimmings	C	Pl
9104	Same	Same	C-N	Pl
9105	Same	Same as obverse of No 7332	C	Pl
9106	Same	Same	Br	Pl
9107	Same	Same as obverse of No 7417	C	Pl
9108	Same	Same	Br	Pl
9109				
9110	Webster Dumm & Co/tobacconists/Zanesville O	469	C	Pl
9111	Same	471	C	Pl

PENNSYLVANIA

Allegheny City

NUMBER	OBVERSE	REVERSE	METAL	EDGE
9200	Wm Carson/leather/merchant/40/ Ohio/St/Allegheny City	418	C	R
9201	Same	Same	Br	R
8202				
9203	Same	419	C-N	R
9304	Same	629	C	Pl
9205				
9206	Gregg & Dalzell/National/Planing/ Mill/Allegheny City	Flooring/mouldings / sash/ blinds/doors/&c	C	Pl
9207	Same	412	C	Pl
9208	Same	418	C	R
9209	Same	Same	Br	R
9210				
9211	Same	420	C-N	R
9212				
9213	Hahn & Riddle/grocers/diamond/ Allegheny Pa	City/tea/house/No 20/dia- mond/Allegheny Pa	C	Pl
9214	Same	418	C	R
9215	Same	Same	Br	R
9216				
9217	Same	420	C	R
9218	Same as reverse of No 9213	418	C	R
9219	Same	Same	Br	R
9220	Same	420	C	R
9221	R & W Jenkinson/tobacco/dealers/ Allegheny Pa	30	C	Pl
9222	Same	467	C	Pl
9223	Same	518	C	Pl
9224	Same	546	C	Pl
9225	Same	Same	W-M	Pl
9226	Same	565	C	Pl
9227	R & W Jenkinson/tobacconists/ No 6/Federal/St/Allegheny City	418	C	R
9828	Same	Same	Br	R
9829	Same	Same	Z	R
9830	Same	420	C	R
9831	Same	617	C	Pl
9232	Same	661	C	Pl
9233				
9234	John Sherer/tobacco/dealer/75/ Federal St/Allegheny City	30	C	Pl
9235	Same	Same	Br	Pl
9236	Same	Same	C-N	Pl
9237	Same	467	C	Pl
9238	Same	468	C	Pl
9239	Same	Same	C-N	Pl
9240	Same	470	C	Pl
9241	Same	518	C	Pl
9242	Same	546	C	Pl
9243	Same	Reymer & Bros/confec- tioners/Pittsburg/Pa	C	Pl
9244				

PENNSYLVANIA—Continued
Bakerstown

NUMBER	OBVERSE	REVERSE	METAL	EDGE
9245	James Maines/gallery/Main St/ Bakerstown Pa	444	C	Pl
9246	Same	469	C	Pl
9247				

Erie

9248	For/bargains/in/dry goods/go to/ Wm Bell's/5 Exchange/Erie Pa	The reverse of this card is the obverse of the cent of '1859'	C-N	Pl
9249				

Honesdale

— 9250	Petersen's/Honesdale/Scranton/ Pittston/Pa/Jewelers	29	C	Pl
9251				
9252	Same	Same	Br	Pl
9253	Same	Same	N	Pl
9254	Same	Same	C-N	Pl
9255				
9256	Same			
9257	Same	99	C	Pl
9258	Same	Same	Br	Pl
9259	Same	Same	N	Pl
9260	Same	Same	C-N	Pl
9261		Same	W-M	Pl
9262	Same			
9263	Same	108	C	Pl
9264	Same	Same	Br	Pl
9265	Same	Same	N	Pl
9266	Same	Same	C-N	Pl
9267		Same	W-M	Pl
9268				
9269	Same	185	Br	Pl
9270				
9271	Same			
9272	Same	Same	C-N	Pl
9273		Same	W-M	Pl
9274				
9275	Same			
9276	Same	302	Br	Pl
9277	Same	Same	N	Pl
9278	Same	Same	C-N	Pl
9279		Same	W-M	Pl
9280				
9281	Same	645	Br	Pl
9282	Same	Same	N	Pl
9283	Same	Same	C-N	Pl
9284				

PENNSYLVANIA—Continued

Johnstown

NUMBER	OBVERSE	REVERSE	METAL	EDGE
9285	Columbia Hotel/Wm/Bock/Prop/ Johnstown Pa	Good for/5/cents/in trade	Br	Pl

Lancaster

9286	S H Zahm/dealer/in/coins/tokens/ medals &c/Lancaster Pa	494	C	Pl
9287	Same	Same	Br	Pl
9288	Same	Same	W-M	Pl
9289	Same	Same	S	Pl

Lawrenceville

9290	Wm Smith/grocer/Lawrenceville/ Pa	468	C	Pl
9291	Same	470	C	Pl
9292	Same	518	C	Pl
9293	Same	546	C	Pl
9294				

Meadville

9295	G C Porter & Co/clothing &/gents furnishing/goods/Meadville Pa	'Go to G C Porter & Co' above—Indian head to left in centre—'For your dry goods' below	C	Pl
9296				

Philadelphia

9297	Small helmeted head with 'Adams' below in a laurel wreath	ton Hall/457/North 3d St/ Phila	C	Pl
9298	Same	Same	Br	Pl
9299	Same	Same	Bronze	Pl
9300	;			
9301	M E Allebach/watch/maker/& jeweler/126/N 2nd St/Philadelphia	430	C	Pl
9302	Same	Same	Br	Pl
9303	Same	Same	N	Pl
9304	Same	Same	C-N	Pl
9305	Same	Same	W-M	Pl
9306	Same	Same	S	Pl
9307				
9308				
9309				
9310	Same	466	N	Pl
9311	Same	Same	W-M	Pl
9312				
9313				
9314	'Amon' above—sheaf of wheat in centre—'1863' below	Bakery/1011/Beach St/Phila	C	Pl
9315				

1342a Dr. Fleming + Leidy Blood Purifier   WM

1343a Idler's Lord Baltimore taken

PENNSYLVANIA—Continued

Philadelphia—Continued

NUMBER	OBVERSE	REVERSE	METAL	EDGE
9316	'Baltz & Stilz/importers of 'above —bunch of grapes in centre— 'Wines/Philadelphia Pa' below	586	C	Pl
9317	Baltz & Stilz/importers of/333/ wines/North 3 St/Phila	586	C	Pl
9318				
9319	M F Beirn/Magnolia/Hotel/100 So 8th St/Philadelphia	466	C	Pl
8320	Same	Same	Br	Pl
9321	Same	Same	N	Pl
9322	Same	Same	C-N	Pl
9323	Same	Same	W-M	Pl
9324				
9325	Same	430	C	Pl
9326				
9327	Same	114	C	Pl
9328	Same	Same	Br	Pl
9329	Same	Same	C-N	Pl
9330	Same	Same	W-M	Pl
9331				
9332	Same	Same as die No 114—no inscription	W-M	Pl
9333				
9334	'M O Campbell's' above—'cor 8 and/Sp/Garden/St/Phila' in centre—'dancing Academy' below	Skating / Academy / Washington Hall	C	Pl
9335				
9336	'Coombs/1863' within a wreath	Second St Exchange/432/ N Second/St/Phila	C	Pl
9337				
9338	Central National D V S Home for	Good for 5 cents at store	C	Pl
9339	Same	Good for 10 cents at store	C	Pl
9340				
9341	'R Flanagan's/Punch' above—goblet in centre—'112 156/North 6th St' below	Pure copper/preferable/to/ paper/money	C	Pl
9342	Same	Same	C	R
9343	Great/Central/Fair/Philadelphia/ June 1864	658	C	R
9344	'North Military Hall' above—lyre in centre—'F & L Ladner/532 N 3 St' below	584	C	Pl
9345	Same	585	C	Pl
9346				
9347	Lambert/Cor 4th/and/Library St/ Philada	429	C	Pl
9348	Same	Same	Br	Pl
9349				
9350	'H Mulligan' above—watch and chain in centre—444 N 2nd St Phila' below	Importer/of/watches/manufacturer of/jewelry/Agent/ for/Eastern jewelry	Br	Pl

PENNSYLVANIA—Continued

Philadelphia—Continued

NUMBER	OBVERSE	REVERSE	METAL	EDGE
9351	Same	Same	N	Pl
9352	Same	Same	C-N	Pl
9352	Same inscription as preceding—portrait in centre instead of watch	Same	Br	Pl
9354	Same	Same	N	Pl
9355				
9356	'F P Rogers 937 S 10th St Phila Pa' around border—milk can dividing date '1863' in centre	Manufacturer/of/milk cans/dairy/fixtures/roofing & Gutter tin	C	Pl
9357	Same	Same	N	Pl
9358	Same inscription and design as preceding—comma instead of period after 'Rogers'	Same	C	Pl
9359	Same	Same	N	Pl
9360	Same	Obverse incused	N	Pl
9361	Same as obverse of No 9356	Same	C	Pl
9362				
9363	'G J Ruelius/319/North 4 St/Phila' in a circle of 14 stars	Building with staff and flag in centre—'Philada City Hotel' above—'1863' below	C	Pl
✗ 9364	Same	Same	Br	Pl
9365				
✗ 9366	Steppacher/Agt/Orleans/House/531/Chestnut St/Phila	586	C	Pl
9367				
9368	'N & G Taylor Co/1863' above—Bust of Washington to right in centre—'303/Branch St/Philadelphia' below	Tin plates/files/metals/steel/wire copper &c Size 28 M M	C	Pl
9369				
9370				

Pittsburgh

9371	Allegheny Valley/railroad/hotel/opposite/depot/Pittsburg Pa	418	C	R
9372	Same	Same	Br	R
9373				
9374	Same	419	C-N	R
9375	Same	634	C	R
9376	Same	Same	Br	R
9377	Same	Same	C	Pl
9378				
9379	F Beilsteine/butcher/105/Diamond/St/ E Side/Pittsburg	30	C	Pl
9380	Same	468	C	Pl
9381	Same	Same	W-M	Pl
9382	Same	582	C	Pl
9383				
— 9384	Buffums/mineral/water/Pittsburg	Bottle within a circle of 27 crosses	C	Pl

✗ 9364a	S. Ruskin	1 New Market + Popular		B
✗ 9365a	John Schmidt	leather findings	Capital	E
— 9365b	" "	" "	—	E
— 9369a	Taylor Apothecary	Drugs Medicines		C
— 9369b	A.B Taylor	Soda Water		WM.

PENNSYLVANIA—Continued

Pittsburgh—Continued

NUMBER	OBVERSE	REVERSE	METAL	EDGE
9385				
9386	J A Eckert/butcher/111/Diamond/ market/Pittsburg	30	C	Pl
9387	Same	467	C	Pl
9388	Same	468	C	Pl
9389	Same	518	C	Pl
9390	Same	546	C	Pl
9391				
9392	Jos Fleming/druggist/cor Market St/& the/Diamond/Pittsburg	418	C	R
9393	Same	Same	Br	R
9394				
9395	Same	419	C-N	R
9396	Same	617	C	Pl
9397	Same	659	C	Pl
9398				
9399	W A Gildenfenney/books/papers/ &/stationery/45 Fifth St/Pittsburg	210	C	Pl
9400	Same	Same	C	R
9401	Same	418	C	R
9402	Same	Same	Br	R
9403	Same	420	C	R
9404	Same	660	C	Pl
9405				
9406	D A Hall & Co/tea/dealers/27/ Fifth St/Pittsburg	30	C	Pl
9407	Same	582	C	Pl
9408				
9409	J W Hannah/81/Liberty/St/Pittsburg Pa	468	C	Pl
9410	Same	621	C	Pl
9411				
9412	J C & W H Lippincott/grocers/ No 19/Diamond/Pittsburg/Pa	30	C	Pl
9413	Same	467	C	Pl
9414	Same	468	C	Pl
9415				
9416	A Ludewig/dealer in / tobacco snuff/and/cigars/310 & 312/Liberty St/Pittsburg Pa	Full sized portrait of man in centre—'Coppers 20 pr ct Premium'	C	Pl
9417				
9418	J W McCarthy/Bill/Poster/Pittsburg	418	C	R
9419	Same	Same	Br	R
9420				
9421	Same	617	C	Pl
9422				
9423				
9424	JMc Kain/grocer/Mount/Washington	593	C	Pl

PENNSYLVANIA—Continued

Pittsburgh—Continued

NUMBER	OBVERSE	REVERSE	METAL	EDGE
9425				
9426	Henry Miner/news/dealer/71 & 73 Fifth St/Pittsburg	574	Br	Pl
9427				
9428	Henry Miner/news/dealer/71 & 73/ Fifth St/Pittsburg	30	C	Pl
9429	same	same	C-N	Pl
9430	same	340	C	Pl
9431	same	400	C	Pl
9432	same	467	C	Pl
9433	same	470	C	Pl
9434	same	518	C	Pl
9435	same	546	C	Pl
9436				
9437	Pekin/tea/store/No 50/St Clair St/Pittsburg	412	C	Pl
9438	same	415	C	Pl
9439	same	same as Die No. 453—dated '1863'	C-N	Pl
9440	same	629	C	Pl
9441	same	656	C	Pl
9442	same	673	C	Pl
9443	same	418	C	R
9444	A C Pentz/tin copper &/sheet iron ware/stoves/20/Penn, St/Pittsburg	408	C	Pl
9445	same	418	C	R
9446	same	420	C	R
9447	same	same as die No 453-dated '1863'	C-N	R
9448				
9449	Pittock/news/dealer/Pittsburg	210	C	Pl
9450	same	415	C	Pl
9451	same	418	C	R
9452	same	same	Br	R
9453				
9454	same	same as die No 453-dated '1863'	C-N	R
9455				
9456	Pittock's/news/depot/opp/post/office/Pittsburg	30	C	Pl
9457	same	same	C-N	Pl
9458	same	467	C	Pl
9459	same	same	C-N	Pl
9460	same	same	W-M	Pl
9461	same	470	C	Pl
9462	same	509	C	Pl
9463	same	same	W-M	Pl
9464	same	518	C	Pl
9465				
9466	Pittock/news/dealer/opposite P O/ Pittsburg Pa	'Pittock's/card'/in a wreath	C	Pl

PENNSYLVANIA—Continued

Pittsburgh—Continued

NUMBER	OBVERSE	REVERSE	METAL	EDGE
9467	same	same	Bronze	Pl
9468				
9469	Pittock's/news/dealer/opp/post office/Pittsburg	30 470	C C	Pl Pl
9470	same	540	C	Pl
9471	same			
9472				
9473	John W Pittock/news/dealer/opposite/Post Office/Pittsburg	same as obverse of No 7886	C	Pl
9474	same	406	C	Pl
9475	same	418	C	R
9476	same	same	Br	R
9477	same	420	C	R
9478	same	622	C	Pl
9479	same	634	C	Pl
9480				
9481	Pittsburgh/dry goods/groceries/hardware & notions	603	C	Pl
9482	same	604	C	Pl
9483				
9484	Drugs/dry goods/groceries/hard-	601	C	Pl
9485	same	602	C	Pl
9486				
9487	Pittsburgh/gazette/84/Fifth/St	467	C	Pl
9488	same	468	C	Pl
9489	same	546	C	Pl
9490	same	670	C	Pl
9491				
9492	Reymers & Bros/confectioners/Pittsburg/Pa	468	C	Pl
9493	same	546	C	Pl
9494	same	Same as obverse on No 3035	C	Pl
9495	same	Also cutlery notions &c	C	Pl
9496				
9497	Sinclair & Wilson/clothing/store/120/Market St/Pittsburg	468	C	Pl
9498				
9499	Frank Snyder/tobacco/and/sugars/43/Fourth St/Pittsburg	30	C	Pl
9500	same	329	C	Pl
9501	same	468	C	Pl
9502	same	546	C	Pl
9503				
9504				

West Greenville

9505	Packard & Co/hardware/&/iron/West Greenville Pa	D E Packard & Co/grocery/West Greenville Pa	Br	Pl
9506				

231

RHODE ISLAND

Providence

9507	Arcade/House/62/Broad St/Providence R I	493	C	Pl
9508	same	same	Br	Pl
9509	same	same	N	Pl
9510	same	same	L	Pl
9511	same	same	Ger-S	Pl
9512				
9513	same	496	C	Pl
9514	same	same	Br	Pl
9515	same	same	N	Pl
9516	same	same	L	Pl
9517	same	same	Ger-S	Pl
9518				
9519	same	581	C	Pl
9520	same	same	Br	Pl
9521	same	same	N	Pl
9522	same	same	L	Pl
9523	same	same	Ger-S	Pl
9524				
— 9525	same	'H Dobson' above- 'Union/		
9526	same	1864' in centre-wreath below	C	Pl
		same	Br	Pl
9527	same	same	N	Pl
9528	same	same	C-N	Pl
9529	same	same	Ger-S	Pl
9530	same	same	L	Pl
9531	Anchor on shield in centre- 'Charnlay' and 13 stars above—No 11 Orange St/Providence R I 'below	493	C	Pl
9532	same	same	Br	Pl
9533	same	same	N	Pl
9534	same	same	L	Pl
9535	same	same	Ger-S	Pl
9536				
9537	same	496	C	Pl
9538	same	same	Br	Pl
9539	same	same	N	Pl
9540	same	same	C-N	Pl
9541	same	same	L	Pl
9542	same	same	Ger-S	Pl
9543				
— 9544	same	581	C	Pl
9545	same	same	Br	Pl
9546	same	same	N	Pl
9547	same	same	C-N	Pl
9548	same	same	Ger-S	Pl
9549	same	same	L	Pl
9550				
9551	same	same as reverse of No 9525	C	Pl
9552	same	same	Br	Pl
9553	same	same	N	Pl
9554	same	same	C-N	Pl

RHODE ISLAND—Continued

Providence—Continued

NUMBER	OBVERSE	REVERSE	METAL	EDGE
9555	same	same	Ger-S	Pl
9556	same	same	L	Pl
9557				
9558	same	'Frank L Gay 140 Westminster St' around border-'bookseller & Stationer/Prov/R I' in centre C		Pl
9559	same	same	Br	Pl
9560	same	same	N	Pl
9561	same	same	C-N	Pl
9562	same	same	Ger-S	Pl
9563	same	same	L	Pl
9564	same	same	S	Pl
9565				
9566	Same as reverse of No 9519	'Good for/one/cent/1863/redeemed' in open wreath	C	Pl
9567	same	same	Br	Pl
9568	same	same	N	Pl
9569	same	same	C-N	Pl
9570	same	same	Ger-S	Pl
9571	same	same	S	Pl
9572	same	same	L	Pl
9573				
9574	Same as reverse of No 9558	same	C	Pl
9575	same	same	Br	Pl
9576	same	same	N	Pl
9577	same	same	C-N	Pl
9578	same	same	Ger-S	Pl
9579	same	same	S	Pl
9580	same	same	L	Pl
9581				
9582	same	'Billiard room & restaurant' around border-'No/27-31/Pleasant/Street' in centre	C	Pl
9583	same	same	Br	Pl
9584	same	same	N	Pl
9585	same	same	C-N	Pl
9586	same	same	Ger-S	Pl
9587	same	same	S	Pl
9588	same	same	L	Pl
9589				
9590	City Fruit Store/No 4/Weybosset/St Prov R I/redeemed by/Phillips	581	C	Pl
9591	same	same	Br	Pl
9592	same	same	N	Pl
9593	same	same	C-N	Pl
9594	same	same	Ger-S	Pl
9595	same	same	L	Pl
9596				
9597	Same	493	C	Pl
9598	same	same	Br	Pl
9599	same	same	N	Pl

RHODE ISLAND—Continued

Providence—Continued

NUMBER	OBVERSE	REVERSE	METAL	EDGE
9600	same	same	Ger-S	Pl
9601	same	same	L	Pl
9602				
— 9603	same	496	C·	Pl
9604	same	same	Br	Pl
9605	same	same	N	Pl
9606	same	same	C-N	Pl
9607	same	same	Ger-S	Pl
9608	same	same	S	Pl
9609	same	same	L	Pl
9610				
9611	same	same as reverse of No 9525	C	Pl
9612	same	same	Br	Pl
9613	same	same	N	Pl
9614	same	same	C-N	Pl
9615	same	same	Ger-S	Pl
9616	same	same	L	Pl
9617				
9618	same	'Rhode Island/in/the/field/first/1864' surrounded by 13 stars	C	Pl
9619				
9620	F W Shattuck/Prov/1864/R I/13 Weybosset St	'Burnside' above- 'S' in wreath in centre- 'Fruit store' below	C	Pl
9621	same	same	Br	Pl
9622	same	same	N	Pl
9623	same	same	Ger-S	Pl
9624	same	same	L	Pl
9625				
9626	'Pohle' above—bunch of grapes in centre- '1863' below	'Elmwood Vineyard' around border-goblet in centre	C	Pl
9627	same	same	Br	Pl
9628	same	same	L	Pl
9629				
9636	Same as Die No 493	Large anchor on shield in centre- 'Hope' above- '1864' Rhode Island coat of arms	C	Pl
9631	same	same	Br	Pl
9632	same	same	N	Pl
9633	same	same	Ger-S	Pl
9634	same	same	L	Pl
9635				
9636	Same as Di eNo 493	East/Boston/1837-same as the reverse of Low's H T Token No 116	C	Pl
9637	same	same	Br	Pl
9638	same	same	N	Pl
9639	same	same	Ger-S	Pl
9640	same	same	L	Pl
9641				
9642	same	same as reverse of No 9630	C	Pl

RHODE ISLAND—Continued

Providence—Continued

NUMBER	OBVERSE	REVERSE	METAL	EDGE
9643	same	same	Br	Pl
9644	same	same	N	Pl
9645	same	same	Ger-S	Pl
9646	same	same	L	Pl
9647				
9648	same	same as reverse of No 9566	S	Pl
9649				
9650	496	same as reverse of No 9630	C	Pl
9651	same	same	Br	Pl
9652	same	same	N	Pl
9653	same	same	Ger-S	Pl
9654	same	same	L	Pl
9655				
9656	same	504	C	Pl
9657	same	same	Br	Pl
9658	same	same	N	Pl
9659	same	same	Ger-S	Pl
9660	same	same	L	Pl
9661				
9662	581	'Billiard room & restaurant' around border- 'No/27-31/Pleasant/St' in centre	C	Pl
9663	same	same	Br	Pl
9664	same	same	N	Pl
9665	same	same	C-N	Pl
9666	same	same	Ger-S	Pl
9667	same	same	S	Pl
9668				
9669	same	504	C	Pl
9670	same	same	Br	Pl
9671	same	same	N	Pl
9672	same	same	C-N	Pl
9673	same	same	Ger-S	Pl
9674	same	same	L	Pl
9675				
9676	same	477	C	Pl
9677	same	same	Br	Pl
9678	same	same	N	Pl
9679	same	same	C-N	Pl
9680	same	same	Ger-S	Pl
9681	same	same	L	Pl
9682				
9683				
9684				
9685				
9686				
9687				
9688				
9689	same	'X' on shield in centre-'Eureka good for 10' around shield-all in circle of 23 stars	C	Pl

RHODE ISLAND—Continued

Providence—Continued

NUMBER	OBVERSE	REVERSE	METAL	EDGE
9690	same	same	Br	Pl
9691	Same as reverse of No 9525	477	C	Pl
9692	same	same	Br	Pl
9693	same	same	N	Pl
9694	same	same	C-N	Pl
9695	same	same	Ger-S	Pl
9696	same	same	L	Pl
9697				
9698	same	504	C	Pl
9699	same	same	Br	Pl
9700	same	same	N	Pl
9701	same	same	Ger-S	Pl
9702	same	same	L	Pl
9703				
9704	same	same as reverse of No 9630	C	Pl
9705	same	same	Br	Pl
9706	same	same	N	Pl
9707	same	same	Ger-S	Pl
9708	same	same	L	Pl
9709				
9710	493	504	C	Pl
9711	same	same	Br	Pl
9712	same	same	N	Pl
9713	same	same	Ger-S	Pl
9714	same	same	L	Pl
9715				
9716	496	same as reverse of No 9636	C	Pl
9717	same	same	Br	Pl
9718	same	same	N	Pl
9719	same	same	C-N	Pl
9720	same	same	Ger-S	Pl
9721	same	same	S	Pl
9722				
— 9723	'H-Y Le Fevre, Pro Empire Saloon' around border-'Union' in wreath in centre	517	C	Pl
9724	same	'N 49½ North Main St' in a circle in centre-surrounded by 12 large stars-'1864' below	C	Pl
9725	same	same	Br	Pl
9726	same	same	N	Pl
9727	same	same	Ger-S	Pl
9728	same	same	W-M	Pl
9729				
9730				

I

TENNESSEE

Clarksville

NUMBER	OBVERSE	REVERSE	METAL	EDGE
9731	Andrew King Merch't Clarksville Tenn	See best stock in city at King's Franklin St	C	Pl
9732	Same	419	C	R
—9733		420	C	R
9734				

Dedham

—9735	N O Underwood/good for/25/cents/Dedham/Tenn	426	Br	Pl
9736	Same as preceding—'10' instead of '25'	478	C	Pl
—9736A / —9737	Same as preceding—'5' instead of '10'	462	c	Pl
9738		Same	C	Pl
9739				

Knoxville

—9740	Barry & M'Dannel premium confectioners Knoxville Tenn	420	C	R
9741	Same	419 Arctic soda water good for 1 glass	C	R
—9742	Same	Same	Br	R
9743	Same	Same	C	Pl
9744				

Memphis

9745	B E Hammar & Co/drayage/25/cents/Memphis Tenn	418	C	R
—9746	Same	Same	Br	R
9747				
9748	Same	420	C-N	R
—9749	Same	Good/for/25/cents/1862	C	R
9750				
—9751	Wm Mc Donald/drayage/25/cents/Memphis Tenn	418	C	R
9752	Same	Same	Br	R
9753	Same	Good for/25/cents/1862	C	R
9754	Same	Good for/25/cents/payable in bank bills	C	R
9755				

Nashville

9756	Gold Pen/depot/72/Cherry St/Nashville Tenn	Blank	Br	Pl
9757	Harris & Pearl/Nashville/Tenn	'20' on plain planchet	L	Pl
9758	D L Lapsley & Co Nashville Tenn	Same as die No 453—dated '1863'	C-N	R
9759	Same	598	C	R
9760	Same	608	C	R

237

TENNESSEE—Continued

Nashville—Continued

NUMBER	OBVERSE	REVERSE	METAL	EDGE
9761	Same	609	C	R
9762	Mc Kay & Lapsley/Nashville/Tenn	'15' on plain planchet	Br	R
9763	Same	'20' on plain planchet	Br	Pl
9764	Same	'50' on plain planchet	Z	Pl
9765	Same	'500' on plain planchet	C	R
9766	Same	Same as die No. 453—dated '1863'	C-N	R
9767	Same	419	C	R
9768	Walker & Napier/Nashville/Tenn	Same as die No 453—dated '1863'	C-N	R
9769	Same	'500' on plain planchet	C	R
9770	Same	419	C	R
— 9771		420	C	R

VIRGINIA

Norfolk

9772 'Pfeiffer & Co' above—'Va' in a beaded circle in centre— 'Norfolk' below   503   L   Pl

NOTE—This is the only Civil War card known to have been issued in Virginia.

WEST VIRGINIA

Glen Eaton

NUMBER	OBVERSE	REVERSE	METAL	EDGE
9773	Bassett's/cheap/dry goods/groceries/etc/Glen Eaton/W Va	Bassett's/cheap/dry goods/ 35Main St/Wheeling/W Va	C	Pl
9774	Same	Dealers in hoop skirts hats caps and notions	C	Pl
9775	Same	117	C	Pl
9776	Same	445	C	Pl
9777	same	462	C	Pl
9778				

Hartford City

9779	In merchandise/Kelly's/store/ Hartford/City/W Va	664	Br	R

Wheeling

9780	Bassett's/cheap/dry goods/35 Main St/Wheeling/W Va	117	C	Pl
9781	Same	423	C	Pl
9782	Same	426	C	Pl
9783	Same	Same	Br	Pl
9784	Same	445	C	Pl
9785	Same	446	C	Pl
9786	Same	447	C	Pl
9787	Same	462	C	Pl
9788	Same	469	C	Pl
9789	Same	478	C	Pl
7890	John Eckhart/Manuf'r/of/Hosiery &c/187/Main St/Wheeling/W Va	117	C	Pl
9791	Same	445	C	Pl
9792	Same	479	C	Pl
9793	Same	560	C	Pl
9794				
9795	Jas Graves & Co/wall paper/and/ news dealers/30/Monroe St/Wheeling/W Va	538	C	Pl
9796				
9797	R C Graves/periodical/and/news dealer/78/Market St/Wheeling/ W Va	425	C	Pl
9798	Same	442	C	Pl
9799	Same	538	C	Pl
9800	Same	591	C	Pl
9801	D Nicoll & Bro/variety/store/109/ Main St/Wheeling/W Va	445	C	Pl
9802	Same	462	C	Pl
9803				
9804	J W C Smith/dealer/in/leather/ and/findings/189 Main St/Wheeling West Va	462	C	Pl
9805	Same	478	C	Pl
9806				

WEST VIRGINIA—Continued

Wheeling—Continued

NUMBER	OBVERSE	REVERSE	METAL	EDGE
9807				
9808	C E Stifel/tin/and/sheet iron/ware/Wheeling/W Va	117	C	Pl
9809	Same	462	C	Pl
9810	Same	464	C	Pl
9811	Same	469	C	Pl
9812	Same	521	C	Pl
9813	Same	524	C	Pl
9814				

WISCONSIN

Appleton

NUMBER	OBVERSE	REVERSE	METAL	EDGE
9825	Parsons & Barlow/grocers/Appleton Wis	118	C	Pl
9826	Same	Same	Br	Pl
9827	Same	Same	C-N	Pl
9828	Same	Same	W-M	Pl
9829				
9830	Same	157	C	Pl
9831	Same	Same	Br	Pl
9832	Same	Same	C-N	Pl
9833	Same	Same	W-M	Pl
9834				
9835	Same	483	C	Pl
9836				
9837				

Baraboo

NUMBER	OBVERSE	REVERSE	METAL	EDGE
9838	Peck & Orvis/druggists/&/grocers/Baraboo/Wis	102	C	Pl
9839	Same	Same	Br	Pl
9840	Same	Same	N	Pl
9841	Same	Same	C-N	Pl
9842	Same	Same	W-M	Pl
9843	Same	Same	S	Pl
9844				
9845	Same	181	C	Pl
9846				
— 9847	Same	202	C	Pl
9848	Same	Same	C-N	Pl
9849				
9850	Same	217	C	Pl
9851				
9852	Same	218	C	Pl
9853				

WISCONSIN—Continued
Baraboo—Continued

NUMBER	OBVERSE	REVERSE	METAL	EDGE
9854	Same	335	C	Pl
9855				
9856	Same	'Washington Market' above —gobbler in centre—'Exchange' below	C	Pl
9857				

Barton

9858	John Reisse/dealer/in/dry goods/groceries/clothing/hats/Barton Wash Co Wis	482	C	Pl
9859				
9860				

Beaver Dam

9861	F Krueger/dry goods/groceries/boots & shoes/hardware/&c/ Beaver Dam Wis	482	C	Pl
9862	Same	157	C	Pl
9863				
9864	A P Redfield/hardware/iron/tin ware/stoves/nails &c/Beaver Dam Wis	482	C	Pl
9865				
9866	O M Warren/hardware/iron/tinware/stoves/nails/&c/Beaver Dam Wis	157	C	Pl
9867	Same	324	C	Pl
9868				

Beloit

9869	Peck & Pratt/dealers/in/wines/liquors/& Segars/Beloit Wis	614	C	Pl

Columbus

9870	Ph Carpeles & Co/dry/goods/&/groceries/Columbus Wis	482	C	Pl
9871				
9872	Frank Huggins/drugs/&/medicines/Columbus Wis	482	C	Pl
9873				
9874	D F Newcomb/dry goods/&/groceries/Columbus Wis	482	C	Pl
9875				
9876	Williams Bros/chemists/& Druggists/Columbus/Wis. Mortar and pestle in centre	25	C	Pl
9877	Same	209	C	Pl
9878	Same	435	C	Pl

WISCONSIN—Continued

Columbus—Continued

NUMBER	OBVERSE	REVERSE	METAL	EDGE
9879	Same	611	C	Pl
9880				
9881				

Cross Plains

9882	C Dahmen & Son/dealers/in/dry goods/groceries/&c/Cross Plains/Wis	25	C	Pl
9883				

East Troy

9884	C W Smith/dealer/in/dry goods/groceries/hardware &/crockery/East Troy Wis	118	C	Pl
9885	Same	Same	Br	Pl
9886	Same	Same	C-N	Pl
9887	Same	Same	W-M	Pl
9888				
9889	Same	157	C	Pl
9890	Same	Same	Br	Pl
9891	Same	Same	C-N	Pl
9892	Same	Same	W-M	Pl
9893				
9894	Same	182	C	Pl
9895				
9896	Same	324	C	Pl
9897	Same	482	C	Pl

Edgerton

9898	C C Root & Bro/dry goods/clothing/boots/shoes crockery/groceries/&c/Edgerton/Wis	459	C	Pl
9899				

Fond Du Lac

9900	C L Alling/grocer/Fond du lac/Wis	421	C	Pl
9901	Same	478	C	Pl
9902	Same	Lanpheer's Card	C	Pl
9903				
9904				
9905	A R Brass/general/dealer in/produce/Fond Du Lac/Wis	446	C	Pl
9906	Same	478	C	Pl
9907				
9908	Carpenter & Pier/call/at the/Farmers/store/Fond Du Lac/Wis	421	C	Pl
9909				
9910	Clarke & Carpenter/dealers/in/dry goods/and/groceries/Fond Du Lac/Wis	471	C	Pl

WISCONSIN—Continued

Fond Du Lac—Continued

NUMBER	OBVERSE	REVERSE	METAL	EDGE
9911				
9912	F Fritz/groceries/crockery/provisions &c/Fond Du Lac Wis	118	C	Pl
9913	Same	Same	Br	Pl
9914	Same	Same	C-N	Pl
9915	Same	Same	W-M	Pl
9916				
9917	Same	157	C	Pl
9918	Same	Same	Br	Pl
9919	Same	Same	C-N	Pl
9920				
9921	Same	482	C	Pl
9922				
9923	J C Lowell/druggist/&/grocer/Fond Du Lac/Wis	421	C	Pl
9924	Same	426	C	Pl
9925	Same	478	C	Pl
9926				
9927	T Mason/grocer/Fond Du Lac/Wis	T Mason/crockery/and/glassware	C	Pl
9928				
—9929	Nye & Youmans/dealers/in/groceries/& Crockery/Fond Du Lac/Wis	.447	C	Pl
9930				
9931	A T Perkins/city/bakery/Fond Du Lac/Wis	A T Perkins/manufacturer/of/crackers/and/confectionery	C	Pl
9932	Same	421	C	Pl
9933				
9934	Perkins & Smith/dealers/in/stoves/and/tinware/Fond Du Lac/Wis	426	C	Pl
—9935	Same	524	C	Pl
9936				
9937	J Pettibone & Co/dry goods/house/Fond Du Lac/Wis	421	C	Pl
9938	Same	Boots/shoes/and/yankee/notions	C	Pl
9939				
9940	A Raymond/grocer/Fond Du Lac/Wis	426	C	Pl
9941	Same	478	C	Pl
9942				
9943	T S Wright/chemist/and/druggist/Fond Du Lac/Wis	T S Wright/books/&/stationery	C	Pl
9944				

Green Bay

—9945	A Detrich/dealer/in/groceries/provisions/liquors &c/Green Bay/Wis	446	C	Pl

WISCONSIN—Continued

Green Bay—Continued

NUMBER	OBVERSE	REVERSE	METAL	EDGE
9946				
9947	Hoffman & Lewis/merchant/tailors/Green Bay/Wis	446	C	Pl
9948	Same	Same	Br	Pl
9949				
9950	A Kimboll/dealer/in/hardware/Green Bay/Wis	423	C	Pl
9951				
9952	Philip Klaus/Yankee notions/and/toys/Green Bay/Wis	426	C	Pl
9953				
9954	Drs Rhode & Hicks/eagle/drug/store/Green Bay/Wis	532	C	Pl
9955				
9956	F R Schettler/dealer/in/hardware/Green Bay/Wis	423	C	Pl
9957	Same	465	C	Pl
9958	Same	480	C	Pl
9959				
9960	Sam Stern/merchant/tailor/& dealer in/clothing/Green Bay/Wis	591	C	Pl
9961				
9962	Z Z St Lewis/dealer/in/hardware/Green Bay/Wis	478	C	Pl
9963	Same	560	C	Pl
9964	Same	591	C	Pl
9965				
9966	J J St Louis/dealer/in/hardware/Green Bay/Wis	478	C	Pl
9967	Same	591	C	Pl

Hales Corner

9968	J Siegel/dry goods/&/groceries/Hales Corner	482	C	Pl
9969				

Janesville

9970	E S Barrows/seeds/&/farming/tools/Janesville Wis	Plow in centre—'stoves hardware iron &c' around border	C	Pl
9971	Same	Same	Br	Pl
9972				
9973	L R Carswell/confectionery/toys &/groceries/Janesville/Wis	26	C	Pl
9974				
9975	'Chapmans one price store' around border—'Lappins/Bl'k/Janesville/Wis' in centre	'Dry goods clothing boots & shoes' around border—'hats/& caps/groceries/&c/at/low prices' in centre	C	Pl
9976	Same	209	C	Pl

244

WISCONSIN—Continued

Janesville—Continued

NUMBER	OBVERSE	REVERSE	METAL	EDGE
9977	Same	485	C	Pl
9978				
9979	E Connell & Co/groceris/liquors/ lime &/wood/Janesville Wis	26	C	Pl
9980	E Connell & Co/groceries/liquors/ lime & wood/Janesville/Wis	26	C	Pl
9981	Same	446	C	Pl
9982				
9983	H L Muth/iron/hardware/wagon stuff &c/Janesville Wis. Padlock in centre	436	C	Pl
9984				
9985	H L Smith/iron/hardware/wagon stuff &c/Janesville Wis. Padlock in centre	436	C	Pl
9986	Same	Same	Br	Pl
9987	M Marsh Young America clothing house Janesville Wis	209	C	Pl
9988				

Jefferson

9989	Philip Johnson/drugs/paints oils/ books/stationery &c/Jefferson/Wis	532	C	Pl
9990				
9991	John Yung/dry goods/groceries &/hardware/Jefferson/Wis	463	C	Pl
9992				
9993	J F W Meyer/groceries/provisions/ &/notions/Jefferson Wis	425	C	Pl
9994				
9995	D Ostrander/grocer/&/insurance/ Agt/Jefferson Wis	520	C	Pl
9996				
9997	S Steinhart/dry goods/&/groceries /Jefferson/Wis	552	C	Pl
9998				

Juneau

9999	S H Coleman Dealer in dry goods Juneau Wis	446	C	Pl
10000				

Kenosha

10001	N A Brown's/cream/ale/stock porter/&/rennet/Kenosha Wis	25	C	Pl
10002	same	435	C	Pl
10003				
10004	Gerkan & Ernst/dealers/in/groceries/&/provisions/Kenosha/Wis	25	C	Pl

WISCONSIN—Continued

Kenosha—Continued

NUMBER	OBVERSE	REVERSE	METAL	EDGE
10005	same	206	C	Pl
10006	same	632	C	Pl
10007	same	633	C	Pl
10008				
10008-a	Hohn Simmons & Co/boots/shoes /&/leather/Kenosha Wis	26	C	Pl
10008-b				
10008-c	Lyman Mowry & Co/boots/shoes /& leather/Kenosha/Wis	26	C	Pl
10008-d	same	627	C	Pl
10008-e				
10008-f				

Kilbourne City

10008-g	J E Dixon & Sons/dry/goods/ groceries/boots/& shoes/Kilbourn City/Wis	209	C	Pl
10008-h				
10008-i	'T Hoffmann' above-barrel in centre- 'Kilbourn City Wis' below	482	C	Pl

La Crosse

10009	Mons Anderson/dealer/in/dry goods/ clothing/boots shoes&c/La Crosse /Wis	499	C	Pl
10010	same	500	C	Pl
10011				
10012	Geo E Stanley/LaCrosse/Wis/1863	537	C	Pl
10013	Same	same	Br	Pl
10014				

Madison

10015	Jas Fr Bodtker/Madison/Wis/photographer	206	C	Pl
10016	same	209	C	Pl
10017				
10018	Emigranten/office/King St/Madison/Wis	The only/Norwegian/news paper/published/in/America	C	Pl
10019				
10020	R K Findlay & Co/druggist/and/ grocers/Madison/Wis	528	C	Pl
10021	same	The celebrated/tea/establishment	C	Pl
10022				
10023	S Klaub & Co/dry goods/clothing/&/furnishing/goods/Madison/Wis	479	C	Pl
10024				
10025	Huntley & Steenland/groceries/ and/crockery/Madison/Wis	422	C	Pl

WISCONSIN—Continued

Madison—Continued

NUMBER	OBVERSE	REVERSE	METAL	EDGE
10026				
10027	J J Lawrence/groceries/crockery/&/glassware/17/King St/Madison Wis	459	C	Pl
10028				
10029	Madison Brewery/Mfgr of/lager beer/stock/&/cream ale	594	C	Pl
10030				
10031	Buy/your/meat/of/E Newcomb/Main St/Madison Wis	479	C	Pl
10032				
10033	George V Ott/Manfr & Dealer/in/leather/hides &c/tannery/Madison Wis	209	C	Pl
10034				
10035	Ramsey & Campbell/stoves/tin/iron &/farming/tools/Madison/Wis	547	C	Pl
10036				
10037	J Rodermund/dealer/in/dry goods/& groceries/Madison/Wis	25	C	Pl
10038	J Rodermund/Madison/Wis-man driving one horse wagon loaded with three kegs	Madison Brewery/Manfr of/lager beer/stock/&/cream ale	C	Pl
10039	Similar-four kegs on wagon	Similar—'K' of 'Stock' almost touches second 'E' of 'Beer'	C	Pl
10040				
10041	Same as preceeding	206	C	Pl
10042	same	594	C	Pl
10043				
10044	Capitol Steam Brewery/by Wm Voight/Mangr of/ale &/lager/beer/Madison/Wis	206	C	Pl
10045	same	209	C	Pl
10046	same	614	C	Pl
10047				

Manitowoc

NUMBER	OBVERSE	REVERSE	METAL	EDGE
10048	W H Horn/produce/dealer/Monitowoc	118	C	Pl
10049	same	same	Br	Pl
10050	same	same	C-N	Pl
10051	same	same	W-M	Pl
10052				
10053	same	324	C	Pl
10054	same	same	Br	Pl
10055	same	same	C-N	Pl
10056	same	same	W-M	Pl
10057	same	482	C	Pl
10058				
10059	Stucke & Co/produce/dealers/Manitowoc Wis	118	C	Pl

WISCONSIN—Continued

Manitowac—Continued

NUMBER	OBVERSE	REVERSE	METAL	EDGE
10060	same	same	Br	Pl
10061	same	same	C-N	Pl
10062	same	same	W-M	Pl
10063				
10064	same	157	Br	Pl
10065	same	same	C-N	Pl
10066	same	same	W-M	Pl
10067				
10068	same	482	C	Pl
10069				
10070	Similar- 'dealer'instead of 'Dealers'	482	C	Pl
10071				

Marshall

10072	I Livingston/dry goods/groceries/ &c/Marshall Wis	482	C	Pl
10073				
10074	W Vosburgh/hardware/stoves/& tin/Marshall Wis	482	C	Pl
10075				

Mauston

10076	J Campbell/hardware/&/groceries/ Mauston/Wis	27	C	Pl
10077				

Mayfield

10078	E Wirth/dealer/in/dry goods/groceries/clothing/ hats/&c/ Mayfield Wis	118	C	Pl
10079	same	same	Br	Pl
10080	same	same	C-N	Pl
10081	same	same	W-M	Pl
10082				
10083	same	157	C	Pl
10084	same	same	Br	Pl
10085	same	same	N	Pl
10086	same	same	C-N	Pl
10087	same	same	W-M	Pl
10088	same	482	C	Pl
10089				

Milwaukee

10090	Indian on pony in centre- 'A Schermann & Co' above- 'Milwaukee' below	Cigars & tobacco/wholesale/&/retail/274/West Water St	C	Pl
10091	same	same	Br	Pl
10092	same	same	C-N	Pl
10093				
10094	same	Obverse incused	C	Pl

WISCONSIN—Continued

Milwaukee—Continued

NUMBER	OBVERSE	REVERSE	METAL	EDGE
10095				
10096	'Wisconsin Brewery' above-barrel in centre—'Ch Bast' below	Mug in double triangle dividing '1863' in centre-'Milwaukee' above-'Wisconsin' below	C	Pl
10097	same	Similar to preceeding-leaf on each side of date	C	Pl
10098				
10099	'Philip Best' above-mug and '1863' in centre'—'Lager Beer' below	Keg, brewing tools, hop and corn stalks in centre-'Empire Brewery' above- 'Milwaukee' below	C	Pl
10100	same	same	Br	Pl
10101	same	same	C-N	Pl
10102				
10103	Best & Co's Beer Hall	large '5' with 'Mil' below-Beer or cash Market Street	C	Pl
10104				
10105	King Gambrinus in centre- 'V Blatz' to left- 'Larger beer' to right	City Brewery/&/malt house /1863/Milwaukee	C	Pl
10106	Same-large planchet	same	C	Pl
10107	same	same	Br	Pl
10108				
10109	M Bodden/Milwaukee/Wisconsin	157	C	Pl
10110	same	482	C	Pl
10111				
10112	City Brewery/Manf'r/Lager Beer/stock/& cream/ale	25	C	Pl
10113				
10114	City Brewery Malt House Milwaukee 1863	Obverse die incused	C	Pl
10115				
10116	A J Cooper/lumber/yard/East Water St/N of Walkers Pt/bridge /Milwaukee	482	C	Pl
10117	same	Obverse die incused	C	Pl
10118				
10119	'D J Doornink' above-bee-hive in centre- '1863/Milwaukee' below	Groceries/&/dry goods/cor of 10th/&/Cherry St	C	Pl
10120	same	Obverse die incused	C	Pl
10121				
10122	A H Filner/corner/of 7th &/Sherman/Street/Milwaukee	Groceries/Kegelbahn/provisions	C	Pl
10123	same	same	C	R
10124				
10125	Joseph Fishbein/Agt/315/West/ Water St/Milwaukee/Wis	saw labeled 'Dont Despair' axe spade and hammer in centre-'stoves & hardware' above—'1863 below	C	Pl
10126	same	Groceries / provisions / Drygoods/1863	C	Pl

WISCONSIN—Continued

Milwaukee—Continued

NUMBER	OBVERSE	REVERSE	METAL	EDGE
10127	same	Obverse die incused	C	Pl
10128	same	same as reverse of No 10125- pick instead of axe	C	Pl
10129				
10130	'Wm Frankfurth' above-Indian head to left in centre-'Milwaukee Wis' below	Same as reverse of No10125	C	Pl
10131	same	Blank reverse	C	Pl
10132				
10133	'Goes & Falk' above-three kegs in centre dividing '1863'-'Milwaukee below	Wisconsin/Malt House/&/Bavaria/Brewery	C	Pl
10134				
10135	Goll & Frank's/retail store/319/ Third St/Milwaukee/J H Hantzsch /Agt	Dry Goods/fancy/goods/yankee/notions/feathers/&c	C	Pl
10136				
10137	C B Graff/dealer/in/all kinds of/ machinery/Milwaukee Wis	118	C	Pl
10138	same	same	Br	Pl
10139	same	same	C-N	Pl
10140	same	same	W-M	Pl
10141				
10142	same	157	C	Pl
10143	same	same	Br	Pl
10144	same	same	C-N	Pl
10145	same	same	W-M	Pl
10146				
10147	same	324	Br	Pl
10148	same	Same	C-N	Pl
10149	same	same	S	Pl
10150				
10151	same	482	C	Pl
10152	same	same	Br	Pl
10153	same	same	C-N	Pl
10154	same	same	W-M	Pl
10155				
10156	Hambach/Milwaukee	482	C	Pl
10157				
10158	C Hambach/cor/Huron &/Jefferson/Sts/Milwaukee	482	C	Pl
10159				
10160	T W Hart Supt	M W M Plank Road Company	C	Pl
10161				
10172	'Ch Hermann & Co' above-jug crossed brooms and '1863' in centre-'Milwaukee' below	Brooms &/stone ware/factory /318/East Water St	C	Pl
10173	same-large '&' in legend	same	C	Pl
10174				

WISCONSIN—Continued

Milwaukee—Continued

NUMBER	OBVERSE	REVERSE	METAL	EDGE
10175	Same	118	C	Pl
10176	same	same	Br	Pl
10177	same	same	C-N	Pl
10178	Same	same	W-M	Pl
10179				
10180	same	157	C	Pl
10181	Same	same	Br	Pl
10182	same	same	C-N	Pl
10183	same	same	W-M	Pl
10184				
10185	same	324	C	Pl
10186	same	same	Br	Pl
10187	same	same	C-N	Pl
10188	same	same	W-M	Pl
10189				
10190	GeorgeKane/dealer/in/fine family/groceries/No 10/Spring St/Wilwaukee	482	C	Pl
10191				
10192	Threshing/machine/works/Kirby/Langworthy/& Co/Milwaukee/Wis	435	C	Pl
10193				
—10194	'A Kleinsteiber/1863' above-hat and sprays in centre---'Milwaukee below	Milinery/&/fancy goods/5th/betw Popular/&/Chestnut St	C	Pl
10195	same	Blank Planchet	C	Pl
10196				
10197	'Chas Kleisteuber' above-portrait to left in centre dividing '1863' 'Mechanic' below Thick planchet	Small machinery/models/engraving/stencil-cutting/No 24/Tamarack St/Milwaukee	C	Pl
10198	Same—thin planchet	same	C	Pl
10199	same	same	W-M	Pl
10200	same	Obverse die incused	C	Pl
10201				
10202				
—10203	HKurt/grocer/cor of/Hanover &/Florida St/Milwaukee	482	C	Pl
10204	same	same	Br	Pl
10205				
10206	Louis Kurz/pictorial/lithographer/Milwaukee	157	C	Pl
10207	same	482	C	Pl
10208				
10209	A Lederer & Co/dry/goods/cor/E Water/&/Michigan/Sts/Milwaukee	26	C	Pl
10210	same	435	C	Pl
10211	same	633	C	Pl
10212	same	641	C	Pl
10213				

WISCONSIN—Continued

Milwaukee—Continued

NUMBER	OBVERSE	REVERSE	METAL	EDGE
10214	M C Meyer/M G B Pl Road/Milwaukee	482	C	Pl
10215				
10216	A Miller & Co/produce/&/commission/Milwaukee	118	C	Pl
10217	same	same	Br	Pl
10218	same	Same	C-N	Pl
10219	same	same	W-M	Pl
10220	same	Obverse die incused	C	Pl
10221				
10222	same	157	C	Pl
10223	same	same	Br	Pl
10224	same	same	C-N	Pl
10225	same	same	W-M	Pl
10226				
10227	same	324	C	Pl
10228	same	same	Br	Pl
10229	same	same	N	Pl
10230	same	same	C-N	Pl
10231				
10232	same	482	C	Pl
10233				
10234	'Frederich Miller' above-brewer's tools in tub in centre dividing '1863'-'Lager Beer' below	Plankroad/brewery/Milaukee	C	Pl
10235	same	same	Br	Pl
10236	same	Blank planchet	C	Pl
10237				
10238	same	'1/glas' on plain planchet	Br	Pl
10239				
10240	F Mitzlaff/grocer/Milwaukee	482	C	Pl
10241	same	same	Br	Pl
10242				
10243	Mossin & Marr/engravers/Milwaukee	157	C	Pl
10244				
10245	Carl Paechke/dry goods/store/Fond Du Lac/Road/Milwaukee	Dry Goods/groceries/&/Provisions	C	R
10246	same	same	C	Pl
10247	same	Groceries/provisions/&/Dry Goods/1863	C	R
10248	same	Same	C	Pl
10249	same	157	C	Pl
10250	same	482	C	Pl
10251				
10252	Planer & Kayser's/sewing/machine cor of/Main & Mason/St's/Milwaukee Wis	482	C	Pl
10253				
10254	'J Pritzlaff & Co' above-cooking stove in centre—'No 303, 3d St/Milwaukee' below	Hardware/iron/nails glass/&stoves/1863	C	R

WISCONSIN—Continued

Milwaukee—Continued

NUMBER	OBVERSE	REVERSE	METAL	EDGE
10255	same	same	C	Pl
10256	same	same	Br	Pl
10257				
— 10258	J Scheidhouer/manufacturer/of/ soap/&/candles/Milwaukee Wis	482	C	Pl
10259				
— 10260	J B Schram/wholesale/grocer/ Milwaukee	482	C	Pl
10261				
— 10262	Severn & Jones/produce/&/commission/Milwaukee Wis	482	C	Pl
10263.	same	Obverse die incused	C	Pl
10264				
10265	C T Stamm & Co/stoves/tin/& hardware/Reed St/Milwaukee	435	C	Pl
10266	same	482	C	Pl
10267	same	same	Br	Pl
10268				
— 10269	A H Steinmann/groceries/dry goods/&/Millinery/corner of 11 &/Galena St/Milwaukee	482	C	Pl
10270				
—10271	D Stoffel/groceries/&/provisions/ 7th/street/Milwaukee	482	C	Pl
10272				
10273	Frederick Thiele/Meat/market	157	C	Pl
— 10274	same	482	C	Pl
10275				
10276	I Teller/Milwaukee	118	W-M	Pl
10277	same	Obverse die incused	C	Pl
10278				
— 10279	same	482	C	Pl
10280				
— 10281	H Upmeyer/jeweller/Milwaukee	115	C	Pl
10282	same	same	Br	Pl
10283				
10284	H Upmeyer/jeweller/ 258/W Water St/Milwaukee	115	C	Pl
10285	same	same	Br	Pl
10286				
10287	H Upmeyer/jeweller/Milwaukee	Bust of Douglass on plain planchet- 'S A D' under bust	C	Pl
10288	Same as reverse die of No 10281	Same as obverse die incused	C	Pl
10289				
10290				
10291	'Hermann Voigt/1863' above-cooking stove in centre- 'Milwaukee' below-small planchet	Stoves/& tinware/329/West Water St	C	Pl

WISCONSIN—Continued

Milwaukee—Continued

NUMBER	OBVERSE	REVERSE	METAL	EDGE
10292	Large planchet-same	same	C	Pl
10293				

Neenah

10294	John Hunt/groceries/& provisions/ Neenah/Wis	Mc Cabe/coral/mills/Manash/Wis	C	Pl
10295				
10296	C W Leavens & Co/groceries/ Neenah/Wis	532	C	Pl
10297				

Newburg

10298	Franckenberg & Keller/dealers/in/ dry goods/groceries/hard/ware/ Newburg Wis	482	C	Pl
10299				

New Lisbon

10300	J Ramsey/dry/goods/groceries/& general/merchandise/New Lisbon Wis	209	C	Pl
10301				

North Prairie

10302	W H Bogardus/dealer/in/dry goods /groceries/hard/ware/North Prairie	482	C	Pl
10303				
10304	J Remington/Sons/dry/goods &/ groceries/North/Prairie/Wis	26	C	Pl
10305				
10306	JSmart/steam/flouring &/planing/ Mills/North Prairie Wis	209	C	Pl
10307				

Oconomowoc

10308	Mrs J Tate Milliner/Oconomowoc	118	C	Pl
10309				

Oconto Co

— 10310	Stiles Gang Mills/dealer/in/lumber /lath/&/shingles/Oconto Co Wis	482	C	Pl
10311	same	Obverse die incused	C	Pl
10312				

Oshkosh

10313	Jos Boles/merchant tailor/and/ dealer in/clothing/Oshkosh/Wis	553	C	Pl

WISCONSIN—Continued

Oshkosh—Continued

NUMBER	OBVERSE	REVERSE	METAL	EDGE
10314				
10315	City Hotel/C Bock/proprietor/ Oshkosh/Wis	The nearest/hotel/to/the/steam boat/landing/Perry St	C	Pl
10316				
10317	Fraker Bro's/dealers/in/boots & shoes/51 Ferry St/Oshkosh/Wis	Fraker Bros/dealers/in/leather /hides/wool & furs	C	Pl
10318				
10319	Andrew Haben & Co/dealers/in/ clothing/Oshkosh/Wis	459	C	Pl
10320	same	469	C	Pl
10321	same	471	C	Pl
10322	same	553	C	Pl
10323				
10324	Hasbrouck & Francher/dealers/in/ stoves &/tinware/Oshkosh/Wis	521	C	Pl
10325				
10326	Hay & Clark/dealers/in/hardware /Oshkosh/Wis	469	.C	Pl
10327	same	471	C	Pl
10328				
10329	Jeanicke & Klotzsch/manufacturers /&/dealers/ in/ leather/ hides/&c/ Oshkosh Wis	482	C	Pl
10330				
10331	Kellog & Hughes/dry goods/Oshkosh/Wis	446	C	Pl
10332	same	same	Br	Pl
10333				
10334	Levy & Duncan/dealers/in/clothing /Oshkosh/Wis	421	C	Pl
10335	same	444	C	Pl
10336	same	446	C	Pl
10337	same	447	C	Pl
10338	same	560	C	Pl
10339				
10340	Lines & Russell/harness/maker/Oshkosh/Wis	Saddlery/hardware	C	Pl
10341				
10342	A Neff/dealer in/hardware/groceries/Oshkosh/Wis	521	C	Pl
10343				
10344	S B & J A Paige/grocers/Oshkosh/Wis	423	C	Pl
10345	same	424	C	Pl
10346	same	469	C	Pl
10347				
10348	H Rans/dealer/in/clothing/Oshkosh/Wis	423	C	Pl
10349	same	446	C	Pl
10350	same	447	C	Pl
10351	same	621	C	Pl

WISCONSIN—Continued

Oshkosh—Continued

NUMBER	OBVERSE	REVERSE	METAL	EDGE
10352				
10353	B H Soper/dealer/in/furniture/ Oshkoch/Wis	421	C	Pl
10354	same	446	C	Pl
10355	same	479	C	Pl
10356				
10357	Allen Vosburg & Co/music/store/ Oshkosh Wis	Steinway's/ pianos/ Smith's/ melodeons/&/tremolo/Harmoniums	C	Pl
10358				
10359	Wm L Williams/chemist/and/druggist/45 Ferry St/Oshkosh/Wis	446	C	Pl
10360				

Portage City

10361	T M Mc Millan/groceries/&/crockery/Portage/City/Wis	209	C	Pl

Port Washington

10362	J Druecker/dealer/in/dry goods/ groceries/clothing/ hats/&c/ Port Washington Wis	482	C	Pl
10363				

Racine

10364	J I Case & Co/thrashing/machine/ Manufacturers/Racine Wis	209	C	Pl
10365				
10366	J I Case & Co/thrashing/machine/ Manfrs/Racine Wis	25	C	Pl
10367	same	433	C	Pl
10368				
10369	J Clough/fine/family/groceries/ nuts/&c/Racine Wis	25	C	Pl
10370	same	435	C	Pl
10371	same	633	C	Pl
10372				
10373	John Elkins/dealer/in/watches/ jewelry/pianos/&c/Racine Wis	25	C	Pl
10374	same	26	C	Pl
10375	same	209	C	Pl
10376	same	627	C	Pl
1$377	same	628	C	Pl
10378				
10379	F Elmlinger/merchant/tailor/Racine Wis	26	C	Pl
10380				
10381	J W English/trunk/&/harness/ dealer/cor Main & 3d St/Racine Wis	25	C	Pl

WISCONSIN—Continued

Rcine—Continued

NUMBER	OBVERSE	REVERSE	METAL	EDGE
10382	same	484	C	Pl
10383	same	485	C	Pl
10384				
10385	Erhardt & Raps/Auctioners/Racine Wis	157	C	Pl
10386				
10387	Thos Falvey/Manfr'r/of/reapers &/mowers/Racine/Wis	25	C	Pl
10388	same	26	C	Pl
10389	same	594	C	Pl
10390	same	627	C	Pl
10391	same	628	C	Pl
10392				
10393	D H Jones/staple &/fancy/dry goods/136/Main St/Racine Wis	25	C	Pl
10394	same	209	C	Pl
10395	same	435	C	Pl
10396	same	627	C	Pl
10397	J & H Miller/dealers/in/boots/&/shoes/Racine Wis	25	C	Pl
10398	same	611	C	Pl
10399	same	627	C	Pl
10400				
10401	Thelen & Dietrich/dealers/in/dry/goods/&/groceries/Racine/Wis	206	C	Pl
10402	same	435	C	Pl
10403				

Ripon

10404	Greenway & Co's/restaurant/&/billiard/rooms/Ripon Wis	Greenway's/immense/concert/hall/Ripon/Wis/seats 1000 people	C	R
10405	same	same	Br	R
10406	same	same	Z	R
10407				
10408	same	419	C	R
10409				
10410	same as reverse of No 10364	419	C	R
10411				

Sauk City

10412	C Nebel/steam/Mills/Sauk City Wis	482	C	Pl
10413				

Sheboygan

10414	Trowbridge's /watch/clock/&/jewelry/store/Sheboygan Wis	419	C	R
10415				
10416	same	535	C	R

WISCONSIN—Continued

Sheboygan—Continued

NUMBER	OBVERSE	REVERSE	METAL	EDGE
10417	same	same	Br	R
10418	same	same	Z	R
10419				
10420				

Sparta

10421	Hamilton & Co/grocers/Sparta/Wis	27	C	Pl
10422	W S Newton/dealer/in/hardware/&/stoves/Sparta Wis	27	C	Pl

Stoughton

10423	T P Camp/watch/maker/Stoughton/Wis	536	C	Pl
10424	same	Blank	Br	Pl
10425	Dearborn/&/Root/grocers/Stoughton/Wis	459	C	Pl
10426				
10427	H Peterson/dry goods/clothing/boots shoes/&c/Stoughton Wis	471	C	Pl
10428				

Tomah

10429	Eaton & Barns/dealer/in/dry goods/groceries/&c/Tomah Wis	482	C	Pl
10430				
10431	Wm Runkel/dealer/in/dry/goods/&c/Tomah & New Lisbon	482	C	Pl
10432				

Two Rivers

10433	R Suettinger/Manufact'r/& dealer/in/stoves tin &/sheet iron/ware/Two Rivers Wis	482	C	Pl
10434				

Waterloo

10435	Ph Carpeles & Co/dry/goods/&/groceries/Waterloo Wis	478	C	Pl
10436	same	482	C	Pl
10437				

Watertown

10438	H Bellack/dry goods/groceries &/provisions/Watertown/Wis	478	C	Pl
10439				
10440	Bertram & Co/boots & shoes/sign/of the/mammoth/boot/Watertown Wis	533	C	Pl

WISCONSIN—Continued

Watertown—Continued

NUMBER	OBVERSE	REVERSE	METAL	EDGE
10441				
10442	Cordes & Platz/dry goods/groceries/liquors/Watertown/Wis	423	C	Pl
10443				
10444	T Dervin/dry goods/groceries/&/clothing/liquors/Watertown/Wis	118	C	Pl
10445	same	same	Br	Pl
10446	same	same	C-N	Pl
10447	same	same	W-M	Pl
10448				
10449	same	157	C	Pl
10450	same	same	Br	Pl
10451	same	same	C-N	Pl
10452	same	same	W-M	Pl
10453				
10454	same	324	Br	Pl
10455	same	same	C-N	Pl
10456				
10457	same	482	C	Pl
10458				
10459	Patrick Duffy/grocer/Watertown Wis	482	C	Pl
10460				
10461	Fischer & Rohr/clothiers/Watertown/Wis	482	C	Pl
10462				
10463	Fisher & Rohr/ready/made/clothing/35 Main St/Watertown/Wis	556	C	Pl
10464	same	Blank	C	Pl
10465	W C Fountain/drugs/paints oils/books/stationary/Watertown/Wis	532	C	Pl
10466	same	same	Br	Pl
10467				
10468	same	539	C	Pl
10469	same	same	Br	Pl
10470				
10471	Chas Goeldner/musical/instruments/and/notions/Watertown/Wis	428	C	Pl
10472	same	539	C	Pl
10473	same	same	Br	Pl
10474	same	555	C	Pl
10475				
10476	Chas Goeldner/Manuf's/of/harness/childrens/carriages/&c/Watertown Wis	555	C	Pl
10477				
10478	John Heymann/oyster/restaurant/&/beer hall/Watertown Wis	482	C	Pl
10479				
10480	Daniel Kusel/hardware/Watertown Wis	482	C	Pl

WISCONSIN—Continued

Watertown—Continued

NUMBER	OBVERSE	REVERSE	METAL	EDGE
10481				
10482	J Moulton/groceries/flour & feed/Watertown/Wis	425	C	Pl
10483				
10484	Theodore Racek/restaurant/Watertown Wis	518	C	Pl
10485	same	same	Br	Pl
10486				
10487	Good for one glass beer T Racek Watertown Wis	568	C	Pl

Waukesha

10488	Charles Cork/groceries/crockery/& notions/Waukesha/Wis	446	C	Pl
10489				
10490	J A Dunbar/groceries/provisions/fruits/&c/Waukesha Wis	446	C	Pl
10491				
10492	H W Sherman Agt/dry goods/hats/caps and/groceries/Waukesha/Wis	533	C	Pl
10493				

White Water

10494	Gallt & Cole/dry/goods/groceries/boots &/shoes &c/White Water Wis	436	C	Pl
10495	same	447	C	Pl
10496	same	612	C	Pl
10497	J S Lathrop/groceries/and/provisions/White Water/Wis	447	C	Pl
10498				
10499	J T Smith/jeweler/White Water/Wis	536	C	Pl
10500	same	537	C	Pl
10501				
10502	Dr Van Valkenburgh/druggist/and/grocer/White Water/Wis	528	C	Pl
10503	same	532	C	Pl
10504				
10505	A Wahlstedt/dry goods/groceries/and/liquors/White Water/Wis	423	C	Pl
10506	A Wahlstedt/dry/goods/groceries/&/liquors/White Water Wis	436	C	Pl

ALPHABETICAL INDEX

A

Adam's 'Ton Hall'	Philadelphia	Pennsylvania
Adams James & Co	Buffalo	New York
Adams & Hatch	La Salle	Illinois
Adderly W J	Detroit	Michigan
Adleta M	Cincinnati	Ohio
Agens J L & Co	Newark	New Jersey
Alberger's Meat Store	Buffalo	New York
Albright P G	Massillon	Ohio
Alden & Fink	Cohoes	New York
Alenburg W	Cincinnati	Ohio
Allebach M B	Philadelphia	Pennsylvania
Allegheny Valley Railroad Hotel	Pittsburgh	Pennsylvania
Allegre & Wroughton	Albany	Indiana
Allen I & Son	Schoolcraft	Michigan
Alling C L	Fond Du Lac	Wisconsin
Alschuler A & H	Ottawa	Illinois
Alvord Caldwell & Alvord	Indianapolis	Indiana
Alward A M	Dowogiac	Michigan
Ambruster J	Lancaster	Ohio
American Coffee Mills	Detroit	Michigan
Ames George B	Belvidere	Illinois
Ames J	Hastings	Michigan
Amon	Philadelphia	Pennsylvania
Anderson C	Ft Wayne	Indiana
Anderson & Evans	Ft Wayne	Indiana
Anderson & Morris	La Crosse	Wisconsin
Andrew & Cooper	Dowogiac	Michigan
Andrews F W	Rochester	Minnesota
Antisdel & Hills	Detroit	Michigan
Applegate & Co	Bellevue	Ohio
Arbeiter Halle	Covington	Kentucky
Arcade House	Providence	Rhode Island
Armbruster J	Lancaster	Ohio
Armstrong B B	Cincinnati	Ohio
Armstrong F H	Detroit	Michigan
Arnold F	Cincinnati	Ohio
Arnold O	Ligonier	Indiana
Aschermann E & Co	Milwaukee	Wisconsin
Ash C H P	Bowling Green	Indiana
Ash & Black	Bowling Green	Indiana
Atlantic Garden	New York	New York
Atwood E W	Bridgeport	Connecticut
Austin J S	Cincinnati	Ohio
Autenrieth Cafe	New York	New York
Avermaat H	Cincinnati	Ohio

B

Babcock Chas	Troy	New York
Babcock & Cobb	Kalamazoo	Michigan

ALPHABETICAL INDEX—Continued

Bacciocco	Cincinnati	Ohio
Bach Philip	Ann Arbor	Michigan
Bacher E	Cincinnati	Ohio
Bahr C	New York	New York
Baierle Chicago Saloon	Chicago	Illinois
Bailey J D	Gallipolis	Ohio
Baker & Brown	Hudson	Michigan
Baldwin & Sweet	Greensboro	Indiana
Baltz & Stilz	Philadelphia	Pennsylvania
Bamlet G	Detroit	Michigan
Bang H J	New York	New York
Barie L W	Detroit	Michigan
Barker & Illsley	Chicago	Illinois
Barnard G P	Grand Rapids	Michigan
Barnes A & W H	Martinsburg	Ohio
Barnes J P	Anderson	Illinois
Barnes Roswell	Brighton	Michigan
Barney Bros	Ligonier	Indiana
Barrett G B	Cadiz	Ohio
Barrows E G	Buffalo	New York
Barrows E S	Janesville	Wisconsin
Barry & Mc Donnell	Knoxville	Tennessee
Bartels H	Syracuse	New York
Bartholomew & McAllan	Valpariso	Indiana
Bartlett Goble & Co	Chesterville	Ohio
Bartlett & Rigby	Frederickstown	Ohio
Bassett's	Glen Eaton	West Virginia
Bast Ch	Milwaukee	Wisconsin
Bathgate R	Cincinnati	Ohio
Bauder & Button	Lyons	Michigan
Bauer John	Cincinnati	Ohio
Baughman C D & Bro	Lisbon	Indiana
Baum Walter & Co	Avilla	Indiana
Beach G	Perrysburg	Ohio
Beach P E	Wooster	Ohio
Beane W A	Goshen	Indiana
Beard George & Son	Detroit	Michigan
Beck Sam'l	Corunna	Indiana
Beer C H	Cincinnati	Ohio
Beers Isaac	Marshall	Michigan
Beeson H W	Detroit	Michigan
Beilstein F	Pittsburgh	Pennsylvania
Beirn M F	Philadelphia	Pennsylvania
Bell Wm	Erie	Pennsylvania
Belknap B P	Cincinnati	Ohio
Bellack H	Watertown	Wisconsin
Bellaire Ferry Ticket	Bellaire	Ohio
Bement W W	South Bend	Indiana
Benjamin & Herrick	Albany	New York
Benner & Bendinger	New York	New York
Bennett Dr	Cincinnati	Ohio
Bennett C H	Cincinnati	Ohio
Bennett Thomas	New York	New York

ALPHABETICAL INDEX—Continued

Benson C	Winona	Minnesota
Beresford Frank	Cincinnati	Ohio
Bernacki Chas W	East Saginaw	Michigan
Bertram & Co	Watertown	Wisconsin
Best J C	Ligonier	Indiana
Best Philip	Milwaukee	Wisconsin
Best & Co	Milwaukee	Wisconsin
Betts O S	Hillsdale	Michigan
Meyer Meyer & Bro	Kendallville	Indiana
Bickel Wm	Huntington	Indiana
Beiler F J	Buffalo	New York
Bier Jno F & Bro	Chillicothe	Ohio
Binder Wm	Saginaw City	Michigan
Binder & Co	Bay City	Michigan
Bingham & Jarvis	Cooperstown	New York
Bippus & Morgan	Huntington	Indiana
Birge R H	Oberlin	Ohio
Bishop Giles	Flint	Michigan
Bishop Sam	North Liberty	Ohio
Black & Kibler	Hillsboro	Ohio
Blackman & Dibble	Adrian	Michigan
Blain I W	New York	New York
Blaisdell W R	Lowell	Michigan
Blakeslee C C	Jonesville	Wisconsin
Blatz V	Milwaukee	Wisconsin
Block J	Lancaster	Ohio
Blome Fred C	Detroit	Michigan
Blood Jno H Agt	St Louis	Missouri
Blowney & Johns	South Bend	Indiana
Bock G	Oshkosh	Wisconsin
Bock Wm	Johnstown	Pennsylvania
Bodden M	Milwaukee	Wisconsin
Bode J L	New York	New York
Bodtker Jas	Madison	Wisconsin
Bogar D S	Freeport	Illinois
Bogardus W H	North Prairie	Wisconsin
Boger I	Findlay	Ohio
Bohm John	Chillicothe	Ohio
Boles Jos	Oshkosh	Wisconsin
Bollinger W J	Lena	Illinois
Boman Lew	Cincinnati	Ohio
Bonbright J S	Bellaire	Ohio
Bond C	Cadiz	Indiana
Boose R	Lima	Ohio
Booth & Sturgis	Logansport	Indiana
Boston Store	Indianapolis	Indiana
Bosworth & Whitford	Kendallsville	Indiana
Boutwell Oliver	Troy	New York
Bowen Ira	Corunna	Indiana
Bowen M M	Kendallsville	Indiana
Bowman J R	Wooster	Ohio
Bowne C L	Cooperstown	New York
Brackenridge T K	Ft Wayne	Indiana

ALPHABETICAL INDEX—Continued

Brady P	Bellevue	Ohio
Brain W G	Springfield	Ohio
Brandiff A D & Co	Ft Wayne	Indiana
Brass A R	Fond du lac	Wisconsin
Braun & Schellworth	Brooklyn	New York
Brennan Jas	New York	New York
Brewer C M	Marshall	Michigan
Brewster D S	Freeport	Illinois
Bridgen's	New York	New York
Brimelow T	New York	New York
Bristor J H	Steubensville	Ohio
Broas Bros	New York	New York
Broeg & Gerber	Detroit	Michigan
Brooks Wm	Battle Creek	Michigan
Brooks Wm	Elkhart	Indiana
Brooks W H Jr	Ft Wayne	Indiana
Brower H & Bro	Grand Haven	Michigan
Brown Ira	Chicago	Illinois
Brown J J	Chicago	Illinois
Brown M S	New York	New York
Brown N A	Kenosha	Wisconsin
Brown W S	New York	New York
Brown & Dill Drs	Piqua	Ohio
Bruce C G	Cleveland	Ohio
Bruggeman A	Cincinnati	Ohio
Brumter S	Wooster	Ohio
Brunson J M	Kenton	Ohio
Buchanan Sam	Huntington	Indiana
Buck & Farrar	Adrian	Michigan
Buffums Mineral Water	Pittsburgh	Pennsylvania
Buhl C C	Richmond	Indiana
Bunyan N & J R	Kendallsville	Indiana
Burkhart F A	Detroit	Michigan
Burkholder P	Beverly	Ohio
Burleson A	Litchfield	Michigan
Burritt H	Maumee City	Ohio
Burton's Exchange	Portsmouth	Ohio
Busch Chas	Detroit	Michigan
Butcher J	Newport	Kentucky
Butler Witter & Co	Lyons	Michigan
Button A	Ravenna	Ohio

C

Cadot J J & Bro	Gallipolis	Ohio
Cain J C	Dayton	Ohio
Camp T P	Stoughton	Michigan
Campbell D	Mauston	Wisconsin
Campbell J	Cincinnati	Ohio
Campbell M C	Philadelphia	Pennsylvania
Campbell & Calmon	Detroit	Michigan
Campbell Linn & Co	Detroit	Michigan

ALPHABETICAL INDEX—Continued

Card Pearce & Co	Hillsdale	Michigan
Carland's	New York	New York
Carle P & Son	Collinsville	Ohio
Carlile D	Warsaw	Indiana
Carpeles & Co	Columbus	Wisconsin
Carpeles & Co	Waterloo	Wisconsin
Carpeles Ph & Co	Beloit	Wisconsin
Carpenter & Pier	Fond Du Lac	Wisconsin
Carr Ryon & Co	Greenfield	Indiana
Carson Wm	Allegheny City	Pennsylvania
Carswell L R	Janesville	Wisconsin
Cary H G O	Zanesville	Ohio
Case J I & Co	Racine	Wisconsin
Castle J A	Adrian	Michigan
Castle W B	Sandwich	Illinois
Cefandorf G A	New York	New York
Central Coal Co	Cincinnati	Ohio
Central National D V S Home	Philadelphia	Pennsylvania
Chadwick C	Camden	Ohio
Chamberlain Bros	Cincinnati	Ohio
Chandler A	Chicago	Illinois
Chandler C	Cleveland	Ohio
Chaney & Harris	Hillsboro	Ohio
Chapman's One Priced Store	Janesville	Wisconsin
Chestnut John	Jackson	Ohio
Childs Die Sinker	Chicago	Illinois
Childs James B	Wooster	Ohio
Childs John	Corunna	Indiana
Chord S M	South Bend	Indiana
Christiansen H A	Detroit	Michigan
Cin & Cov Ferry Co	Cincinnati	Ohio
City Brewery	Chicago	Illinois
City Brewery Malt House	Milwaukee	Wisconsin
City Hosiery Store	Allegheny	Pennsylvania
City Tea House	Cincinnati	Ohio
City of New York	New York	New York
Clark's Drugs	Flint	Michigan
Clark G & W	Detroit	Michigan
Clark M H	Clarkston	Michigan
Clark & Carpenter	Fond Du Lac	Wisconsin
Clark N M & Co	East Saginaw	Michigan
Clark's C E	Cincinnati	Ohio
Cleveland Detroit & La Salle	Detroit	Michigan
Close P	Fremont	Ohio
Clough J	Racine	Wisconsin
Cobb Wm R	Brighton	Michigan
Cobb & Fisher	Kalamazoo	Michigan
Cochran A C	Cambridge	Ohio
Cochran H M	Mc Connelsville	Ohio
Coe & Hayden	Winona	Minnesota
Coffin C M	West Newton	Ohio
Cohen A	Leavenworth	Kansas
Cohen S	Detroit	Michigan

ALPHABETICAL INDEX—Continued

Colby G A & Co	Niles	Michigan
Coleman S H	Juneau	Michigan
Coles Bekery	Cincinnati	Ohio
Collier V P	Battlecreek	Michigan
Collins Bro's	Paris	Illinois
Commission Boots & Shoes	Cincinnati	Ohio
Comstock & Bro	Albion	Michigan
Congdon Bros	Chelsea	Michigan
Connecticut Mutual Life Ins Co	Cincinnati	Ohio
Connell E & Co	Janesville	Wisconsin
Connely A C	Paris	Illinois
Connely's New York Store	Brazil	Indiana
Conroy Chas	Cincinnati	Ohio
Conry T J	Buffalo	New York
Coombs	Philadelphia	Pennsylvania
Cooper A J	Milwaukee	Wisconsin
Copland A W	Detroit	Michigan
Cordes & Platz	Watertown	Wisconsin
Cork Chas	Waukeska	Wisconsin
Corle J F	Kendallville	Indiana
Costello's	Cincinnati	Ohio
Cotteral W W	Middletown	Indiana
Countiss R H	Chicago	Illinois
Courlander & Pressgood	Grand Rapids	Michigan
Coutts & Bro	Perth Ambo	New Jersey
Cov & Cin Ferry Co	Covington	Kentucky
Cox & Landers	Brooklyn	Indiana
Craddick & Homan	Danville	Indiana
Craig & Foy	Birmingham	Ohio
Crane H A	Corunna	Michigan
Crew B L	Richmond	Ohio
Crittenden Shades	Cincinnati	Ohio
Crooks C & Co	Granville	Indiana
Crosby C L	Detroit	Michigan
Crosby Joseph	Zanesville	Ohio
Cullen J V	Kokomo	Indiana
Cullen N W	Middletown	Indiana
Cullen Tom	New York	New York
Culley R C	Cairo	Illinois
Cummings C	Charlotte	Michigan
Cummings & Anderson	Shelby	Ohio
Curtis C P	Toledo	Ohio
Curtis Geo E	Detroit	Michigan

D

Daggett J M & Co	Cincinnati	Ohio
Dahmen C & Son	Cross Plains	Wisconsin
Dale J M	Plymouth	Indiana
Danforth L	Buffalo	New York
Dangler J B	Massillon	Ohio
Darling W	Saranac	Michigan

ALPHABETICAL INDEX—Continued

Dartt H	Almond	New York
Davenport J & Son	Elkhart	Indiana
Davies Jesse	Huntington	Indiana
Davies & Maxwell	West Unity	Ohio
Davis A J	Rockford	Illinois
Davis A M	New Paris	Indiana
Davis & Bates	Kalamazoo	Michigan
Davis & Whiteman	Wappakoneta	Ohio
Dayton M	Martinsburg	Ohio
Dean & Co	Ann Arbor	Michigan
Dean & Slade	Palatine	Illinois
Dean Godfrey & Co	Detroit	Michigan
Dearborn & Root	Stoughton	Wisconsin
Dechand & Engelhart	Cleveland	Ohio
Decker J	Ligonier	Indiana
Deinzer John	Hamilton	Ohio
Dehner & Maples	Pontiac	Michigan
Dervin T	Watertown	Wisconsin
Detrich A	Green Bay	Wisconsin
Detroit City Flour Mills	Detroit	Michigan
Dickinson Comstock & Co	Utica	New York
Dickson A M & Co	Dowagiac	Michigan
Dickson D	Detroit	Michigan
Dickson H B & Co	Plymouth	Indiana
Diehl J J	New York	New York
Diem Carl	New York	New York
Diffenbaugh J D	Freeport	Illinois
Dillon Dr E & Son	Freemont	Ohio
Dixon Geo R & Co	Cincinnati	Ohio
Dixon J E & Sons	Kilbourne City	Wisconsin
Dobson H	Providence	Rhode Island
Dodd's Elgin Dairy	Chicago	Illinois
Dolman J	Covington	Kentucky
Doniphan J N	Cincinnati	Ohio
Doornink D J	Milwaukee	Wisconsin
Dorland Garrett T	Cincinnati	Ohio
Doscher C	New York	New York
Downing R	Cincinnati	Ohio
Drover's Hotel	St Louis	Missouri
Druecker J	Fort Washington	Wisconsin
Drury E A	Detroit	Michigan
Dryer D & Co	Chicago	Illinois
Dryfoos M	Fremont	Ohio
Dubois F N	Chicago	Illinois
Duburn A M	Buffalo	New York
Duden J S	Wooster	Ohio
Duffy Patrick	Watertown	Wisconsin
Dunbar J A	Waukesha	Wisconsin
Dunlap Wm	Steubenville	Ohio
Dunn & Co	Boston	Massachusetts
Dunn Goudy & Bro	Cleveland	Ohio
Durst J	Dayton	Ohio
Dutton A C	Eaton Rapids	Michigan
Dynes J M	Morrow	Ohio

ALPHABETICAL INDEX—Continued

E

E A W	Red Wing	Minnesota
Eager W B	Elyria	Ohio
Early C & Co	Brownstown	Indiana
Eastman H	Niles	Michigan
Eastman Business College	Poughkeepsie	New York
Eaton & Barnes	Tomah	Michigan
Eccard Francis	Detroit	Michigan
Eckert J A	Pittsburgh	Pennsylvania
Eckert L	Cincinnati	Ohio
Eckhart John	Wheeling	West Virginia
Eckley O J	Hillsboro	Ohio
Eckstein David	Lansing	Michigan
Edwards	Chicago	Illinois
Eisenlord Wm	Detroit	Michigan
Eliel L	La Porte	Indiana
Elkins John	Racine	Wisconsin
Elliot & Hinshaw	Lynn	Indiana
Elliot & Swain	Mechanicsburg	Indiana
Ellis C W	Cincinnati	Ohio
Ellsworth & Halsey	Lacon	Illinois
Elwood I L	De Kalb	Illinois
Emigraten Office	Madison	Wisconsin
Emlinger F	Racine	Wisconsin
Emmert W P	Freeport	Illinois
Emrich & Co	Fremont	Ohio
Emswiler G P & Co	Richmond	Indiana
Endly H	Mansfield	Ohio
Eingel John	Elizabethport	New Jersey
Engert V C	Covington	Kentuckey
English J M	Racine	Wisconsin
Epting & Eaton	Saganaw City	Michigan
Erhardt & Raps	Racine	Wisconsin
Erlenborn A	Mendota	Illinois
Escherich A W	Chicago	Illinois
Evans S C	Kendallville	Indiana
Evans & Allen	Binghamton	New York
Evericks & Barton	Zanesville	Ohio

F

Fairbanks & Scriver	Lawton	Michigan
Faller J & Son	La Porte	Indiana
Falvey Thos	Racine	Wisconsin
Fanley & Brechbill	Uniontown	Ohio
Farmer's Clothing Store	Detroit	Michigan
Farnhain's Bronchial Tablet	Hillsdale	Michigan
Farnham D & Co	Edgertown	Ohio
Felix Dining Rooms	New York	New York
Fenton & Beck	Cincinnati	Ohio
Ferguson J	Cincinnati	Ohio
Fickhart C H	Circleville	Ohio

ALPHABETICAL INDEX—Continued

Fiedler E	Cincinnati	Ohio
Filner A H	Milwaukee	Wisconsin
Findlay R K & Co	Madison	Wisconsin
Fischer F	Cincinnati	Ohio
Fishbein Jos	Milwaukee	Wisconsin
Fisher J	New York	New York
Fisher & Hendryx	Tecumseh	Michigan
Fisher & Rohr	Watertown	Wisconsin
Fisler & Chance	Cincinnati	Ohio
Fitch Ira H	Aurora	Illinois
Fitzgerald J W	Cincinnati	Ohio
Fitzsimmons C & Co	Detroit	Michigan
Flach Chas	Cincinnati	Ohio
Flagg Cheap Store	Chicago	Illinois
Flagg & McDonald	Chicago	Illinois
Flanagan R	Philadelphia	Pennsylvania
Fleming Jos	Pittsburgh	Pennsylvania
Fleming Wm & Bro	Lansing	Iowa
Follett G W	Fremont	Indiana
Foote J R	Paw Paw	Michigan
Ford D	Cairo	Illinois
Fornshell J P	Camden	Ohio
Fort P V & Co	Albany	New York
Foster James Jr & Co	Cincinnati	Ohio
Foster & Metcalf	Grand Rapids	Michigan
Fountain W C	Watertown	Wisconsin
Fox W G	Buffalo	New York
Fox & Smith	Pontiac	Michigan
Fraker Bros	Oshkosh	Wisconsin
Francis E P	Fall River	Massachusetts
Franckenberg & Keller	Newbury	Wisconsin
Frank John	Cincinnati	Ohio
Frankfurth Wm	Milwaukee	Wisconsin
Frechtling H & W	Hamilton	Ohio
Freedman & Goodkind	Chicago	Illinois
Freedman Goodkind & Co	Chicago	Illinois
Freeman L	Detroit	Michigan
Freise Fr	New York	New York
French	Clarksburg	Ohio
French & Parson	Hillsdale	Michigan
French & Swonger	Piqua	Ohio
Frisbie	Detroit	Michigan
Fritz F	Fond Du Lac	Wisconsin
Frost's Medicines	Cincinnati	Ohio
Frost H M	Eaton Rapids	Michigan
Frost & Daniels	Eaton Rapids	Michigan
Fry & Johnston	Sidney	Ohio

G

Gaffney P	Chicago	Illinois
Gaffney & McDonnell	Columbia City	Indiana
Gage Lyall & Keller	Lyons	Iowa

ALPHABETICAL INDEX—Continued

Gage D W	Cleveland	Ohio
Gage Geo	Buffalo	New York
Gale A & H	Jonesville	Michigan
Gale A W	Concord	New Hempshire
Gall F	Chicago	Illinois
Gallagher & Hess	Saginaw City	Michigan
Gallt & Cole	White Water	Wisconsin
Galvagni John	Cincinnati	Ohio
Gardner H R & Co	Jonesville	Michigan
Gardner J F	New York	New York
Gates & Trask	Aurora	Illinois
Gavron A	New York	New York
Gay Frank L	Providence	Rhode Island
Geilfus L	Cincinnati	Ohio
Geis F & Bro's	Detroit	Michigan
Geisendorf C E & Co	Indianapolis	Indiana
Geisendorff G W & Co	Indianapolis	Indiana
Geiser J	Cincinnati	Ohio
Geiss F	Detroit	Michigan
Geitgey Samuel	Wooster	Ohio
Gentry's	Centreville	Indiana
Gentsch Charles	New York	New York
Gentsch W	Cincinnati	Ohio
Gerdts H D	New York	New York
Gerken & Ernst	Kenosha	Wisconsin
Gerts G E & Co	Chicago	Illinois
Giaugue D	Mt Eaton	Ohio
Gies F	Detroit	Michigan
Gilbert & Hotchkiss	Cincinnati	Ohio
Gildenfenny W A	Pittsburgh	Pennsylvania
Gillett & Niles	Hudson	Michigan
Glatte G C	Kendallville	Indiana
Glacier's Pharmacy	Parma	Michigan
Gleason A	Hillsdale	Michigan
Goeldner Chas	Watertown	Michigan
Goes & Falk	Milwaukee	Wisconsin
Goetz S	Gallipolis	Ohio
G O (O Goffery)	Cincinnati	Ohio
Gold Pen Depot	Nashville	Tennessee
Goll & Frank	Milwaukee	Wisconsin
Good M H	Indianapolis	Indiana
Goodell G W	Corunna	Michigan
Gooder Rob't	Jonesboro	Indiana
Goodhue H & G	Waterloo	Iowa
Goodrich C B	Detroit	Michigan
Goodrich & Gay	Grand Rapids	Michigan
Gordon & Thurston	Wabash	Indiana
Gorham J H & A S	Cleveland	Ohio
Gotsch J H	Kendallville	Indiana
Gottlieb J	Hillsdale	Michigan
Gould D S	Rochester	Indiana
Graden E	Kendallville	Indiana
Graff C E	Milwaukee	Wisconsin

ALPHABETICAL INDEX—Continued

Graham G	New York	New York
Grant Alex'r & Co	Zanesville	Ohio
Graves Jas & Co	Wheeling	West Virginia
Graves R C	Wheeling	West Virginia
Gray J W	Steubenville	Ohio
Great Central Fair	Philadelphia	Pennsylvania
Green C T & Co	Elkhart	Indiana
Green & Wardsworth	Hudson	Michigan
Greenman A G	Sandwich	Illinois
Greenleaf D G	St Paul	Minnesota
Greenway & Co	Ripon	Wisconsin
Gregg & Dalzell	Allegheny City	Pennsylvania
Gretcher John	Columbus	Ohio
Gridley M H	Logansport	Indiana
Griffee G W	Zanesville	Ohio
Griffin A E	Marion	Ohio
Grimes & Griner	Canaan	Ohio
Griswold H & Co	Lapeer	Michigan
Grossius J	Cincinnati	Ohio
Grout J B	Indianapolis	Indiana
Groyen Jacob	Como	Indiana
Grube J A C	New York	New York
Gruber John P	New York	New York
Guipe John	Elkhart	Indiana
Gunning S W	Portsmouth	Ohio
Guth Jacob	Cincinnati	Ohio

H

Haas Carl	Cincinnati	Ohio
Haas & Rowell	Chicago	Illinois
Haben Andrew & Co	Oshkosh	Wisconsin
Hafer F H & Co	Greenville	Ohio
Hahn & Riddle	Allegheny City	Pennsylvania
Haines G	Wolf Creek	Indiana
Haines D H & Bro	Swan	Indiana
Hall E W	White Hall	New York
Hall J	Troy	Ohio
Hall D A Co	Pittsburgh	Pennsylvania
Hall & Frymire	Navarre	Ohio
Halls F J	Xenia	Ohio
Hambach	Milwaukee	Wisconsin
Hambach C	Milwaukee	Wisconsin
Hamblin G W	Stryker	Ohio
Hamilton & Co	Sparta	Wisconsin
Hamman F & Co	Detroit	Michigan
Hammar B F & Co	Memphis	Tennessee
Hammond Shoe Store	South Bend	Indiana
Hanley W W	Cincinnati	Ohio
Hanna Co	Detroit	Michigan
Hannah J W	Pittsburgh	Pennsylvania
Harley Linville	Columbia City	Indiana
Harley Wm	Chicago	Illinois

ALPHABETICAL INDEX—Continued

Harley & Johnson	Chicago	Illinois
Harpel	Cincinnati	Ohio
Harris W B & Bro	Zanesville	Ohio
Hart T W	Milwaukee	Wisconsin
Hart's Arcade Gallery	Watertown	New York
Harter E K	Troy	Ohio
Hartman C G	Cincinnati	Ohio
Hartman M	North Hampton	Ohio
Hartzel M	Cincinnati	Ohio
Harvey & Co	Ft Edwards	New York
Hasbrouch & Francher	Oshkosh	Wisconsin
Hascall Alderman & Brown	Goshen	Indiana
Haskell & Co	Kokomo	Indiana
Hasse E E	Yonkers	New York
Hastings Wm	New York	New York
Hatch & Craw	Lowell	Michigan
Hauck C I	Brooklyn	New York
Hause Dr E	Tecumseh	Michigan
Hawkins John	Cleveland	Ohio
Hawley C C	Hastings	Michigan
Hay & Clark	Oshkosh	Wisconsin
Hayes J & Bro	Cincinnati	Ohio
Heath L F	Lyons	Michigan
Heilbroner R	Chicago	Illinois
Heinman	Cincinnati	Ohio
Heintz & Henkle	Columbus	Ohio
Heinzman E	Cincinnati	Ohio
Helmeg J	Cincinnati	Ohio
Hempleman B	Cincinnati	Ohio
Hendrick B	Cincinnati	Ohio
Hendrie W A	Chicago	Illinois
Hendry Frank	Oberlin	Ohio
Henning A J	New York	New York
Herendeen & Witter	Zanesville	Ohio
Hereth J C	Indianapolis	Indiana
Herinton	Detroit	Michigan
Hermann Ch & Co	Milwaukee	Wisconsin
Herron & Amen	Hillsboro	Ohio
Herschman Bros	Binghampton	New York
Hertrich Helena	Freeport	Illinois
Hetzel Charles E	New York	New York
Hewitt Isaac	Maples Rapids	Michigan
Hewitt E & Bro	Ypsilanti	Michigan
Heyl V	Cincinnati	Ohio
Heyman John	Watertown	Wisconsin
Hiatt & Showalter	Cadiz	Indiana
Higby & Bro	Charlotte	Michigan
Higby & Stearn	Detroit	Michigan
Higgins H D	Mishawaka	Indiana
Hill Dr H H & Co	Cincinnati	Ohio
Hilterscheid Bros	Detroit	Michigan
Hind J H	Steubenville	Ohio

ALPHABETICAL INDEX—Continued

Hinshaw J A	Lynn	Indiana
Hintrick B & C Glaser	Cincinnati	Ohio
Hirst E F	Richmond	Indiana
Hochstadt Jacob	Detroit	Michigan
Hochstetter & Strause	Buffalo	New York
Hoegner Martin	Piqua	Ohio
Hoffman T	Kilbourne City	Wisconsin
Hoffman & Lewis	Green Bay	Wisconsin
Hohn Simons & Co	Kenosha	Wisconsin
Holcomb B	Mishawaka	Indiana
Holker J	Oldenburg	Indiana
Holland S & Son	Jackson	Michigan
Holmes C L	Indianapolis	Indiana
Holmes & Norton	Rockford	Illinois
Holthofer C I	Detroit	Michigan
Hoot & Meng	Freemont	Ohio
Hoover & Camp	Wellsville	Ohio
Hope & Clow	Rockford	Illinois
Horn W H	Manitowac	Wisconsin
Hough & Hall	Toledo	Ohio
Howard R R	Kalamazoo	Michigan
Howe H & Co	Hudson	Michigan
Howe Wm B	Detroit	Michigan
Hubbard Geo E	Grand Have	Michigan
Huggins Frank	Columbus	Wisconsin
Hughes J A	Cincinnati	Ohio
Hughes P	Cincinnati	Ohio
Hulsman & Alexander	Franklin	Indiana
Humrichouser H	Plymouth	Indiana
Hunt John	Neenah	Wisconsin
Hunt J W	Delphos	Ohio
Huntley & Steenland	Madison	Wisconsin
Hussey's	New York	New York
Hustler S E	Troy	Ohio
Hyatt C C	Cincinnati	Ohio
Hyenlein Geo	New York	New York

I

Ibert M	Brooklyn	New York
Icenhour & Co	Columbiana	Ohio
Idler G	Ogdensburg	New York
Ingram S A	Chicago	Illinois
Insworth J H & Co	Huntington	Indiana
Irwin John	Zanesville	Ohio
Ismon H S	Jackson	Michigan
Ivory T	Brooklyn	New York

J

Jackson Wm	Jackson	Michigan
Jacobs A	Van Wert	Ohio
Jacobs & Co	Kendallville	Indiana

ALPHABETICAL INDEX—Continued

Jaenicke & Klotzsch	Oshkosh	Wisconsin
Jahr B	Cincinnati	Ohio
Jahr B & Co	Cincinnati	Ohio
James & French	Clarksburg	Ohio
Jaxon W	Jackson	Michigan
Jenkens Henry	St Louis	Missouri
Jenkinson R & W	Allegheny	Pennsylvania
Jenks A	Dublin	Indiana
Jennings Dr D R	Ravenna	Ohio
Joergers John	Brooklyn	New York
Johnson F M	St Paul	Minnesota
Johnson J B	Indianapolis	Indiana
Johnson J F	Seymour	Indiana
Johnson Philip	Jefferson	Wisconsin
Johnson S & Bro	Henderson	Kentucky
Johnson & Oursler	Plainfield	Indiana
Johnston A M	Buffalo	New York
Johnston H	Cincinnati	Ohio
Johnston W	Cincinnati	Ohio
Jones D H	Racine	Wisconsin
Jones & Mosher	Kendallville	Indiana
Joyce J J	Kendallville	Indiana
Judd & Corthell	Chicago	Illinois
Judkins S H	Mishawaka	Indiana
Julian & Co	Troy	Ohio
Jung John	Jefferson	Wisconsin

K

Kahn L & Co	Cincinnati	Ohio
Kane George	Milwaukee	Wisconsin
Kanter Ed	Detroit	Michigan
Karl Christopher	New York	New York
Karmann A	Cincinnati	Ohio
Katzenstein J	Cincinnati	Ohio
Kaufman & Co	Springfield	Ohio
Keating E C	Hillsdale	Michigan
Keim H	Chillicothe	Ohio
Keitteridge Dr O G	Williamantic	Connecticut
Kellog & Co	Kalamazoo	Michigan
Kellogg & Hughes	Oshkosh	Wisconsin
Kelly David	Troy	Ohio
Kelly R T	New York	New York
Kelly's Store	Hartford City	West Virginia
Kendall A	Logansport	Indiana
Kendall O Sons & Co	Chicago	Illinois
Kennedy James	Iona	Michigan
Kennedy Warren	Cincinnati	Ohio
Kepner W W & Son	Columbia City	Indiana
Kern Frank	Cincinnati	Ohio
Ketcham G T	Tecumseh	Michigan
Ketcham & Barker	Toledo	Ohio
Killeen A	Greenpoint	New York

ALPHABETICAL INDEX—Continued

Kimboll A	Green Bay	Wisconsin
Kinderman Dr C	Columbia City	Indiana
Kindig J L	Goshen	Indiana
King Andrew	Clarksville	Tennessee
King J L	Circleville	Ohio
King's	Cincinnati	Ohio
King & Reed	Logansport	Indiana
Kingsland John S	Stryker	Ohio
Kingsley & Whipple	Waukegan	Illinois
Kipp G	Columbiana	Ohio
Kirby Langsworthy & Co	Milwaukee	Wisconsin
Kercherschlager J	Cincinnati	Ohio
Kirchner M J	Tiffin	Ohio
Kirker J & Co	Cincinnati	Ohio
Kitteredge B & Co	Cincinnati	Ohio
Klauber S & Co	Madison	Wisconsin
Klaus Philip	Green Bay	Wisconsin
Klein J	Cincinnati	Ohio
Kleine Henry	Dayton	Ohio
Kleinsteuber A	Milwaukee	Wisconsin
Kleinsteuber Chas	Milwaukee	Wisconsin
Knapp I J	Utica	New York
Knapp Wm	Rockford	Illinois
Knauber Jacob	Cincinnati	Ohio
Knecht Wm	Cincinnati	Ohio
Kneeland P N	Detroit	Michigan
Knoblock H	Masillon	Ohio
Knobloch J C	South Bend	Indiana
Knoop's Cigars	New York	New York
Koch John	Cincinnati	Ohio
Koerner J M & V	Columbus	Ohio
Kolb Charles	Newark	New Jersey
Koos	Cincinnati	Ohio
Kramer A S	Chillicothe	Ohio
Kreager B	Cincinnati	Ohio
Kreber H	Cincinnati	Ohio
Krebs D	Perrysbury	Ohio
Krebs D W & Co	Fremont	Ohio
Krengel A	Cincinnati	Ohio
Kreuger F	Beaver Dam	Wisconsin
Kreutzer J	Peru	Indiana
Krug & Reed	Logansport	Indiana
Kruger & Booth	Grand Repids	Michigan
Kuhn Charles	Indianapolis	Indiana
Kurt H	Milwaukee	Wisconsin
Kurz Louis	Milwaukee	Wisconsin
Kusel Daniel	Watertown	Wisconsin
Kusterer C	Grand Rapids	Michigan

L

Ladner F & L	Philadelphia	Pennsylvania
Lake V A	Rockton	Illinois
Lambert A	Philadelphia	Pennsylvania

ALPHABETICAL INDEX—Continued

Lane H M	New York	New York
Lane John	Warsaw	Indiana
Lang Charles	Worcester	Massachusetts
Langdon's Hardware Store	Belmont	New York
Langhorn J	Cleveland	Ohio
Lanphear W K	Cincinnati	Ohio
Lants J	Kendallville	Indiana
Lapham & Thayer	Detroit	Michigan
Lapsley D L & Co	Nashville	Tennessee
Larwell J F	Cincinnati	Ohio
Larzelere D & Co	Dowagiac	Michigan
Lash Wm H & Co	Goshen	Indiana
Lasurs S	Cincinnati	Ohio
Lallemand's Specific	St Louis	Missouri
Lathrop J S	White Water	Wisconsin
Lauferty Joseph	Goshen	Indiana
Lauferty I	Ft Wayne	Indiana
Lavey S S	Columbia City	Indiana
Lawrence J J	Madison	Wisconsin
Lawrence Wm	Wellsville	Ohio
Lawrence & Noble	Goshen	Indiana
Lazaress H	Cincinnati	Ohio
Leas William	Sonora	Ohio
Leavens C W & Co	Neenah	Wisconsin
Leavitt F A	Chicago	Illinois
Leavitt & Bevis	Cincinnati	Ohio
Lederer A & Co	Milwaukee	Wisconsin
Lee John W	Lexington	Kentucky
Le Fevre H Y	Previdence	Rhode Island
Leggett S T	East Saganaw	Michigan
Leis John	Wooster	Ohio
Lembert E L	Frazensburg	Ohio
Lenour J F	Indianapolis	Indiana
Leonard J B	Battle Creek	Michigan
Leonard P	Eaton Rapids	Michigan
Levy E	Morrow	Ohio
Levy & Duncan	Oshkosh	Wisconsin
Lewis J S	Jonesville	Michigan
Lewis Jas & Co	La Porte	Indiana
Lewis & Moses	Detroit	Michigan
Linch H	Brookville	Indiana
Lindenmueller Gustavus	New York	New York
Lindermann M	Cincinnati	Ohio
Lines & Russell	Oshkosh	Wisconsin
Lininger & Bro	Peru	Illinois
Lippincott J C & W H	Pittsburg	Pennsylvania
Livingston I	Marshall	Wisconsin
Lochary P	Morristown	Ohio
Loeffler Fred	Massilon	Ohio
Loewenstein H	Cincinnati	Ohio
Longwell G W	Paw Paw	Michigan
Loomis J M	Kendallville	Indiana
Lord D H & Co	Hillsdale	Michigan

ALPHABETICAL INDEX—Continued

Lott & Warner	Sycamore	Illinois
Lotz C	Detroit	Michigan
Loveday J L & Co	Waukegan	Illinois
Low J W	Springfield	Ohio
Lowell J C	Fond Du Lac	Wisconsin
Ludewig A	Pittsburg	Pennsylvania
Ludlow & Bushnell	Springfield	Ohio
Luhrs Charles A	New York	New York
Luk F W	Cincinnati	Ohio
Lutes J	Butler	Indiana
Lyman Moury & Co	Kenosha	Wisconsin
Lyons Jas	Hartford	Indiana

M

Madison Brewery	Madison	Wisconsin
Magnus C	New York	New York
Mahnken J	New York	New York
Maines James	Bakerstown	Ohio
Maloney B	New York	New York
March C C	Goshen	Indiana
March George	Hillsboro	Ohio
March & Miner	Chicago	Illinois
Markham R T	Cincinnati	Ohio
Marsh & Miner	Cincinnati	Ohio
Marshall M L	Oswego	New York
Martin's	Cincinnati	Ohio
Martin R C	Monroeville	Ohio
Martin S C	Wooster	Ohio
Martin S T	Columbus	Ohio
Martin Bros	Detroit	Michigan
Marvin C L	Cleveland	Ohio
Marz M	Detroit	Michigan
Mason T	Fond Du Lac	Wisconsin
Mason & Son	Circleville	Ohio
Mather & Shefferly	Detroit	Michigan
Matthews James	Centreville	Ohio
Maumee & Perrysburg Bridge Co	Manumee City	Ohio
May C M	Steubenville	Ohio
Mayhew Ira	Albion	Michigan
Melville H B	New York	New York
Merchant's Exchange	Columbus	Ohio
Meredith L Phil & N McClung	Cincinnati	Ohio
Merriam Jos A	Boston	Massachusetts
Merril L A	Grand Rapids	Michigan
Mesing F W	Kendallville	Indiana
Messmore & Lucking	Detroit	Michigan
Mester A & Co	Eaton Rapids	Michigan
Metcalf O G	Belmont	Ohio
Metz Adam	Cincinnati	Ohio
Metz J & D	Cincinnati	Ohio
Metzger George	Cincinnati	Ohio
Meyer A	Chicago	Illinois
Meyer C E	Chicago	Illinois

ALPHABETICAL INDEX—Continued

Meyer G R	Chicago	Illinois
Meyer J A	Canton	Ohio
Meyer L	Cincinnati	Ohio
Meyer J F W	Jefferson	Wisconsin
Meyer M C	Milwaukee	Wisconsin
Meyer C & Co	Cincinnati	Ohio
Mickesell J & Bro	Charlotte	Michigan
Mickey Thos	Shelby	Ohio
Miedeking	Cincinnati	Ohio
Miehling Edward	New York	New York
Mier S & Co	Ligonier	Indiana
Miles A C	Wappakoneta	Ohio
Miles & Sperry	Chesterville	Ohio
Millar Robt	Detroit	Michigan
Millen C H	Ann Arbor	Michigan
Millen D P	Waukegan	Illinois
Miller Frederick	Milwaukee	Wisconsin
Miller James	Paris	Illinois
Miller J & H	Racine	Wisconsin
Miller Jeff	Bryan	Ohio
Miller L	New York	New York
Miller & Co	Wooster	Ohio
Miller A & Co	Milwaukee	Wisconsin
Miller H & Co	Louisville	Kentucky
Miller & Crow	Kendallville	Indiana
Miller's Hair Dye	New York	New York
Miner Henry	Pittsburg	Pennsylvania
Minger J U	Chicago	Illinois
Mitchell C T & Co	Hillsdale	Michigan
Mittnacht G M & Co	New York	New York
Mitzlaff F	Milwaukee	Wisconsin
Moe Geo	Detroit	Michigan
Monarch S B	Cincinnati	Ohio
Monk's Metal Signs	New York	New York
Montz Henry C	New York	New York
Moore J T	Cincinnati	Ohio
Moore Wm	Chemung	Illinois
Morgan & Ferry	Cincinnati	Ohio
Moritz Bro & Co	Indianapolis	Indiana
Morris & Messinger	Pontiac	Michigan
Morse E C	Mussey	Ohio
Moseley H L	Durand	Illinois
Moser H J	Cincinnati	Ohio
Mosin & Marr	Milwaukee	Wisconsin
Mosure Bro & Lemon	Fredericstown	Ohio
Mott & Bros	Hillsdale	Michigan
Mott C E & Co	Hillsdale	Michigan
Motter Rufus	Chillicothe	Ohio
Moulton J	Watertown	Wisconsin
Mulligan H	Philadelphia	Pennsylvania
Murdock A J	Logansport	Indiana
Murdock James	Cincinnati	Ohio

ALPHABETICAL INDEX—Continued

Murdock Jas Jr	Cincinnati	Ohio
Murdock Spencer	Cincinnati	Ohio
Murphy & Bro	Springfield	Ohio
Murray & Bro	Pierceton	Indiana
Muth H L	Janesvile	Wisconsin
Myers E & Co	Cincinnati	Ohio
Mc Burney Jas	Albany	New York
Mc Carthy J W	Pittsburg	Pennsylvania
Mc Carty Washington	Urbana	Ohio
Mc Cauley J	Steubenville	Ohio
Mc Caw & Richey	Oxford	Ohio
Mc Clenahan W C & Co	Cincinnati	Ohio
Mc Conville D	Steubenville	Ohio
Mc Creery Joseph	Indianapolis	Indiana
Mc Culloch T & H C	Anderson	Indiana
Mc Donald T W	Cincinnati	Ohio
Mc Donald Wm	Memphis	Tennessee
Mc Donald & Co	Logansport	Indiana
Mc Grew W H	West Unity	Ohio
Mc Kain J	Pittsburg	Pennsylvania
Mc Kay	East Saginaw	Michigan
Mc Kay & Lapsley	Nashville	Tennessee
Mc Laughlin Jas	London	Ohio
Mc Lean G W	North Hampton	Ohio
Mc Lean G W	Springfield	Ohio
Mc Millan T M	Portage City	Wisconsin
Mc Millans W K	Sharonville	Ohio
Mc Neil M	Elgin	Illinois
Mc Vey Jason	Sidney	Ohio

N

Naper Robert	Naperville	Illinois
Nash G W	Brownsburg	Indiana
Naylor W H	Brighton	Michigan
Nebel C	Sauk City	Wisconsin
Neff A	Oshkosh	Wisconsin
Neuburger & Hamburger	La Porte	Indiana
Neuburger J M	La Porte	Indiana
Newcomb D F	Columbus	Wisconsin
Newcomb E	Madison	Wisconsin
Newton W S	Sparta	Wisconsin
Newton & Kumlers	Oxford	Ohio
New York & Albany Steamboat	New York	New York
New York C R R Trains	New York	New York
New York Store	Waterbury	Connecticut
Nicoll D & Bro	Wheeling	West Virginia
Neibuhr H	Cincinnati	Ohio
Neimer F J	Cincinnati	Ohio
Nill George C	Ligonier	Indiana
Nold & Co	Wooster	Ohio
Nolwer J H	Cincinnati	Ohio
Noris R D	Cincinnati	Ohio
N'pt & Cov	Newport	Kentucky
Nye & Youmans	Fond Du Lac	Wisconsin

ALPHABETICAL INDEX—Continued

O

Oberly C	Canton	Ohio
O'Donoghue & Naish	Cincinnati	Ohio
Oppenheimer & Metzger	Chicago	Illinois
O'Reilly Bros	Cincinnati	Ohio
Orr F B	Mansfield	Ohio
Osborn M	Plainfield	Indiana
Osborne & Bro	Findlay	Ohio
Ostendorf Wm	Chicago	Illinois
Ostrander D	Jefferson	Wisconsin
Ott Geo V	Madison	Wisconsin
Owen & Taylor Mrs	Wilmington	Ohio

P

Packard W & A J	Youngstown	Ohio
Packard & Co	West Greenville	Pennsylvania
Paeschke Carl	Milwaukee	Wisconsin
Page J M & Co	Morenci	Michigan
Paige S B & J A	Oshkosh	Wisconsin
Pairin Chas	Lancaster	Ohio
Palmer F J & F	Atlas	Michigan
Palmer & Goodsall	Hudson	Michigan
Panzer B	Cincinnati	Ohio
Parker A	Pontiac	Michigan
Parker E S	Niles	Michigan
Parker Geo H	Detroit	Michigan
Parker H S & Co	Kalamazoo	Michigan
Parker R R	Indianapolis	Indiana
Parson G	New York	New York
Parson & Barlow	Appleton	Wisconsin.
Patrick James	Wooster	Ohio
Passage Ticket from London to Chicago	Chicago	Illinois
Patterson C S	Tecumseh	Michigan
Patterson I N	Kokomo	Indiana
Patterson N	Barnesville	Ohio
Pearce J	Ligonier	Michigan
Pearce & Co	Hillsdale	Michigan
Pearson & Bro	Troy	Ohio
Pease C A	Ravenna	Ohio
Peck W G	Chicago	Illinois
Peck D & Co	Ironton	Missouri
Peck & Orvis	Baraboo	Wisconsin
Peck & Pratt	Beloit	Wisconsin
Peebles	Cincinnati	Ohio
Pierce J W	Grand Rapids	Michigan
Perkin's Tea Store	Pittsburg	Pennsylvania
Pennoyer & Larkin	Paris	Illinois
Pentz A C	Pittsburg	Pennsylvania
Perkins A T	Fond Du Lac	Wisconsin
Perkins Wm Jr	Detroit	Michigan

ALPHABETICAL INDEX—Continued

Perkins & Smith	Fon du Lac	Wisconsin
Perrin H	Wilmington	Ohio
Perrin L W	Kalamazoo	Michigan
Peter R & J T	Clarkston	Michigan
Petersen's	Honesdale	Pennsylvania
Peterson H	Stoughton	Michigan
Pettibone J & Co	Fond Du Lac	Wisconsin
Pfaff Chas	New York	New York
Pfeiffer & Co	Norfolk	Virginia
Phelps J W & Co	Mason	Michigan
Philip	Cincinnati	Ohio
Phillips	Providence	Rhode Island
Peifer C I	Charlotte	Michigan
Pierce & Son	West Unity	Ohio
Pierr P	Fort Wayne	Indiana
Piper C	Charlotte	Michigan
Pittock's News Dealer	Pittsburg	Pennsylvania
Pittock John W	Pittsburg	Pennsylvania
Pittsburgh Gazette	Pittsburg	Pennsylvania
Planer & Kayser	Milwaukee	Wisconsin
Platt G W & H C	Niles	Michigan
Pleisteiner J G	Cincinnati	Ohio
Plessner & Son	Toledo	Ohio
Plumb Chas	Cincinnati	Ohio
Pogue & Jones	Cincinnati	Ohio
Pohle	Providence	Rhode Island
Pomeroy Fry & Co	Indianapolis	Indiana
Pond C C	Detroit	Michigan
Pond D	Dowagiac	Michigan
Porter Henry	Cincinnati	Ohio
Porter G C & Co	Meadville	Pennsylvania
Post John C	Buffalo	New York
Pottenger D R & Co	Warsaw	Indiana
Potter P L	Middletown	Ohio
Potwin C W & Co	Zanesville	Ohio
Powell M L	New Castle	Indiana
Powers E K	Grand Rapids	Michigan
Prentice W R	Chicago	Illinois
Prentiss A W	Monroeville	Ohio
Prescott's Soda Water	New York	New York
Preston Wm	Wilmington	Ohio
Price Brothers	Sullivan	Indiana
Pritzlaff J & Co	Milwaukee	Wisconsin
Proudy F	Detroit	Michigan
Prusel I W & Co	Schoolcraft	Wisconsin
Pulmonale	Albany	New York
Purdy A M	South Bend	Indiana

Q

Queeby J J	Peru	Indiana
Quinlan T J	Cleveland	Ohio
Quinn John	New York	New York

ALPHABETICAL INDEX—Continued

Schroeder Jno	Detroit	Michigan
Schroeder John & Co	Cincinnati	Ohio
Schubert John	Hamilton	Ohio
Schuch F	Loudenville	Ohio
Schuhs John	New York	New York
Schultze Edw	New York	New York
Schultz & Negley	Cincinnati	Ohio
Sealy H A	Detroit	Michigan
Seas J F	Orville	Ohio
Sedgwick S P & Co	Bloomingdale	Illinois
Seely John	Detroit	Michigan
Seiters PH J	New York	New York
Selby E G	Bryan	Ohio
Selby E G & Co	Bryan	Ohio
Senour J F	Indianapolis	Indiana
Senour Wm	Cincinnati	Ohio
Severn & Jones	Milwaukee	Wisconsin
Seward S B	Buffalo	New York
Shafer Mendal N	Cincinnati	Ohio
Shafer & Bro	Huntington	Indiana
Shagnon J B	Detroit	Michigan
Shattuck C E	Owasso	Michigan
Shattuck F W	Providence	Rhode Island
Shaw G M	New London	Ohio
Shaw H E	Cincinnati	Ohio
Sheen F	Cincinnati	Ohio
Sheldon E H	Constantine	Michigan
Sherer John	Allegheny City	Pennsylvania
Sherman A M	Ogdenburg	New York
Sherman H W	Waukesha	Wisconsin
Sherman J D	Paw Paw	Michigan
Sherwood I P	Cleveland	Ohio
Sherwood J P	Cleveland	Ohio
Sherwood & Hopson	Utica	New York
Shidlers Isaac M	Indianapolis	Indiana
Showerman & Bro	Ypsilanti	Michigan
Shroeder John & Co	Detroit	Michigan
Siegel J	Hales Croner	Wisconsin
Siehler J F	Chicago	Illinois
Sinclair & Wilson	Pittsburg	Pennsylvania
Sisk & Wahlen	Paris	Illinois
Skidmore D	Seneca Falls	New York
Skinner H C	Marengo	Illinois
Sleight H G	Niles	Michigan
Sloan F	Ionia	Michigan
Smart J	North Prairie	Wisconsin
Smart & Co	Piqua	Ohio
Small E & L	Hagerstown	Indiana
Smick's	Atlantic City	New Jersey
Smith C W	East Troy	Wisconsin
Smith E B	Detroit	Michigan
Smith Frank	Cincinnati	Ohio
Smith H L	Janesville	Wisconsin

ALPHABETICAL INDEX—Continued

Smith J	Cincinnati	Ohio
Smith J T	White Water	Wisconsin
Smith J W C	Wheeling	West Virginia
Smith S & L	Cincinnati	Ohio
Smith Wm	Lawrenceville	Pennsylvania
Smith Wm B	Detroit	Michigan
Smith Yankee	Detroit	Michigan
Smith Brothers	Addison	Michigan
Smith & Taylor	Indianapolis	Indiana
Snooks Geo	Detroit	Michigan
Snow S F	West Unity	Ohio
Snow Wm	Detroit	Michigan
Snyder F	Cincinnati	Ohio
Snyder Frank	Pittsburg	Pennsylvania
Sohm & Rohman	Buffalo	New York
Solf	Cincinnati	Ohio
Sommer I	New York	New York
Soper B H	Oshkosh	Wisconsin
Sosman Wm M	Chillicothe	Ohio
Souder & Carpenter	Tiffin	Ohio
Spencer M	Indianapolis	Indiana
Spreen Chas	Cincinnati	Ohio
Squier J J	Cambridge	Ohio
Stalkamp H	Cincinnati	Ohio
Stamm C T & Son	Milwaukee	Wisconsin
Standish J D & C B	Detroit	Michigan
Stanley Geo E	La Crosse	Wisconsin
Stanton John	Cincinnati	Ohio
Staples L J	Detroit	Michigan
Staudinger's	New York	New York
Stearn Chas W	Cleveland	Ohio
Stearn D E	Berea	Ohio
Stebbens & Wilson	Ann Arbor	Michigan
Steer & Bowen	Kendallville	Indiana
Stein C & S	Chicago	Illinois
Steinfeld S	New York	New York
Steinhart S	Jefferson	Wisconsin
Steinman A H	Milwaukee	Wisconsin
Stenton Goff	Detroit	Michigan
Stephenson G W	St Johns	Michigan
Steppacher	Philadelphia	Pennsylvania
Sterling Wm F	Eaton Rapids	Michigan
Stern Sam	Green Bay	Wisconsin
Stevens M D	Woodstock	Illinois
Steward M L	Owasso	Michigan
Stifel C E	Wheeling	West Virginia
Stiles Gang Mills	Oconto Co	Wisconsin
St Charles Billiard Rooms	New York	New York
St Lewis Z Z	Green Bay	Wiconsin
St Louis J J	Green Bay	Wiconsin
Stoffel D	Milwaukee	Wiconsin
Stoner & Schroyer	Adamsville	Onio
Story & Southwark	New York	New York

ALPHABETICAL INDEX—Continued

Straight's Shoe Store	Albany	New York
Strausburger & Nuhn	New York	New York
Strauss Bros	Ligonier	Indiana
Straus Louis & Co	Elmira	New York
Stringer Mrs A	Detroit	Michigan
Strous D H	Adelphia	Ohio
Stuart J & Son	Battlecreek	Michigan
Stucke & Co	Manitowoc	Wisconsin
Stump Jacob	Crestline	Ohio
Stuettinger R	Two Rivers	Wisconsin
Stutz C	Middlebury	Indiana
Sutherland G W	Detroit	Michigan
Sutton C	Cincinnati	Ohio
Swain Ezra	Mechanicsburg	Indiana

T

Tages London Yoke Shirt	Cleveland	Ohio
Talbot W A & Son	Barnesville	Ohio
Tamsey & Ballard	Plainfield	Indiana
Tate Mrs J	Oconomowoc	Wisconsin
Taylor C H	Lodi	Illinois
Taylor I & C	Detroit	Michigan
Taylor R G	Detroit	Michigan
Taylor N & G Co	Philadelphia	Pennsylvania
Tea Store	Detroit	Michigan
Tell Wm	Cincinnati	Ohio
Teller I	Milwaukee	Wisconsin
Terhune Bros	Jersey City	New Jersey
Thelen Dieterich	Racine	Wisconsin
Thew Joseph	Kendallville	Indiana
Thiele Fr	New York	New York
Thierbach Wm	New York	New York
Thomas John	Albany	New York
Thomas J H	Fortville	Indiana
Thomas W S	Kendallville	Indiana
Thompson & Spicer	Fremont	Ohio
Thompson & Wiley	Bethel	Indiana
Thomson Mrs A & Son	Indianapolis	Indiana
Tiemmermeister T H	Wappakoneta	Ohio
Timmins T	Norwalk	Ohio
Titus B W	Trenton	New Jersey
Todd S M & Co	Sidney	Ohio
Tollner & Hamacher	New York	New York
Tompkin's Gallery	Grand Rapids	Michigan
Tompkins P H	El Paso	Illinois
Torry R T	Bangor	Maine
Tou J P	Pomeroy	Ohio
Townley E	Cincinnati	Ohio
Trelleaven W	Chicago	Illinois
Tresler John	West Jefferson	Ohio
Trowbridge's Jewelry Store	Sheboygan	Wisconsin
Tubbs & Spear	Hudson	Michigan

ALPHABETICAL INDEX—Continued

Tunis W E	Detroit	Michigan
Turpen T P	Greenville	Ohio
Turner Hubbel & Co	Detroit	Michigan
Tuttle S S	Fredericktown	Ohio
Tuttles C F	Boston	Massachusetts
Twiford A S	Newcomerstown	Ohio
Tyler R C	Detroit	Michigan
Tyler's Bee Hive	Indianapolis	Indiana

U

Underwood Geo W	Hillsdale	Michigan
Underwood N C	Dedham	Tennessee
Upmeyer H	Milwaukee	Wisconsin

V

Vail C G	Ligonier	Indiana
Van Duyn & Lynch	Manchester	Michigan
Van Houten Mrs M A	Columbus	Ohio
Van Ness & Turner	Jonesville	Michigan
Van Wunder's	Cincinnati	Ohio
Van Valkenburg Dr	White Water	Wisconsin
Venn & Wreford	Detroit	Michigan
Viele A J	Lansing	Michigan
Voegtle & Metzger	Indianapolis	Indiana
Vogel Jacob	Cincinnati	Ohio
Voigt Herman	Milwaukee	Wisconsin
Voight Wm	Madison	Wisconsin
Vosburgh W	Marshall	Wisconsin
Vosburg Allen & Co	Oshkosh	Wisconsin

W

Wade B A & Co	Chemung	Illinois
Wagner's Dining Hall	Columbus	Ohio
Wagner Wm	Ann Arbor	Michigan
Wahlstedt A	White Water	Wisconsin
Waldo & Brandon	Cincinnati	Ohio
Walker C R	Buffalo	New York
Walker & Napier	Nashville	Tennessee
Wallace A	Chillicothe	Ohio
Wallace A W	Bridgeport	Connecticut
Wallace W W	La Porte	Indiana
Walsh M & Sons	Niagara Falls	New York
Walter & Smith	Alton	Illinois
Walton J W	Woodsfield	Ohio
Ward's Lake Superior Line	Cleveland	Ohio
Ward Wm	Ravenna	Ohio
Ward Hahn & Riddle	Allegheny	Pennsylvania
Warmkessel Peter	New York	New York
Warner J H	New York	New York

ALPHABETICAL INDEX—Continued

Warner Wm F	New York	New York
Warren O M	Beaver Dam	Wisconsin
Washburn John	Columbia City	Indiana
Washington Market	New York	New York
Washington Restaurant	New York	New York
Waterman N J	Coldwater	Michigan
Watson John	New York	New York
Weatherby's	Cincinnati	Ohio
Weaver M	Lena	Illinois
Weaver & Fox	Buchanan	Michigan
Weaver & Maguire	Indianapolis	Indiana
Webber L D	La Porte	Indiana
Weber Henry	Detroit	Michigan
Webster B	Detroit	Michigan
Webster & Co	Buffalo	New York
Webster Dumm & Co	Zanesville	Ohio
Wehrman H C	Cincinnati	Ohio
Weidezahn Ed	Dixon	Illinois
Welch D S	Kendallville	Indiana
Wellers	Norwich	Connecticut
Welles Henry C	Waterloo	New York
Wentzel John	North Vernon	Indiana
Wert W W	Cincinnati	Ohio
Wheeler & Wilson	St Paul	Minnesota
Wheelock G A	Dowagiac	Michigan
White Hatter	New York	New York
White Thomas	New York	New York
White & Swann	Huntsville	Alabama
Whitlark W W	Detroit	Michigan
Wiatt & Bro	Columbus	Ohio
Wightman J	Newark	New Jersey
Wilcox Wm S	Adrian	Michigan
Wild S	Dayton	Ohio
Wiles L	Putnam	Ohio
Wilkins & Martin	Detroit	Michigan
Wilkinson	Cincinnati	Ohio
Willard C A	Bellevue	Ohio
Willard & Jackson	New York	New York
Williams Daniel	Brooklyn	New York
Williams Wm L	Oshkosh	Wisconsin
Williams Bros	Columbus	Wisconsin
Williams J G & Co	Wheeling	Indiana
Williamsville Express	Williamsville	New York
Wilson A B	Cincinnati	Ohio
Wilson J B	Indianapolis	Indiana
Winans E B & Co	Bellaire	Ohio
Winckler J W	Detroit	Michigan
Wind H	Cincinnati	Ohio
Winesteiner	Cincinnati	Ohio
Wing F M	Detroit	Michigan
Wing D L & Co	Albany	New York
Winsauer C	Chicago	Illinois
Winter G	Detroit	Michigan

ALPHABETICAL INDEX—Continued

Wirth E	Mayfield	Wisconsin
Wisner D A & Son	Jonesville	Michigan
Witgen A	Detroit	Michigan
Woessner John	Cincinnati	Ohio
Wolfe & Sherman	Alexandria	Indiana
Wolfer C	Cincinnati	Ohio
Wolff Henry	Detroit	Michigan
Wood A D	Indianapolis	Indiana
Woodward W H P	Mooresville	Indiana
Worthington Geo	Cleveland	Ohio
Wraith T R	Wilmington	Ohio
Wright	Cincinnati	Ohio
Wright A & C F	Harvard	Massachusetts
Wright Robert	Cincinnati	Ohio
Wright T S	Fond Du Lac	Wisconsin
Wyman Geo	South Bend	Indiana

X

Xelar H B	Cincinnati	Ohio

Y

Y S (Stephen Yeatman)	Cincinnati	Ohio
Yager J C	Springfield	Illinois
Young L	Cincinnati	Ohio
Young M Marsh	Janesville	Wisconsin
Yung John	Jefferson	Wisconsin

Z

Zahm S H	Lancaster	Pennsylvania
Zandt Jos	Cincinnati	Ohio
Zanone Jos	Cincinnati	Ohio
Zeltner John	Cincinnati	Ohio
Zeltner John E	Cincinnati	Ohio
Zimmercan J C	Ligonier	Indiana

COINS OF THE AMERICAS

By GUTTAG BROTHERS

This book contains the premium on United States Coins with illustrations, and a list of Mexican and Central and South American Coins also with illustrations.

35c. per copy

FOREIGN CURRENCY and EXCHANGE GUIDE

By GUTTAG BROTHERS

This book gives details of about 250 Countries with U. S. Bullion Values, Weights, Fineness, etc., of all current Gold and Silver Coins, denominations of Government and Bank Notes, names of Note-issuing Banks, as well as a host of other information necessary to BANKERS, MERCHANTS, NUMISMATISTS, and all others interested in the Monies of the World.

$1.50 per copy

OTHER NUMISMATIC BOOKS IN STOCK

JOHN KENMUIR MAN'F'G JEWELER ST. JOSEPH, MO.		JOHN KENMUIR WATCH MAKER FELIX ST. ST. JOSEPH, MD		Br	Pl
	401 (9H. 1862)	Indented	C		Pl
	401 (9H. #)		Br		Pl
D. PECK & CO. DEALERS IN GROCERIES DRUGS & MEDICINES IRONTON, MO.	402 (9H 1862)	Indented	C (Bronze)	R	Pl
	419 (1864)		Copper	Medal	
	419 (1864)		Brass	R	
	419 (1864)	Indented	Z	R	(extremely clarified we give Z)
	420 (1864)	Indented	GN	R	
	402 (9H 1862)		Br		Pl
	402 (9H 1862)		C Im Plated		Pl
	417 (9H. 1863)		Br		Pl
DROVERS HOTEL 125 NORTH 4 ST ST. LOUIS, MO. (Bulls Head)	417 (9H 1863)		C (Bronze)		Pl
	418 (9H 1863)		C Die Break		Pl
	418 (9H 1863)		C	R	
	420 (9H 1864)		Br		
	420 (9H 1864)		C		R
	420 (9H 1864)		GN		R
	507 (9H 1865) Standing Bull		C (Bronze)		Pl
	(9H 1865) Prairie Flower		C		Pl

Rankin & Riddle Chad for 25¢   210
Sioux Fox Fiddlers in trade

"   2nd for 50¢   210
                        in trade

                Three me Orbie Fiddler
                Idaho

Dunfee + Peele St.L   2nd for 25¢
                      auto in Winchester
     Wolf Alexander   & Buffalo
     Phila Pa   Leipzig

HENRY JENKENS	582 (wreath 1863)	C	Pl
WHOLESALE RETAIL CLOTHIER ST. LOUIS, MO.	582 (wreath 1863)	C Chowder break head Thick Beaded Pl	Pl
	582 (wreath 1863)	C	Pl
	Same as reverse	C	Pl
	Obverse reversed	C	Pl
	Jos. Zemmert Ice Cream Saloon 285 Central Ave (Cincinnati)	C	R
	Obverse reversed	C	R
	J.C. Yager, Tinner Helen, Springfield below see 245?	C	R

USE LALLEMAND'S SPECIFIC Sold By Druggists Jno. H. Blood, Agt 24 Fifth St ST. LOUIS	LALLEMAND'S RHEUMATISM GOUT NEURALGIA SPECIFIC	C	R
	Same as above	Br	R

Same as reverse of above	The Prairie Flower (Indian Head) 1863	CN	R
	464 (9H 1863)	C	R
	420 (S4 1864)	C	R
	419 (S4 1864)	C	R

Sine as above

(over)

CPSIA information can be obtained
at www.ICGtesting.com
Printed in the USA
BVHW031354220922
647764BV00011B/294